THE RAILROADING HANDBOOK

Facts, figures, history, and operations of North American railroads

Compiled by JEFF WILSON

Kalmbach
Media

ACKNOWLEDGEMENTS

The material in this book comes from hundreds of sources, mainly past articles from *Trains* and *Classic Trains* magazines as well as several Kalmbach books. Some of the material is original, based on industry practices, interviews with railroaders, my own published books, articles from trade publications, advertising and promotional material from railroads and manufacturers, historical society publications, and various books about the industry and individual railroads. Statistics and data come from sources including *Poor's Manual of Railroads, Moody's Transportation Manual, Railway Age,* AAR data sheets, various editions of the *Car Builder's Cyclopedia* and *Locomotive Cyclopedia,* industry trade groups, and several other sources. This data sometimes conflicts depending on sources; every effort has been made to ensure that the information is correct as of the publication date, and any errors that remain are my own.

Jeff Wilson
Waukesha, Wis.
June 2022

On the cover: An eastbound double-stack train rolls on Union Pacific's two-track main line east of Vail, Ariz., in February 2001. Jeff Wilson

Opposite page: New Amtrak Siemens Charger ALC42 diesels lead the *Empire Builder* at Brookfield, Wis., in early 2022. David Lassen

Back cover: Clockwise from top: Santa Fe FT diesels lead a freight in the 1950s (Robert Milner). Pennsylvania's TrucTrain was one of the first dedicated piggyback trains when introduced in 1955 (Pennsylvania Railroad). Genesis diesels lead Amtrak's *Southwest Chief* across a bridge in the Arizona desert in 2001 (Jeff Wilson).

Kalmbach Media
21027 Crossroads Circle
Waukesha, Wisconsin 53186
www.KalmbachHobbyStore.com

Published in 2022
26 25 24 23 22   1 2 3 4 5

Manufactured in China

ISBN: 978-162700-920-1
EISBN: 978-162700-921-8

Editor: Jeff Wilson
Book Design: Lisa Bergman and Lisa Schroeder

Library of Congress Control Number: 2022940077

CONTENTS

INTRODUCTION

A BNSF Dash 9-44CW leads an eastbound piggyback train through Rochelle, Ill., in October 2007. Railroading has evolved into a high-tech industry. Jeff Wilson

The railroad industry has evolved significantly since its beginnings in the early 1800s. Many of the changes are obvious—larger locomotives and cars, longer and faster trains, the move from steam to diesel—but many are more subtle. The way railroad operations have changed, the way trains are dispatched and controlled, and high-tech improvements in locomotives, rolling stock, signals, communications, and track have increased efficiency and kept railroading a dominant mode of transportation.

Knowing how the technology works and understanding how locomotives, freight cars, and other equipment have evolved—and why they changed in the ways they did—will give you a much better understanding of how and why railroads operate the way they do today.

The railroad industry through the years has sometimes been saddled with a reputation for being stuck in the past and slow to adopt new ideas and technology. In part these accusations are made because many things are so long-lasting. Locomotives and freight cars can remain in service for 40 or more years. Rail laid in the 1920s and 1930s is still in use. And railroads were indeed slow to adapt to labor efficiencies, with excessive train crew requirements remaining long after many specific jobs were no longer needed.

It's easy to lose track of the advancements of railroads because much of what today's railroads do aren't in the public eye. No longer do small towns have depots with local agents and operators, with daily trains exchanging passengers and mail. Rail yards, intermodal terminals, and large industries are now largely hidden from public view, with high levels of security.

Railroads, however, deserve credit for adjusting to the times, upgrading their equipment, adopting new technology, and improving efficiency. Railroading has become an extremely high-tech industry. Today's diesel-electric locomotives are powerful, high-efficiency, microprocessor-controlled marvels. Dispatching is done by computer, with direct contact with crews. Positive Train Control tracks all trains, ensuring safety by recognizing when trains are on collision courses. Trackside and track-mounted detectors not only find overheated bearings and dragging equipment before they become problems (and do it better than crews observing from cabooses)—modern detectors use strain gauges as well as optical and sound devices to identify potential problems with wheels and trucks long before they become defective. Imaging detectors can spot shifted or oversize loads before they do damage.

What you'll find

This book is intended to serve several purposes. It provides a brief history of the industry, shows how equipment and railroads have evolved, explains railroading terms, and gives descriptions of common equipment and fixtures. It answers questions about how railroads operate and about locomotives, rolling stock, and infrastructure. What's the weight limit of a freight car? How does freight traffic today compare to the 1940s? How heavy is rail? What are the rules for loading cars? How many miles of track are in operation? When did railroads quit operating their own passenger trains?

You'll also learn how technology has affected railroading: Why did diesels replace steam, and how did it happen so quickly? How do today's diesels work? How do today's Centralized Traffic Control and track warrant dispatching systems differ from timetable-and-train-order dispatching?

Information is divided into four broad categories by chapter: railroad history and operations; locomotives; rolling stock; and railroad rights of way. It's impossible for one book to answer in detail all of the questions you might have—it would take an entire library (and a large one at that) to accomplish that. However, my goal is that this book provide a thorough overview that encourages you to seek further details on areas that interest you.

Railroad history and operations

■ Railroads have been a primary means of moving freight and passengers in the U.S. since the early 1800s. The first U.S. common-carrier railroad—the Baltimore & Ohio—was chartered in 1827, with construction beginning the following year (on July 4 at Baltimore harbor). In 1830, the first regularly scheduled passenger operation behind a steam locomotive (the *Best Friend of Charleston*) ran in South Carolina. Railroads began appearing in many locations, with small lines gradually joining with neighboring railroads to form ever-longer routes. More than 9,000 miles of track were in service by 1850, with the growth of railroads following U.S. population expansion westward to the Mississippi and then Missouri rivers. Lines along the east coast expanded to the Midwest, with Chicago and St. Louis becoming key railroad cities.

A Chicago, Burlington & Quincy freight behind 4-8-4 No. 5634 heads out of Zearing, Ill., in the twilight of steam operations in the late 1950s. The steam locomotive remains an icon of railroading more than 60 years after disappearing from the scene. Jim Shaughnessy

Route-miles of railroad operated in U.S.: 1830-2020	
1830:	23
1840:	2,800
1850:	9,000
1860:	30,600
1870:	52,900
1880:	82,100
1890:	158,100
1900:	192,600
1910:	240,800
1920:	251,000
1930:	249,000
1940:	233,000
1950:	223,900
1960:	217,600
1970:	206,000
1980:	185,000
1990:	175,000
2000:	170,000
2010:	139,000
2020:	138,000
Source: AAR (statistics sometimes conflict; some source data tables include only Class 1 railroads)	

The western gold rush and California's statehood in 1850 led to plans for railroad expansion westward across the continent. The first transcontinental railroad was authorized by President Lincoln in 1862, and the line was completed in 1869 with the driving of the golden spike joining the Central Pacific/Union Pacific route at Promontory Summit, Utah. As western population grew, additional transcontinental lines were completed: the Santa Fe, Southern Pacific, and Northern Pacific in 1883, Union Pacific (Northwest route) in 1884, Canadian Pacific in 1885, Great Northern in 1893, and finally the Milwaukee Road 1909.

The period from the late 1800s into the 1910s saw a huge boom in railroad construction, with main and branch lines crisscrossing populated areas, especially in plains and "granger" states. As an example, Iowa became famous for having a railroad roughly every 12 miles, with a total of 10,500 miles of track in the state in 1915 (a figure down to 3,800 miles today).

The development of air brakes and knuckle couplers in the late 1800s led to longer and faster trains, which led to larger, more-powerful locomotives and bigger freight cars. Railroads were the key means of carrying raw materials and finished products of the expanding industrial age, as well as hauling grain and agricultural products throughout the country.

By the early 1900s, major railroads had firmly established their key high-traffic routes. The busiest included what would become known as the Northeast Corridor (from Boston southward through New York City and Philadelphia to Washington, D.C.); multiple routes linking New York and

Chicago; key transcontinental routes (notably Union Pacific, Santa Fe, and Great Northern); and routes spoking to the south and southeast from Chicago. Chicago, St. Louis, and Kansas City became the key gateways to the West.

Total U.S. railroad mileage peaked in 1916, with 254,037 route-miles of track. By that time, however, the expansion of improved roads, the coming of the affordable automobile, and the emergence of ever-larger trucks began taking passenger and freight revenue from railroads. This was especially true for short-haul travel and shipping, which affected low-traffic branch lines, short-haul freight and passenger service, and interurban passenger lines. Railroads began abandoning marginal lines (many of which should never have been built) and cutting back local service.

Even though railroad mileage began dropping, the amount of freight carried continued increasing, as railroads took advantage of improved technology to remain the most-efficient option for long-haul shipping and travel. (Railroad freight traffic is measured in ton-miles—as it sounds, a ton of freight carried one mile; likewise, passenger traffic is measured in passenger-miles). Freight and passenger traffic both fell through the Depression, but then rose in advance of U.S. entry into World War II and peaked in 1944 at the height of the war.

Diesel locomotives, which had begun making inroads in switching service from the late 1920s into the 1930s, made a big splash with the introduction of several streamlined trains starting in 1934 with Union Pacific's (distillate-powered) M-10000 and Burlington's *Zephyr*. The introduction of General Motors' FT freight diesel, which toured the country in 1939 and entered production in 1940, proved popular and railroads ordered as many as the War Production Board allowed to be built during the war.

The years immediately following the war saw railroads place orders for hundreds of new passenger cars and diesel locomotives—passenger as well as freight. Although some steam builders tried to hang on, the move to total dieselization was well underway. Diesels first outnumbered steam locomotives in 1952; by 1959, steam was gone from Class I railroads.

Freight traffic would drop a bit in the years immediately following World War II, but then continue rising through the 2010s. Intercity passenger traffic grew briefly with the advent of many new streamliners in the late 1940s, but dropped rapidly from the late 1950s through the 1960s, with the coming of Amtrak in 1971 stabilizing the market. Commuter passenger

traffic remains strong in many metro areas.

Trucks took over many traffic segments through the 1960s, including perishable, livestock, and less-than-carload (LCL) and express shipments. Railway Express Agency went bankrupt and was dissolved in 1975. Many railroads found themselves in financial trouble, especially in the Northeast. Large crew sizes, worn-out infrastructure, and the inability to abandon lines or revise rates without government approval drove many lines to bankruptcy—including Penn Central, the ill-fated merger of one-time rivals Pennsylvania and New York Central. The formation of Conrail via government subsidy in 1976 seemed like a temporary fix to a serious problem.

Conrail was created by government order in 1976 to take over several bankrupt Northeast-ern railroads. It began turning a profit in the 1980s, and was privatized in 1987. This train is on the former Erie main line near Wellsburg, N.Y., in May 1988. Brian Solomon

Passage of the Staggers Act in 1980 (discussed in more detail on page 28), which largely deregulated the railroading industry, proved to be the salva-tion railroads needed. Conrail eventually became profitable, and other railroads were able to improve their tracks and equipment while bringing in revenue and increasing business. Railroading remains a healthy industry in 2022, with railroads moving more freight in the 2010s than ever before—and doing it over less trackage.

Railroad ownership

Unlike Canada, Mexico, and many other countries, railroads in the U.S. have historically not been owned by the government, but been privately (corporately) owned. Two exceptions to private ownership in the U.S. have been Amtrak and Conrail. Amtrak (see page 71) is a quasi-public entity that took over most intercity passenger trains in 1971. Conrail, which began operation in 1976, was overseen by a government-owned corporation, the U.S. Railway Association (not to be confused with the World War I era U.S.

Canadian National in the early 1900s comprised several lines, and it was under government control starting in the 1920s. It was recapitalized in 1978 and privatized in 1995. This CN train is at North Vancouver, B.C., in 2008. Kevin Cameron

Railroad Administration). The new USRA was created in 1974 to acquire and operate bankrupt railroads, specifically in the Northeast, merging them to form Conrail (Consolidated Rail Corporation). Conrail began turning a profit in the early 1980s; USRA was dissolved in 1986 and Conrail was privatized in 1987.

Railroads in Canada were a mix, with most railroads in the east falling under Canadian National control; financial difficulty brought CN under government ownership by the 1920s. Canadian Pacific, which operated most lines in the West, remained independent. In 1978, CN went through recapitalization and was run as a for-profit corporation, albeit still owned by the government. The railroad was privatized following the CN Commercialization Act in 1995.

Mexican railroads were also historically government owned. Following the Mexican Revolution of the 1910s and through the late 1930s, most standard and narrow gauge rail lines in the country were absorbed by National Railways of Mexico (NdeM), with four other government-owned lines retaining their own identities. These were all consolidated as FNM (for Ferrocarriles Nacionales de Mexico) in the late 1980s, and the railroads were privatized in 1995.

Two National of Mexico steam locomotives prepare to double-head their train at Cuautla, on their way to Mexico City in the 1950s. Jim Shaughnessy

Railroad classes and sizes

Beginning in the 1910s, the Interstate Commerce Commission divided U.S. common-carrier railroads into three divisions by size: Class I, Class II, and Class III (usually indicated by Roman numerals). The divisions were based on revenue generated, with $1 million as the threshold for Class I status and $100,000 for Class II railroads. Those criteria remained until 1956, when the Class I limit was raised to $3 million and the Class III category was dropped (it would be reinstated in 1978). The revenue limits continued to increase, and as of 2020 were $504.8 million for Class I status, while Class III railroads were those with revenue under $40.4 million.

Since the 1960s, mergers have continually reduced the number of large railroads. In 1956, when the ICC reclassified the revenue divisions, there were 113 Class I railroads; by 1978 the number had dropped to 41, and as of 2022 there are just seven Class I railroads: BNSF, Canadian National, Canadian Pacific, CSX, Kansas City Southern, Norfolk Southern, and Union

Pacific. Class I railroads in 2022 accounted for 94 percent of freight revenue and 68 percent of freight mileage.

Today, Class II and III designations are rarely referred to as such. Class II lines are generally referred to as regional railroads (per the AAR, a regional operates at least 350 miles of track), and Class IIIs are short lines, local railroads, or switching and terminal railroads. Some switching and terminal lines have revenue that would place them as Class II lines, but their physical size puts them in Class III. As of 2022, there were about 630 regional and shortline railroads, operating about 45,000 route-miles of track.

Mergers and spinoffs

Mergers and acquisitions have always been a part of railroading, with small lines joining together to form larger systems. The business end of this can be done in several ways: two or more companies can merge, forming a new railroad; one railroad can buy another (usually through stock acquisition); or one railroad can negotiate a long-term lease of another railroad.

The Penn Central merger of 1968 was ill-fated from the start. The resulting bankruptcy of PC led to Conrail. Here two ex-PC locomotives lead a CR train in Indiana in 1976. Gary W. Dolzall

The net effect of primary concern to railfans is how the merger appears in terms of paint scheme and railroad name, and whether any routes are abandoned. One company may absorb the other (Chicago Great Western effectively vanished when it merged into Chicago & North Western in 1968, with most of its routes abandoned); a new railroad name and paint scheme can be created (Penn Central from the Pennsylvania Railroad and New York Central, also in 1968); or the railroads can retain their basic identities under a new corporate umbrella (Chessie System kept the Baltimore & Ohio, Chesapeake & Ohio, and Western Maryland names alive).

The 1,400-mile-long regional railroad Iowa, Chicago & Eastern in 2002 assumed operations of I&M Rail Link, which had been spun off from Canadian Pacific in 1997. Here an ICE grain train behind second-hand SD40-2s rolls across northern Iowa in November 2006. Jeff Wilson

The 1940s saw the beginning of a trend of larger railroads joining forces. Large mergers tended to be one of two types: end-to-end mergers that gave the new railroad a longer mainline run or access to a new city (such as Louisville & Nashville merging Monon in 1971 to get to Chicago) and allow railroads to better compete against longer neighbors; and side-by-side mergers, where merged railroads can eliminate duplicate lines and services to save money (Illinois Central and Gulf, Mobile & Ohio merging in 1972 to form Illinois Central Gulf). Some—such as Burlington Northern (1970) and ICG—proved quite successful; others (Penn Central) were disastrous.

Class I merger tree

This merger tree shows how major Class I railroads have merged to form larger systems, leading to the seven Class I railroads as of 2022 (continued to next page). Kalmbach Media

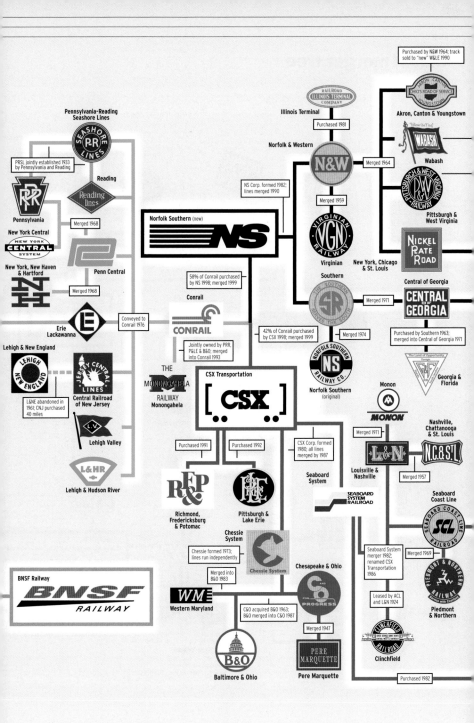

Pennsylvania-Reading
Seashore Lines

SEASHORE P-R LINES

PRSL jointly established 1933
by Pennsylvania and Reading

Reading

Reading lines

Pennsylvania

PRR

New York Central

NEW YORK CENTRAL SYSTEM

Merged 1968

New York, New Haven
& Hartford

NH

Merged 1968

Penn Central

Erie
Lackawanna

E

Conveyed to
Conrail 1976

Lehigh & New England

LEHIGH NEW ENGLAND

L&NE abandoned in
1961; CNJ purchased
40 miles

JERSEY CENTRAL LINES

Central Railroad
of New Jersey

L.V.

Lehigh Valley

L&HR

Lehigh & Hudson River

Norfolk Southern (new)

NS

Conrail

CONRAIL

Jointly owned by PRR,
P&LE & B&O; merged
into Conrail 1993

THE MONONGAHELA RAILWAY
Monongahela

CSX Transportation

[CSX]

Purchased 1991

R F&P

Richmond,
Fredericksburg
& Potomac

Purchased 1992

P&LE

Pittsburgh &
Lake Erie

Chessie
System

Chessie formed 1973;
lines run independently

Chessie System

Merged into
B&O 1983

WM
Western Maryland

BNSF Railway

BNSF RAILWAY

Illinois Terminal

RAILROAD ILLINOIS TERMINAL COMPANY

Purchased 1981

Norfolk & Western

N&W

Merged 1964

NS Corp. formed 1982;
lines merged 1990

Merged 1959

VGN RAILWAY

Virginian

Southern

SR THE SOUTHERN SERVES THE SOUTH

58% of Conrail purchased
by NS 1998; merged 1999

42% of Conrail purchased
by CSX 1998; merged 1999

Merged 1974

NORFOLK SOUTHERN
NS
RAILWAY CO.

Norfolk Southern
(original)

Purchased by N&W 1964; track
sold to "new" W&LE 1990

AKRON CANTON OHIO'S ROAD OF SERVICE YOUNGSTOWN

Akron, Canton & Youngstown

WABASH

Wabash

PW&V RAILWAY

Pittsburgh &
West Virginia

NICKEL PLATE ROAD

New York, Chicago
& St. Louis

Central of Georgia

CENTRAL OF GEORGIA

Merged 1971

Purchased by Southern 1963;
merged into Central of Georgia 1971

G&F

Georgia &
Florida

Monon

MONON

Merged 1971

L&N

Louisville &
Nashville

Nashville,
Chattanooga
& St. Louis

N.C.&St.L

Merged 1957

Seaboard
System

SEABOARD SYSTEM RAILROAD

CSX Corp. formed
1980; all lines
merged by 1987

Seaboard System
merger 1982;
renamed CSX
Transportation
1986

Leased by ACL
and L&N 1924

Chesapeake & Ohio

C&O FOR PROGRESS

C&O acquired B&O 1963;
B&O merged into C&O 1987

Merged 1947

B&O

Baltimore & Ohio

PERE MARQUETTE

Pere Marquette

Seaboard
Coast Line

SCL SEABOARD COAST LINE RAILROAD

Merged 1969

P&N PIEDMONT & NORTHERN RAILWAY

Piedmont
& Northern

CLINCHFIELD RAILROAD

Clinchfield

Purchased 1982

19

Class I merger tree

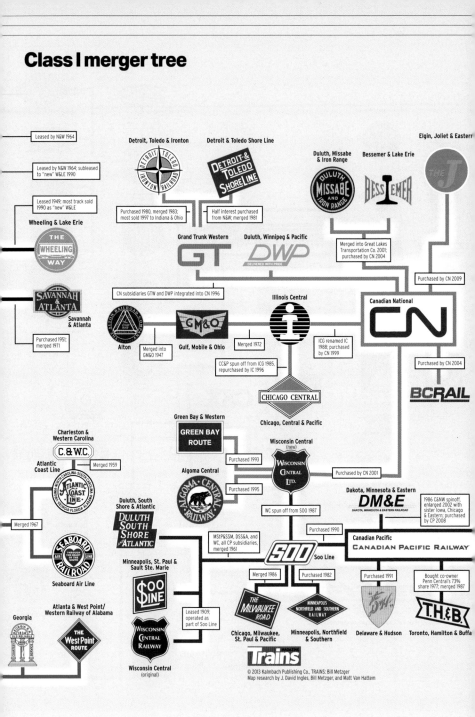

© 2013 Kalmbach Publishing Co., TRAINS: Bill Metzger
Map research by J. David Ingles, Bill Metzger, and Matt Van Hattem

Mergers continued forming larger and larger systems through the 1970s and 1980s, eventually leading to the seven Class I railroads we have today.

Spinoffs are the opposite of mergers. Large railroads—especially upon merging with other lines—often look to rid themselves of portions of their routes that aren't primary traffic generators. These routes remain quite desirable to smaller operators, who can provide service with older equipment, less-frequent (and slower) operation, or smaller crew sizes. These can be quite short—a small branch line—or fairly long. An example is ICG in 1985 selling its 700-plus-mile western line from Chicago across Iowa to Omaha to form Chicago, Central & Pacific. The new railroad became quite successful, inspiring IC to buy the railroad back in 1996.

Into the 1990s, railroad mergers had to be approved by the Interstate Commerce Commission; since 1996, approval comes from the Surface Transportation Board. Conditions were often imposed on mergers to ensure what the ICC termed "fair competition," such as trackage rights granted to a third railroad or a specific line or route being sold to another company.

Common carriers, industrial, and private railroads

Most railroads are common carriers, with the current definition that they "provide transportation or service on reasonable request at a reasonable rate." The specific definition has varied over the years, but the basic premise is common carriers (whether trucking companies, barge/steamship lines, or railroads) are obligated to provide, within reason and at published rates, shipping services to those who desire it.

Non-common-carrier railroads are owned by private companies to serve a specific service, with mines and logging operations prime examples. They are not obligated to provide shipping services to other companies or individuals. Industrial railroads are built to serve a specific owner, and can be short—such as trackage within a multi-building manufacturing plant or complex (Ford's plant railroad at its River Rouge plant near Detroit had nearly 100 miles of track). They can also be quite long; an example is the Northshore Mining (former Reserve Mining) railroad in northern Minnesota, which carries iron ore 47 miles from mines to a taconite pellet plant on the shore of Lake Superior. Some railroads are 100 percent privately owned by a corporation, but still serve as common carriers. An example is Bessemer & Lake Erie: it's owned by U.S. Steel and has a primary responsibility of serving its business, but is a common carrier and carries freight for any number of customers.

Interurbans, streetcars, light rail

An interurban is an electric passenger-service railroad, generally with self-propelled cars, that runs between cities. They became quite popular following the turn of the 20th century. Interurbans were cheaper and faster to build than a conventional steam railroad: they were built with lighter rail, sharper curves, steeper grades, and limited roadbed and subgrade. More than 15,000 miles of interurban lines were in service in the U.S. by 1915, and they were especially popular in the upper Midwest from Ohio and Indiana upward through Illinois and Iowa. They typically had their own rights of way in rural areas, with street running in towns and cities. Although primarily

Northshore Mining is an example of a privately owned, non-common-carrier railroad. It hauls iron ore from a northern Minnesota mine to a processing plant on Lake Superior. John Leopard

built to carry passengers, some carried freight (some carload freight, but mainly less-than-carload and express parcels). The growing popularity of the automobile and improved highways doomed most interurbans, and by the 1920s many were being abandoned. The Depression finished off most remaining interurban lines during the 1930s, although a few survived and were converted to conventional railroads (the Illinois Terminal was among the best known). The Chicago South Shore & South Bend is the last surviving interurban.

Streetcar lines (often called "trolleys") are electric passenger railroads that operate within cities or urban areas, with track often sharing right-of-way with vehicles on streets. Some cities (Chicago, New York, Philadelphia, others) have had elevated ("El") lines, with tracks on bridgework above streets. Early streetcar lines, from the early to late 1800s, featured horse-drawn cars, but by the 1890s, streetcars were self-propelled electric cars, drawing power from an overhead electric wire. All major cities (and many smaller cities and towns) had them; they were sometimes connected to and

Interurbans featured electric operations over tracks built to lighter standards than steam lines. This is the Cedar Rapids & Iowa City (CRANDIC) at Cedar Rapids. Trains magazine collection

operated in conjunction with interurban lines. As with interurbans, streetcar lines were abandoned in large numbers through the 1930s, with some hanging on into the early 1950s.

Light rail is the term for modern urban passenger rail (mass-transit) systems that use self-propelled electric cars. Like streetcars, they can operate on their own rights of way, in streets with vehicular traffic, or a mix. Many cities rebuilt older streetcar systems or added new routes, using self-propelled multiple-unit cars, with electricity coming from either an overhead

wire or third rail next to the running rails. The American Public Transportation Association currently lists about 30 U.S. cities with light rail systems. These systems are government owned.

Industry trade organizations

The American Railway Association (ARA) was the first major railroad industry trade group, formed in 1892 following regular meetings of railroad representatives at the General Time Convention. The ARA represented the industry at large, with standing committees for various aspects of railroading including operations and equipment. The ARA in 1934 merged with several

Electric streetcar lines were common from the 1890s through the 1930s. This is Beloit, Wis., in 1908. They shared rights-of-way with vehicular traffic. Library of Congress

Modern light transit lines serve many cities. Here a six-car San Diego Trolley runs on the south side of San Diego in 1984. The city has three lines with 54 miles of track. J.W. Swanberg

other groups (including the Master Car Builders Association, the Association of Railway Executives, the Association of Railway Executives, and others) to form the:

Association of American Railroads (AAR). The AAR remains the industry's major trade group today, setting standards for equipment specifications and interchange rules, representing the railroad industry to Congress and government regulators, and compiling statistics and publishing reports and other information regarding railroading. The AAR's subsidiaries include Railinc, which transmits waybills and other information and compiles information and data (including the Umler database of rolling stock), and the Transportation Technology Center, Inc. (TTCI), which operates a testing facility at Pueblo, Colo., under the auspices of the Federal Railroad Administration.

The American Short Line and Regional Railroad Association (ASLRRA) is similar to the AAR, but is a trade group representing and providing services for smaller (Class II and III) railroads. As of 2022, the association covers 603 railroads that operate a total of 47,500 route-miles.

Government agencies

Interstate Commerce Commission (ICC). The ICC was was created by the Interstate Commerce Act of 1887. Its main duties were setting and approving rates (for coach lines, ships, and eventually trucking and bus lines as well as railroads) and establishing safety regulations. A major ICC duty that grew in importance through the 1960s and later was approving or denying railroad merger requests. The ICC was abolished in 1995.

Federal Railroad Administration (FRA), Department of Trainsportation (DOT). The FRA was created by the Department of Transportation Act of 1966. It falls under the DOT, which was formed at the same time. The FRA assumed many of the duties of the ICC, and is responsible primarily for safety regulations involving infrastructure, hazardous materials transport, and operating rules (some hazmat transportation administration comes from the PHMSA, the Pipeline and Hazardous Materials Safety Administration).

Surface Transportation Board (STB). Formed in 1996, the STB is the federal agency overseeing economic regulations involving railroads and other businesses, including rates, abandonments, and railroad mergers. The STB succeeded the ICC, and was under the DOT until 2015, when it became an independent federal agency.

National Transportation Safety Board (NTSB). The NTSB is an independent federal agency formed in 1967. It investigates significant accidents on railroads (and other modes of transport), determining probable cause and issuing recommendations for avoiding future accidents.

Federal Transit Administration (FTA). The FTA provides financial and technical assistance to local public transit systems, including light rail, subway, and heavy rail commuter systems as well as other non-rail transit systems. It's an agency of the DOT, established in 1964 as the Urban Mass Transit Administration (UMTA) and renamed in 1991.

Staggers Act

The Staggers Rail Act, passed in 1980, is one of the most significant milestones in railroad history, as it largely deregulated the industry. The main portion of Staggers dealt with shipping charges. Historically, railroads had not been free to set their own rates. With the formation of the Interstate Commerce Commission in 1887, railroads became subject to federal regulation. Among the most contentious of the ICC's oversight duties was approving rates. Railroads couldn't simply charge rates based on the cost of providing services—the ICC was empowered to change any rate to one it considered "just and reasonable." Railroads were often stuck having to provide services at rates that were unprofitable (or marginally so), or were unable to discount rates that would undercut rates charged by other transportation modes—regardless of the actual cost of providing the services. A classic case was the Southern Railway's purchase of the first jumbo covered hoppers for grain in 1960. The railroad's attempt to offer shippers discounted rates for using the efficient cars (instead of traditional inefficient boxcars) was denied by the ICC. The railroad had to extend its appeal all the way to the U.S. Supreme Court to gain the right to set its rates, finally making it

This 0-8-0 switcher was one of several locomotive designs developed by the United States Railroad Administration during its time of control over U.S. railroads. TRAINS magazine collection

worthwhile to own the cars.

The Staggers Act largely deregulated pricing in the industry, allowing railroads in most cases to set their own rates and establish contracts with shippers without ICC approval (the main exception was where the ICC determined that there was no direct competition for a railroad's services). Railroad traffic and profits had been dropping steadily, even though the industry provided the most-efficient mode of transport in many cases. Staggers reversed this: Following the act's passage, railroads were able to recover much of their lost business, increasing profitability while lowering rates. The Staggers Act was related to the Motor Carrier Act of 1980, which likewise deregulated much of the trucking industry, with similar effects.

United States Railroad Administration

The United States Railroad Administration (USRA) was the governmental body that took over operations and direction of all U.S. railroads during World War I. Rail traffic (freight and passenger) had increased substantially, even before the U.S. entered the war in March 1917, especially with materials heading to Europe via Eastern ports. Railroads were unable to efficiently move goods and people, with heavy traffic, clogged main lines and yards, inefficient interchange and dispatching practices, manpower shortages, and aging equipment. Through the USRA, the government guaranteed the railroads a rental rate based on their net operating incomes for the three previous years, raised minimum wages for workers, and guaranteed that control of railroads would revert to their owners within 21 months of the end of the war.

The USRA coordinated operations and, most notably, designed and ordered 2,000 new locomotives and 50,000 freight cars (more on those in Chapters 2 and 3) to committee-designed standards, assigning them to railroads as need was determined. This provided the most lasting legacy of the USRA, as any manufacturer could build equipment to USRA designs. Thousands of cars and locomotives were built to these designs long after USRA control ended (some USRA-design locomotives were built into the 1940s). Following the end of the war in November 1918, the USRA passed control back to the railroads in March 1920.

Railroad jobs

Specific railroading jobs have evolved significantly since the 1800s. A few jobs have remained relatively unchanged, but many others have come and gone as technology has evolved. Steam locomotives required an army of laborers, boilermakers, and maintenance workers to keep them running; the coming of diesels eliminated hundreds of thousands of workers. Computer-based systems likewise eliminated the need for many agent and clerk positions. Train crews in the steam and early diesel era typically comprised four to six members; the elimination of cabooses in the 1980s and elimination of many positions means most trains today have two-person crews. Overall railroad employment peaked in 1920 at 2.1 million; it fell below a million in 1957 (999,000) and today is around 151,000.

Railroading has always been a dangerous profession, even moreso from the 1800s into the early 1900s. In the peak year of 1907, 4,534 railroad employees were killed on the job. Better equipment, improved training, and more stringent safety rules have greatly improved working conditions, and the number of on-duty deaths was 11 in 2020.

Jobs on locations—such as operators, agents, and shop workers—typically are assigned in eight-hour shifts called "tricks" (first trick: 8 a.m.-4 p.m.; second trick: 4 p.m.-midnight; third trick: midnight-8 a.m.). Historically, many of these jobs were seven-day-a-week positions. Train crews typically work on specific routes (often divisions or subdivisions) and are limited to 12 consecutive hours of service (this was 16 hours in the early 1900s). Their call times and specific hours on duty vary by train frequency and schedules.

Many jobs were based on seniority: As jobs opened, employees could bid on them. For train crews, passenger trains paid the best and were the most sought-after posts, followed by scheduled freight trains and yard jobs (yard jobs were generally by tricks). Employees could "mark off" to take vacation; they would be temporarily replaced by employees on the "extra board," who—again by seniority—would be called to work extra trains and shifts.

Following is a summary of the most-common railroad positions. Railroads also employ a broad variety of clerks, laborers, maintenance workers, and administrators to keep trains moving.

Dispatcher. The dispatcher is responsible for getting trains over a defined stretch of railroad (often a subdivision). Working from a central office, the dispatcher uses one of several operating systems (timetable/train order, Centralized Traffic Control, track warrants, or manual blocks—see page 76) to coordinate train movements by issuing instructions to train crews.

Engineer. The engineer drives the train, sitting on the right side of the cab while operating the controls in the locomotive. Although the types of locomotives have certainly changed, the basic job of the engineer hasn't changed much since the early days of railroading.

Road Foreman of Engines (RFE). The RFE is responsible for overseeing engineers on a railroad, including training and evaluation. The RFE often rides with (and operates) locomotives while working with engineers.

Fireman. On a steam locomotive, the fireman tended the boiler, making sure the fuel, fire, and water were in good condition. In the diesel era, the job evolved to an engineer's assistant position; the title and job were eliminated on most railroads starting in the 1980s when the conductor moved to the cab.

This dispatcher is at a traditional mechanically interlocked Centralized Traffic Control panel in the 1940s. By the 1990s, these largely gave way to computer terminals. Union Pacific

An engineer is at the controls of an EMD E unit in 1950. The locomotives and trains have changed, but the engineer's job is largely the same. William A. Akin

Conductor. The conductor is in charge of the train, directing movements as needed. On passenger trains, the conductor is responsible for passenger ticketing as well. On freight trains the conductor rode in the caboose, which served as his office. With the elimination of the caboose, the conductor became one of two positions in the cab, together with the engineer.

Brakeman (trainman). In the 1800s, a brakeman had a hazardous job, walking the tops of cars to set and release brakes by hand, as well as coupling cars with link-and-pin couplers. By the early 1900s the main duty was to throw turnouts and couple and uncouple cars. Through the 1960s, most freight trains had head- and rear-end brakemen; the position was largely eliminated by the 2000s, with duties added to the conductor position.

Passenger conductors are responsible for the train itself, as well as passenger seating and ticketing (and tracking money from ticket sales). Trains magazine collection

A Pennsylvania freight conductor uses a fusee to give a highball to the head end in 1960. Cabooses are now gone and radio has changed how crews do their jobs. Don Wood

Station agent. The station agent was responsible for working with shippers and local passengers, ordering freight cars for loading, and dealing with passenger ticketing. At small stations, the position was sometimes combined with the operator.

Operator. In the days of timetable and train-order operations, the operator at each station was responsible for passing train orders from the dispatcher to the crews on passing trains. This was typically done by telegraph through the 1940s (later in many locations). At small stations, this position was sometimes combined with the station agent.

A brakeman is ready at a switch stand in 1943. Jack Delano, Library of Congress

Hooping up train orders to crews was a key duty of station operators in the era of timetable-and-train-order operations. The job has since vanished. Jim Shaughnessy

Towerman. A towerman (or "leverman") was an operator stationed at an interlocking tower, with the additional duties of controlling an interlocking plant via levers or CTC-panel switches.

Hostler. The hostler is responsible for moving locomotives within engine servicing and terminal areas as they are fueled and maintained.

Yardmaster. The yardmaster coordinates operations in a yard, working to ensure switch crews get inbound trains sorted and outbound trains assembled and ready to depart and that clerks and other personnel have paperwork ready.

Roadmaster. The roadmaster has overall authority for train movements on a specific portion of railroad (usually a division or subdivision), ensuring that the line is properly maintained.

Trainmaster. The trainmaster is the manager overseeing train crews (usually over a subdivision), including scheduling. The trainmaster is responsible for training and testing crews on safety and operational procedures.

Interlocking tower operators were responsible for setting the levers that controlled signals and turnouts at junctions. Most towers were gone by the 2000s. Wallace W. Abbey

Umler (railroad equipment database), *Official Railway Equipment Register*

Umler—now the Umler Equipment Management Information System—is the electronic database for all North American rail equipment. It's managed by Railinc, which is a division of the Association of American Railroads, and is the official manner of accepting equipment for interchange. Railroads and private car owners maintain their entries for every piece of rolling stock, including freight and passenger cars, locomotives, non-revenue equipment, containers and trailers, container chassis, and end-of-train devices. The data for each entry includes reporting marks and number, tare weight, gross rail load (GRL), clearance (Plate) restrictions, equipment specifications, capacity/dimensions, and inspection dates, along with instructions on loading and

Yardmasters are in charge of train operations in yards. Trains magazine collection

A yard clerk chalks a note on a boxcar in the 1940s. Library of Congress

routing. Railroads use the database for billing, assigning cars, determining clearance restrictions along routes, calculating train weights, and maintenance schedules. The printed version is the *Official Railway Equipment Register,* published quarterly.

Cabooses

Cabooses were a railroading icon from the 1840s through the 1970s, trailing virtually every freight train in North America. The caboose served as a rolling office for the conductor to do paperwork and as an observation post

The caboose was a staple of railroading through the 1970s. Crew reductions and the end-of-train device have since eliminated them from trains. Russ Porter; Don Heimburger collection

where the conductor and rear brakeman could observe the train for potential problems while in motion. Crewmen could also monitor the brake-pipe pressure and, if needed, use a brake valve in the caboose to apply the emergency brakes. Cabooses were equipped with bunks, allowing crews to sleep in them if other accommodations weren't available. Through the 1950s, cabooses were typically assigned to individual conductors, meaning cabooses were swapped on trains whenever crews changed. This changed to unassigned (pool) cabooses by the 1960s, which led to a drop in caboose numbers.

Changes in operation, the adoption of roller bearing trucks, and the increased number of defect detectors lessened the need for a rear-end crew, and by the 1970s, railroads were lobbying to reduce crew sizes and eliminate

cabooses. Cabooses were a major expense item—both in initial cost as well as the cost of operation. The number of cabooses dropped from a high of 34,000 in the late 1920s to 15,000 by the late 1960s. The development of the end-of-train device, or ETD (see below) in the 1970s allowed monitoring rear brake pressure remotely from the locomotive. A 1982 agreement between railroads and the United Transportation Union allowing a reduction in crew sizes was the effective end for cabooses, first on unit trains and other through freights, then on other trains. By the late 1980s, cabooses were rare; other than transfer runs and specialized switching jobs, they were virtually eliminated by 2000.

End-of-train devices

The end-of-train device (EOT or ETD; in the 1990s sometimes called

The end-of-train device (EOT or EDT) serves as a marker and also remotely monitors brake-line pressure. Most can now also respond to commands from the engine. Jeff Wilson

flashing rear-end device, or FRED) is a box that mounts on the rear coupler of a train with a connection to the air hose. It monitors brake-pipe pressure and reports data to a receiver on the locomotive, and also has a flashing red light that serves as a marker. Most modern ETDs (since about 2000) can also respond to commands from the locomotive to made a brake application (those with two-way communication are termed "smart" ETDs). The first ETD appeared in 1969, but it was the 1982 agreement between railroads and operating unions that led to an immediate, rapid decline in caboose operations, with widespread use of ETDs on almost all freight trains.

Initially, ETDs were powered by batteries. Most modern devices still have batteries as a backup, but the primary power is from a small turbine powered from the train air system. They communicate with the head-end via a head-of-train (HOT) device called a HOT box. Depending upon handling and use, an ETD will last about 5-7 years.

Brake systems

Early brakes. Through most of the 1800s, trains relied on manual brakes. Each car had brakes that had to be set by turning a brake wheel located at the top of the car. Brakemen on the car roofs applied and released brakes as needed based on whistle signals from the engineer. The method was inexact and difficult to control, and even in an era where speeds were relatively slow and trains were short, being a brakeman was a dangerous and difficult job. Add bad weather, mountain grades, and nighttime operations, and the job became extremely hazardous.

Air brakes. The air brake was patented by George Westinghouse in 1869. His original system ("straight air") used compressed air to apply brakes throughout the train. Although a vast improvement over manual brakes, a broken air hose or other leak could suddenly leave a train without brakes. It was Westinghouse's improved automatic brake system of 1872 that truly revolutionized railroading, adding a fail-safe layer of protection that allowed faster speeds and longer trains. Air brakes have been mandatory since the Railroad Safety Appliance Act of 1893, although it was several years into the 1900s before all cars were equipped. The current ABDW system (standard since 1974) is an upgrade of the AB brake system that became mandatory for all new cars as of 1932, replacing K brakes—all of which trace back to Westinghouse's initial design. The improved designs have increased reliability and response time.

The drawings on the following page shows how brake components are arranged. Specific component locations vary by car: Under the body for flatcars and boxcars, under the slope sheet for hoppers and covered hoppers, and on the end platform or under tank cars. Some cars have truck-mounted brakes, where the cylinder is mounted inside the truck frame.

Here's how the system works: The brake pipe, which terminates at each end of the car at a flexible hose with coupling, forms the train line when connected to other cars. Hose couplings ("glad hands") are connected by hand—they uncouple automatically when cars are pulled apart. At the base of each hose is an angle cock, a valve that opens or closes the line. Air compressors on the locomotive charge the train line, generally with 90 pounds of pressure (70 pounds was typical in the steam era).

The control valve (not "triple valve"—those went away with K-type brakes in the steam era) on each car is connected to the train line. It performs several functions mechanically, based on sensing pressure changes in the train line. Connected to the control valve is the air reservoir, which stores the car's air supply for braking. The reservoir has two halves: auxiliary or service (normal) and emergency. As the train line is charging, the control valve directs air to the reservoir, charging it to the same pressure as the train line.

To make a standard ("service") brake application, the engineer opens the

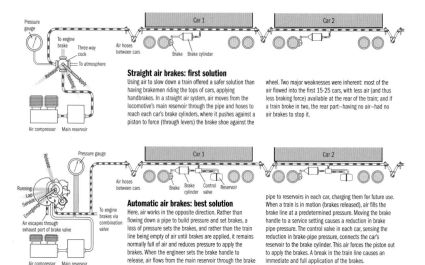

Straight air brakes: first solution

Using air to slow down a train offered a safer solution than having brakemen riding the tops of cars, applying handbrakes. In a straight air system, air moves from the locomotive's main reservoir through the pipe and hoses to reach each car's brake cylinders, where it pushes against a piston to force (through levers) the brake shoe against the wheel. Two major weaknesses were inherent: most of the air flowed into the first 15-25 cars, with less air (and thus less braking force) available at the rear of the train; and if a train broke in two, the rear part—having no air—had no air brakes to stop it.

Automatic air brakes: best solution

Here, air works in the opposite direction. Rather than flowing down a pipe to build pressure and set brakes, a loss of pressure sets the brakes, and rather than the train line being empty of air until brakes are applied, it remains normally full of air and reduces pressure to apply the brakes. When the engineer sets the brake handle to release, air flows from the main reservoir through the brake pipe to reservoirs in each car, charging them for future use. When a train is in motion (brakes released), air fills the brake line at a predetermined pressure. Moving the brake handle to a service setting causes a reduction in brake pipe-pressure. The control valve in each car, sensing the reduction in brake-pipe pressure, connects the car's reservoir to the brake cylinder. This air forces the piston out to apply the brakes. A break in the train line causes an immediate and full application of the brakes.

Similar brake rigging is used in straight and automatic air: the difference is in the valve.

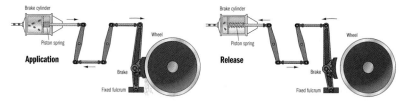

The invention of air brakes by Westinghouse — and the improvement of automatic air brakes — revolutionized railroading, allowing longer trains and higher speeds. Kalmbach Media

brake valve in the locomotive, which allows air to escape from the train line. The amount of braking is regulated by the amount of air released from the train line: A 12-pound reduction, for example, provides stronger braking than an 8-pound reduction.

The control valve on each car senses the drop in pressure and directs a corresponding percentage of air from the service portion of the car's reservoir to the brake cylinder. Air entering the brake cylinder forces the piston out from the end of the cylinder. The piston, via levers, pulls rods attached to the brake beams on each truck, pushing the brake shoes against the wheel treads, which applies the brakes.

To release the brakes, the engineer closes the valve; compressors begin charging the train line. When the control valves sense the increase in pressure, they release the brakes and begin recharging the brake reservoirs. The retaining valve (located next to the brake wheel on the end of each car) is used at times when descending steep or long grades. Setting the valve keeps a certain amount of air in the brake cylinder, allowing the brakes to be applied while at the same time allowing the car's reservoir to recharge.

To make an emergency application, all of the air is released from the train line (known as "big-holing" the brakes). Sensing this, the control valves move all the air from each car's reservoir, including the emergency portion, to the cylinder, providing a maximum application. This is what provides the key safety

Air hoses have a metal casting with rubber gasket on the end ("glad hand"), allowing hoses to be easily connected. Jeff Wilson

feature with automatic brakes: Any broken hose or failure of the air line (such as if a coupler knuckle breaks or a train breaks in two, separating the air hoses) causes an instant drop in pressure, which automatically triggers an emergency brake application.

A power hand brake, consisting of a brake wheel (or lever) mounted on a gearbox, is located on one end of each car. From the gearbox, a vertical rod and lever connect to the end of the piston on the brake cylinder. Turning the wheel pulls out the piston, applying the brakes. The hand brake is used both as a parking brake for cars and by crew members riding moving cars into position to stop them. The end of the car that has the brake wheel is the "B" end; the opposite end is the "A" end. Brake wheels were mounted at the top of car ends until 1966, when the requirement for running boards was eliminated. Brake wheels are now mounted lower on the car end.

Into the 1920s, most cars were equipped with K brakes. The K system worked in similar manner to the AB system, but had a slower response time and no separate emergency section in the reservoir, and the K triple valve had fewer functions than the later AB valve. The components could be coupled together in the K system—called KC, for "K combined." K brakes could not be used on new equipment after 1932, and K brakes were banned from interchange traffic in 1953. Many older cars were converted from K to AB brakes from the 1940s onward.

Locomotives have their own brakes, including dynamic braking on diesels—more on those systems in Chapter 2.

Couplers

Through most of the 1800s, cars were joined by link-and-pin couplers: an oval loop (link) that slid into slots on the end of a car, with a heavy pin that dropped through a hole in the slot on each car to anchor the pin. These couplers were problematic and dangerous, with brakemen regularly losing fingers as they aligned links while dropping pins in place. The solution was the knuckle coupler, first patented by Eli Janney in 1873. Automatic couplers have a moveable knuckle that opens outward. To couple cars, the knuckle on one or both couplers is opened. One car is backed into the other, and the force causes the knuckles to close and lock automatically. To uncouple cars, a crew member pulls the uncoupling lever, which opens the knuckle on that car and releases the couplers. The uncoupling lever (not "lift bar") on each car end extends to the left as you're looking at the car end. Levers are made in a variety of styles depending upon the type of coupler and whether the car has extended draft gear because of a cushioning device.

Knuckle couplers became mandatory with the railroad Safety Appliance Act of 1893. Designs have continually been upgraded, with improvements and variations signified by letters; the current Type E and F couplers were introduced in the 1930s and 1940s. The type E is the standard coupler; the F

Couplers have knuckles that lock in place. The coupler at right is a shelf coupler, mandatory on tank cars. The design helps keep cars from separating in derailments. Jeff Wilson

is based on the type H tightlock coupler used for passenger service, with a design that eliminates most slack space between couplers (and thus minimizes slack action).

Tank cars carrying hazardous materials were first required to be equipped with shelf-type interlocking couplers in 1970. Shelf-style couplers help prevent coupler separation in derailments, minimizing the chance that a coupler from an adjoining car will puncture the end of a neighboring tank in an accident. Many hopper and coal gondola cars were equipped with rotary couplers starting in the early 1960s. These rotate within their draft-gear boxes, allowing the coupler to turn while still coupled to the adjoining cars. The coupler type and style is often indicated in stenciling on the car end.

Whistle and bell signals

Whistle and horn use is prescribed by the rulebook, with various signals indicated by combinations of long ("—") and short ("o") blasts. The best known is the signal for approaching a grade crossing (— — o —) and for a train when starting (— —). Whistle posts (a "W" or "X"on a small signboard) alert crews to upcoming grade crossings. Prior to the era of portable radios, whistle signals let flagmen and other distant workers know of various situations (see the chart at right). Bell use is also specified by rule, and specific situations varied by railroad. Bells are typically rung when trains begin moving, when trains move within passenger station areas, and at grade crossings in some situations. Many railroads used signs with a "B" on a post (similar to a whistle post).

COMMON WHISTLE SIGNALS	
Sound	**Indication**
o	Apply brakes. Stop
— —	Release brakes Proceed.
o o o	When standing, back.
— — o	Approaching meeting or waiting points.
— o o o	Flagman protect rear of train.
o o o —	Flagman protect front of train.
— — — —	Flagman may return from west or south.
— — — — —	Flagman may return from east or north.
— — —	Train parted; to be repeated until answered
o o	Answer to any signal not otherwise provided for.
o o o o	Call for signal.
— — o —	Approaching public crossings at grade.

o = short sound
— = long sound

Helpers, pushers, and DPUs (distributed power units)

To keep from having to restrict train size over an entire subdivision or division because of a stretch of steep grade, railroads have long used helper locomotives to assist trains—situations include climbing a mountain grade or climbing out of a river valley. Passenger trains often had helpers added to the front; for freight trains, helpers (pushers) were typically added at the rear. Areas where helpers are based are called "helper districts," with helper locomotives stationed on a spur at the bottom of the grade. A train heading upgrade stops for the helper locomotive to be added. This was often done in front of the caboose (especially if the caboose was wooden); the helper could also be placed behind the caboose. Some railroads based this decision upon the weight of the helper locomotive. Helper operations are directed by the engineer at the head end (using whistle signals until onboard radio came into wide use). At the top of the grade, the helper is cut off (this could be done while in motion, or "on the fly," if the helper was behind the caboose). The helper then returns to the bottom of the grade to await another train. The number of helper districts has dropped significantly since the end of the steam era.

Remote (radio) control of helper and in-train locomotives became practical by the 1970s, and since the 1990s it has become more common for trains to operate with locomotives spread through the train consist, either in the middle or at the end of a train, with the remote locomotives controlled by the engineer at the head end. These are called distributed power units, or DPUs.

A Western Maryland 4-6-6-4 pushes a train near Cumberland, Md., in 1952. The coming of diesels eliminated many helper districts. George C. Corey

A helper locomotive waits in a spur for its next assignment. The phone box at left was vital for crews to communicate with the dispatcher in the days before radio. Jim Shaughnessy

Railway preservation

Railroads and their equipment are an important part of history, and fortunately many private and public individuals, organizations, and museums, along with active railroads, have worked to preserve equipment, photographs, and information. Among them are the National Railway Historical Society (nrhs.com), the Railway & Locomotive Historical Society (rlhs.org), and the Center for Railroad Photography & Art (railphoto-art. org). Many museums and groups have restored classic steam and diesel locomotives and rolling stock to operating condition. Among railroads, the Union Pacific is best-known for its recent restoration of Big Boy 4-8-8-4 no. 4014 as well as a 4-6-6-4 and 4-8-4; the Norfolk Southern has operated Norfolk & Western J-class 4-8-4 no. 611.

Freight operations

Modern railroads carry more freight than ever before. Ton-miles (one ton of freight carried one mile) for U.S. railroads peaked in 2014 at 1.85 million-million (compared to 1.96MM for trucks and 5.18MM total for all modes). Compare this to about 0.7MM ton-miles during the heavy traffic of World War II. Ton-miles have increased even though railroads have far less track than that period, and carloadings themselves are down. Railroads have become more efficient, with longer hauls, unit trains, and higher-capacity cars (about 110 tons of payload compared to 50 in the 1940s and 1950s).

Waybills, bills of lading

A lot of paperwork (albeit now computerized) is required to move freight cars. There are a number of forms required in the world of shipping, but the two most important and recognizable are the bill of lading and the waybill. When a shipper has material to transport, it contacts an agent of the serving railroad to order a car or cars. The railroad then delivers the cars and the shipper loads them. The shipper then fills out the bill of lading, which serves as the legal contract between the shipper and the railroad carrying the cargo and conveys title to the cargo. Historically this was done with the local agent; today it is done online (through Railinc, a subsidiary of the AAR). Through the late 1900s, the local agent created the waybill, which accompanied the shipment and listed the cargo in detail: it listed the shipper, the consignee, the rate, the origin and destination of the shipment, and the routing. A printed copy of the waybill accompanied the shipment (as part of the paperwork that conductors were required to maintain for the cars in their train). The bill of lading is the contract and title for the cargo being shipped; the waybill is essentially the bill provided to the shipper (often subject to the weight of the cargo, hence "weigh+bill").

U.S. railroad ton-miles, 1882-2020 (in millions of ton-miles)	
1882	39,302
1890	79,193
1900	141,597
1910	255,017
1920	413,699
1930	385,815
1940	379,201
1950	596,940
1960	572,309
1970	764,809
1980	932,000
1990	1,033,969
2000	1,465,960
2010	1,691,004
2020	1,439,814
All-time peak: 2014 (1,851,229); peak during World War II: 1944 (746,912) Source: AAR	

Types of freight trains

Train names. For timetable purposes, scheduled freight trains through the 1960s historically had numbers (one, two, or three digits), just like passenger trains (see Dispatching on page 76). Many had nicknames based on their typical consists, the businesses they served, or the territory they covered (an example was the Cotton Belt-Southern Pacific *Auto Parts West,* a

1970s train carrying GM auto parts and loaded auto racks from St. Louis to Los Angeles). Since the 1980s, it has become more common for railroads to assign train names based on their originating and destination points, the date of origination, priority level, and/or type of traffic carried. This can be a mix of letters and numbers, with each railroad having its own system. As an example, on the BNSF, train E-SUDSCM1-15A is an empty coal train (code E) operating from Superior, Wis. (SUD) to Spring Creek Mine, Mont. (SCM); it's the first section (1) and is scheduled to depart on the 15th of the month. The last letter can vary to indicate route or specific contents.

With the move from timetable-and-train-order operation to Centralized Traffic Control and track warrants, most trains now operate as extras. Thus, to the dispatcher, a train might be Extra 6347 West, but he and the operating department know that it's E-SUDSCM1-15A.

Railroads move freight using a variety of types of freight trains. Some handle specific types of freight or are dedicated to a specific commodity or shipper, others handle a variety of cars and traffic, and all vary in their priority level. Here's a summary of the main types of freight trains:

Local (way) freight. The local freight is responsible for picking up and setting out cars at industries along a specific route. Along main lines, locals generally operate as out-and-back operations from a main city, or run between two cities (usually at ends of subdivisions), often going outward one day and returning the next. They are often run as extras, allowing flexibility in scheduling. Their schedules are generally slow, allowing for time to switch cars at intermediate locations.

Merchandise. Through the 1950s, when railroads carried a lot of less-than-carload (LCL) freight (see page 53), merchandise trains were dedicated trains carrying all boxcars of LCL. These were high-speed, high-priority trains, and the cars they hauled were each on a regular, dedicated route and schedule operating between specific freight terminals and freight houses. Some railroads named their LCL service and had cars dedicated to the service, wearing special paint schemes (examples were New York Central's Pacemaker and Missouri Pacific's Eagle services).

Manifest. Manifest freights comprise multiple types of cars and shipments, operating from a specific origin to destination (which can be across a subdivision or an entire railroad). These can be regularly scheduled priority (fast freight) trains moving non-stop between major yards or cities, or slow trains carrying more empty cars or responsible for more en-route switching

Local freights set out and pick up cars at businesses along the line, as this Canadian Pacific train is doing at a grain elevator at Headingley, Man., in 1980. John Uckley

(the slowest of these are often called "junk trains"). Railroads prioritize trains by listing their specific duties; high-priority trains generally have tonnage limits and horsepower minimums (and get the newest, best locomotives) to ensure making their schedules.

Commodity. Commodity trains are non-unit trains that still carry a single product or type of product (grain, automobiles, auto parts, perishables, iron ore, coal). They can be high priority, such as auto parts or (historically) perishables and livestock, or low priority. Solid trains of coal cars from the steam era through the early 1960s often looked like unit trains, but they were not: they included cars collected from multiple mines and/or billed to a number of final destinations. Commodity trains carrying coal and grain can be low or high priority depending on the season and needs of the consignees.

Merchandise trains carried less-than-carload (LCL) freight. The New York Central had dedicated cars for this, which it called Pacemaker service. New York Central

Unit trains. A unit train is more than a train carrying the same commodity in all cars—it has all cars in its consist billed to the same consignee under a single waybill. Examples include a 110-car coal train loaded at a Wyoming mine destined for a power plant or a 100-car grain train loaded at a Midwestern elevator and billed to an export elevator in New York. The first true unit trains ran in the 1960s, and they became common starting in the 1970s, first with coal, then with other commodities including grain, taconite pellets, and ethanol. The shipper benefits from a lower rate, and the railroad gets a complete train that requires no en route switching or yard work.

Intermodal. The growth of trailer-on-flatcar (TOFC, or piggyback) in the 1950s led to dedicated trains. An early example was Pennsylvania's Chicago-New York (Kearny, N.J.) TrucTrain in 1955. By the 1960s and '70s, piggyback trains were often the hottest trains on a railroad, especially those carrying mail, LCL, UPS parcels, auto parts, and perishables. The 1980s saw big increases in international as well as domestic container traffic carried on double-stack well cars. Railroads began scheduling dedicated stack trains, many of which were devoted to single shipping companies such as American President Lines and Maersk. Container trains are generally slower (and longer and heavier) than piggyback trains.

Manifest freights carry a mix of shipments, usually in a variety of cars. A Union Pacific SD9043MAC leads an eastbound manifest train near North Bend, Neb., in 2004. Jeff Wilson

Commodity trains carry single products or classes of products, but with cars billed individually to multiple consignees. This is a Santa Fe perishable train in the 1950s. Santa Fe

Unit trains have all cars traveling under a single waybill to a single consignee. This is a unit train of ethanol cars on BNSF in 2006. The covered hopper is a buffer car. Jeff Wilson

Transfers. Cars are often interchanged as entire trains, especially at large cities where the railroads involved both have yards. The railroad possessing the cars is responsible for getting them to the receiving railroad, and does this with a transfer run that delivers the cars and returns as just a locomotive (or locomotive/caboose, called a "caboose hop"). Into the late 1900s, car per diem payments were calculated at 12:01 a.m., which led railroads to run transfers late at night to get them to the receiving railroad before that deadline.

Special movements: Railroads sometimes carry loads requiring special handling. These are usually oversize (tall/wide/long) or overweight loads such as electrical transformers and generators, boilers and other vessels, components for cranes and other heavy equipment, or long components such as girders, trusses, and wind-generator equipment. A special movement travels as its own train, even though it might be a single locomotive and a car or two. These generally have slow speed limits (often 25 mph or less) and may require

special rules such as not being able to pass cars on adjoining tracks.

Mixed trains. These are freight trains that also provide passenger accommodations (see Passenger Operations on page 63).

Less-than-carload (LCL) freight

Less-than-carload freight traffic is any package, parcel, or item that takes up less than a full car. Railroads began carrying LCL freight from their earliest days of operation, and it remained a major part of traffic into the 1950s. Parcels collected at stations and freight houses were consolidated, sorted and grouped at large freight terminals, then distributed across the country via a system of regularly scheduled boxcars that connected freight terminals of all railroads. The coming of the interstate highway system and the flexibility of highway transport led to trucking companies taking more and more of this traffic by the end of the 1950s. Most railroads had exited the LCL freight business by 1970.

Freight forwarders are independent companies that handle LCL parcels, billing shippers and collecting parcels, then shipping them as a carload lot via rail (or trailer). Railroads have always handled a great deal of forwarder traffic (in boxcars and trailers), but as carload shipments, since the forwarder (and not the railroad) bills the shippers of individual packages.

Intermodal

Intermodal is a type of traffic that can move between two transportation modes. For railroads, this means primarily truck trailers carried aboard flatcars and containers that can be moved among railcars, truck chassis, and ships. In railroading this is called of trailer-on-flatcar (TOFC, or piggyback) and container-on-flatcar (COFC) traffic.

The idea of securing a truck trailer to a flatcar—instead of transloading the contents from a trailer to a boxcar—was tried a few times in the early 1900s, but it was the Chicago Great Western carrying trailers of trucking companies between Chicago and Minneapolis starting in 1936 that led to modern intermodal transport. Piggyback traffic increased in the 1950s, leading in 1955 to the first dedicated piggyback flatcars—75-footers that could carry two trailers—and the formation of Trailer Train (TTX). This company, owned by several railroads, provides intermodal railcars on a pool basis to its owners. By the 1960s, piggyback traffic was booming, with 89-foot cars carrying pairs of 40-foot trailers in dedicated TOFC priority trains of merchandise, mail, and perishables.

Containers that could be moved from ship to truck and railroads were developed in 1956 by Malcolm

McLean, a trucker who formed Sea-Land. A number of container designs and systems were developed, including New York Central's Flexi-Vans, which used specialized flatcars and containers with bogies (wheel assemblies) that were added and removed at terminals.

The specialized containers and flatcars required for these systems were inefficient, and it was the adoption of standardized (ISO) container sizes and connectors for international shipping that led to a huge growth in railroad

Intermodal trains are solid trains of trailers and/or containers. They are often the highest-priority trains on modern railroads, especially those carrying mail and trailers of UPS and other LTL (less-than-truckload) carriers. This is a UPS train on Union Pacific Jeff Wilson

container traffic from the 1970s into the 1980s, continuing through today. Double-stack (well) cars improved efficiency, and by the 1980s and 1990s railroads were operating dedicated stack trains for international as well as domestic traffic. Container traffic continued increasing, passing TOFC in 1992. Today, containers account for more than 90 percent of rail intermodal traffic, and intermodal traffic today is just over half of total rail traffic, with dedicated yards and terminals to handle the traffic both inland and at international ports.

Workers unload LCL parcels from a boxcar ("peddler car") to a station on the Rutland in 1958. Jim Shaughnessy

A double-stack container train moves on Union Pacific. Jeff Wilson

Switching and car handling

Freight cars are handled in a number of ways. Individual cars (or groups of cars) can be picked up and dropped off on tracks at large and small industries and businesses. This can be a single tank car dropped off at a local fuel distributor, a cut of 10 cars to a large propane distributor, or a full train of 110 cars at a coal-fired power plant. As the "Types of freight trains" entry shows, cars carrying the same commodity are often grouped together in their own trains; unit trains are solid trains billed to a single customer under a single waybill.

Handling individual cars that are under their own waybills is called "loose-car railroading." Servicing local industries has historically been the job of the local, or way freight; on some lines today, switching is done by trains that carry through cars as well. Leaving a car at an industrial siding is called making a setout; collecting a car is a pickup.

When a local arrives at its terminating yard, all of the cars it has picked up are sorted by destination and grouped in through freights that take them in

A Chicago, Burlington & Quincy switcher on a local freight shoves two stock cars toward a livestock loading pen in Wyoming in 1955. William A. Akin

the proper direction. This might involve re-sorting cars at multiple intermediate yards and interchanging them among two or more railroads. When a car arrives at a classification yard near its destination, it is placed in a local freight, which sets it out at the customer.

Interchange traffic

Cars traveling long distances often originate on one railroad and terminate on another. Additional railroads may haul the cars between these carriers—especially true in the period when there were more than 100 Class I railroads, when it wasn't unusual for a car to travel over five or more railroads. The railroad originating the shipment is responsible for providing the car and billing the shipper; the originating railroad then divides the revenue among the carrying railroads based on mileage. The railroads originating and terminating the traffic get a higher proportion of the fee. A shipper can specify a specific routing and/or railroad(s); otherwise the originating railroad will generally keep the car online as long as possible before handing it off to the second railroad. The car's waybill specifies the routing. Railroads have contractural agreements with each other regarding when, where, and how cars are interchanged. This can mean a car or two at a rural junction, or a 100-car cut at an urban yard. How freight cars are supplied to shippers is governed by a set of rules (see freight car use rules on page 197 in Chapter 3).

Marine operations

It's sometimes more efficient to move cars across bodies of water than run trains around them. For this, railroads used both car ferries—self-propelled

A Central Vermont freight has pulled across the Conrail main line at Palmer, Mass., in 1993, and is now shoving a cut of cars onto the interchange track at the junction. Jeff Wilson

boats that docked at land terminals—and car floats, which are flat-top barges equipped with tracks that are moved by tugboats. Ferries were generally used for longer journeys (several operated on the Great Lakes). The most-famous car float operations were in New York City, where several railroads operated fleets of tugboats to carry car floats across the Hudson River to Manhattan.

Joint rate/route, trackage rights, haulage rights

Along with regular interchange traffic, railroads work together to get new business and handle cars together in different ways: sometimes by choice, sometimes ordered as conditions of a merger. The first method is with a joint rate and/or route. With this, two railroads agree to establish a single rate from an origin on one railroad to a destination on the other. The shipper pays one bill to one railroad, which divides the revenue in a negotiated split with the second railroad.

With trackage rights, one railroad (tenant) secures the right to operate its trains over a portion of a second railroad (the owner). The tenant pays the owner a fee based on amount of traffic (often by ton-mile). Each agreement specifies whether the tenant may or may not serve online customers on the route. Trackage rights are sometimes mutually agreed upon by railroads; they may also be granted by the FRA (earlier, ICC) as a condition of a merger or line sale. With trackage rights, the tenant and owner each operate

An Erie Lackawanna tugboat moves carfloats across the Hudson River in New York in 1966.

Richard J. Solomon

their own trains.

Haulage rights are related, but differ in key points. The railroad receiving haulage rights over the railroad granting the rights can negotiate rates with customers over an entire route; it also supplies the cars and assumes all loss/damage risk. The railroad granting the rights provides all service (track, crews, dispatching, and sometimes locomotives). In return, it receives a specified (negotiated) per-unit payment for each car handled. Haulage rights have become popular in the 2000s, with a growing number of agreements among railroads.

Run-through trains, detours

Run-through trains are those originating on one railroad and running through an interchange point to terminate on another railroad, usually with the same locomotives. Each railroad's crews operate the train on their own railroads, swapping at the interchange point. The two railroads involved agree on locomotive use (railroads often trade "horsepower hours") and operating logistics; the advantage is saving time in yard switching and interchanging cars.

If a line closes because of a wreck, flood, or other situation, a railroad may detour its trains over another neighboring railroad. Crews of the detouring railroad ride their trains, but the trains are operated by "pilot" engineers of the host railroad. Locomotives will generally be from the detouring railroad, but some railroads have signal systems that will require the host railroad to place one of its own locomotives in the lead. Rates and guidelines have been established for detour situations.

Precision Scheduled Railroading

Precision Scheduled Railroading (PSR) is an operating scheme where railroads operate trains on fixed schedules regardless of the type of cars or traffic involved, moving away from the focus of fixed unit trains or dedicated intermodal or commodity (such as grain or auto-rack) trains. One railroad describes PSR as a shift to a focus of "moving cars instead of moving trains." The idea was developed by the late Hunter Harrison, then-CEO of the Illinois Central in the 1990s. Canadian National acquired IC in 1998; during Harrison's time at CN (he became its COO in 2003) he implemented PSR on CN. Since then, variations have been adopted by other railroads. Although touted as having a goal of improving service, PSR has been criticized heavily by customers for poorer, delayed service and by operating unions, which claim jobs have been eliminated and employees given more work with less time to do it, with the charge that PSR benefits stockholders more than customers.

Yard operations

A classification yard is a collection of tracks that allows a railroad to sort cars and assemble trains to get them efficiently to their destinations. The goal of a yard is not to store cars: it's to get cars organized. Yards can be large or

In the mid-1960s, the Chicago, Burlington & Quincy entered into run-through agreements with New York Central (owner of the two trailing engines on this train on the CB&Q in the Twin Cities in Minnesota) as well as Union Pacific. J. David Ingles

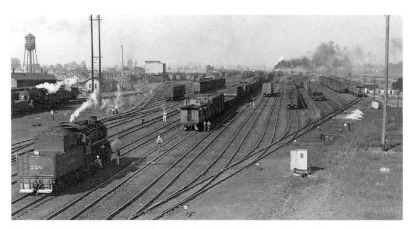

The Nickel Plate Road's Frankfort, Ind., yard in 1944 was busy, with multiple classification tracks and several locomotives and crews working to sort cars. Jay Williams collection

small. Early yards were often in urban areas in terminal cities, but by the 1950s railroads were building their main classification yards larger and away from congested urban areas. Yards follow three basic designs: through (with double-ended tracks); stub, where sorting tracks are single-ended; or combination. Where space allows, railroads use double-ended yards as they are far more efficient. Space limitations—especially in older yards in urban areas—result in yards with shorter, stub-ended tracks.

A typical yard layout features one or more arrival tracks, where inbound trains park prior to being sorted, and another departure track or two, where assembled trains are placed. A number of sorting tracks allow switch engines to shove cars to assemble trains. These tracks are often divided by direction at large yards.

Yards are either flat-ground or hump. In a flat-ground yard, switching locomotives move cuts of cars, pushing and pulling them onto various tracks to sort them. In a hump yard, a cut of cars is pushed over a hill and individual cars (or groups of cars) uncoupled. The car or cut then rolls downhill into one of several sorting (bowl) tracks. The groups of cars are collected at the far end of each bowl track when they're all sorted. Devices called "retarders" grip wheels as they start down the hump to control the speed of cars to ensure they travel the proper distance and provide smooth coupling (early hump yards had retarders operated by manual control; automated retarders, based on car weight, soon became standard). Hump yards became popular with automation in the 1950s and 1960s, but began to fall out of favor by the

Hump yards use gravity to sort cars. Here a boxcar rolls downgrade through the retarders toward the bowl tracks at Southern Pacific's Englewood Yard in Houston. Southern Pacific

2000s. Many railroads today have taken large hump yards out of service.

Engine servicing facilities are often located adjacent to classification yards. These were large complexes in the steam era, usually with a turntable and roundhouse where major and minor repairs could be made. Steam locomotives required frequent servicing and routine maintenance, so were swapped off of trains and serviced at subdivision points. Other servicing terminal features included a coaling tower (and/or fuel oil rack), sand tower, water tower, and ash pit. The coming of diesels greatly simplified engine servicing. They did not require frequent servicing (such as dumping ashes or cleaning flues) as did steam locomotives, so they were able to make longer runs; this led to smaller and fewer engine facilities, spaced more widely apart (usually at major terminals or yards). Most turntables and roundhouses were removed from service with the retirement of steam. With diesels, locomotives are fed at the fueling rack, topped with water and sand, and sent on their way.

Passenger trains and operations

Railroads have carried passengers since the first trains began operating in the 1830s. Passenger trains remained a primary means of transportation well into the 20th century, until the automobile began dominating short-distance travel in the 1930s. By the late 1950s, improved highways and the emergence

Steam-era engine facilities featured ash pits (left), water towers, and numerous shop buildings. TRAINS magazine collection

of jet planes and low-cost airfares doomed most long-distance passenger trains, with the elimination of mail contracts meaning most railroad-operated passenger trains were losing money by the 1960s. Railroads were not free to simply drop passenger service as they desired: the ICC had to grant permission, which often was not granted. The emergence of Amtrak in 1971 saved long-distance trains on major routes. Commuter rail remains a viable and popular option in many cities, metro areas, and regions.

There have been many types of passenger trains, ranging from high-speed luxury trains to slow-moving locals. All were first-class trains by timetable, giving them priority over freight trains.

Commuter totals are in brackets in chart on the following page (the overall total includes inter-city as well as commuter; commuter wasn't counted as a separate category until 1930). The all-time peak (in millions) was 95,663 in 1944, during WWII.

Types of passenger trains

Long-distance flagship (primary). As the name implies, long-distance trains connect terminals in distant cities hundreds or even thousands of miles apart (examples were New York Central's New York-Chicago *20th Century Limited* and Santa Fe's Chicago-Los Angeles *Super Chief*), with overnight (and sometimes multi-day) schedules. Most railroads designated one train on each main route as the primary, or flagship train, which had the fastest schedule with the most luxurious accommodations. These typically stopped only at major cities en route. Some, such as the *Century,* were strictly first-class (all-Pullman) trains. Primary trains carried Railway Post

Chicago, Burlington & Quincy's westbound *Morning Zephyr,* a stainless-steel streamlined day train, passes through Oregon, Ill., behind E5 diesels in the mid-1960s. Craig Willett

Office cars, but rarely carried much (if any) express traffic, leaving that to secondary trains. These trains had a railroad's newest, best-maintained cars and locomotives; as they were re-equipped, their old equipment was bumped to secondary and other trains.

Accommodation (secondary). Secondary or accommodation trains are long-distance trains that travel the same route as a railroad's primary train, but on a slower schedule (usually due to having more stops, not slower speeds). They generally had a mix of coach and sleeping cars, and often carried a great deal of mail and express ("head-end") traffic. An example is Northern Pacific's Chicago-Seattle *Mainstreeter,* the secondary train to the railroad's *North Coast Limited* flagship. Additional secondary trains ran on additional routes (often secondary main lines) not covered by flagship trains.

Day. Day trains depart in the morning and arrive at their destinations in the afternoon or evening, eliminating the need for sleeping cars. An example

U.S. passenger-miles: 1882-2020 (In millions; a passenger-mile is the movement of 1 passenger for 1 mile)	
1882	7,688
1890	12,522
1900	16,038
1910	32,338
1920	47,370
1930	26,876 [commuter: 6,669]
1940	23,816 [3,997]
1950	31,790 [4,990]
1957	25,914 [4,828]
1960	21,300 [4,200]
1970	10,800 [4,600]
1980	11,100 [6,500]
1990	13,200 [7,100]
2000	15,000 [9,400]
2010	17,200 [10,800]
2020	9,500 [6,000]

Sources: USDOT, Bureau of Transportation Statistics; Amtrak annual reports; AAR Railroad Facts

was Chicago, Burlington & Quincy's *Morning* and *Afternoon Zephyrs* between Chicago and Minneapolis/St. Paul). Day trains were often all-coach trains, but many included parlor cars for first-class accommodations, and could include a diner.

Troop. The U.S. military once relied heavily on railroads to move personnel. The peak period for troop trains was World War II, with another spike in operations during the Korean War in the early 1950s. These ran as extras, and were primarily made up of available secondary equipment. They had standard personnel (conductors, porters) plus a railroad-military liaison and an on-board military commander.

Special. Through the 1960s, railroads would often run special trains for groups and events if enough passengers were involved. Examples included extra trains to cities for football games or sporting events; group conventions (such as Boy Scouts and Shriners); and tours and outings. These trains could be run as extra movements or as second sections of existing trains.

Mail/express. Into the 1960s, railroads carried a great deal of stored mail and express (Railway Express Agency) traffic. These cars operated on set schedules, and on busy routes were handled by dedicated trains. These trains sometimes carried a single coach at the rear; others offered no passenger accommodations (but were first-class trains operated as passenger trains). They were usually numbered but sometimes named; many railroads operated express trains named the *Fast Mail.* Mail and express traffic dropped significantly through the 1960s.

The *Panama Limited* was Illinois Central's flagship Chicago-New Orleans train. It's shown here at Homewood, Ill., in June 1969. J. David Ingles

Northern Pacific's *Mainstreeter* carried a lot of head-end traffic. It was the railroad's secondary train to its *North Coast Limited*. It's at St. Paul, Minn., in 1967. J. David Ingles

Milk trains. Milk trains were a type of express train that served dairy operations, primarily in the Northeast and New England (Boston, New York, Philadelphia), but also in Chicago and some other cities. They were first-class trains, sometimes having a trailing coach, but primarily responsible for bringing inbound loaded milk cars to the city in the morning and distributing empties to dairies on the outbound run in the afternoon or evening. Trucks captured most of this traffic by the 1950s.

Local. These were short-distance trains (often between end points of a subdivision or on a branch line). They stopped at all stations, giving them slow schedules, and were responsible for picking up and dropping off mail and express. They were often short, with a coach or two (and possibly a coach-baggage combine). The schedules of many low-ridership local trains were covered by gas-electric motor cars ("doodlebugs") or Rail Diesel Cars (RDCs).

Mixed. Mixed trains were locals that featured a single passenger car (typically a coach-baggage combine) at the end of a local freight train; this

Troop trains ("Mains") were extra trains exclusively for moving military personnel. Trains magazine collection

A westbound Burlington mail-express train rolls near Keenesburg, Colo., in 1949. The train's consist is all express cars except for a single trailing coach. Joe Schick, Jim Seacrest collection

car generally served as the caboose as well. Some railroads provided mixed service by selling seats in a standard caboose, or with cabooses with extra seats and a baggage-express storage area. They were used on low-ridership lines where railroads were obligated to provide passenger service.

Commuter. Commuter trains carry passengers into and out of large cities, with frequent trains inbound in the morning and outbound in the afternoon. Cars are coaches with high-capacity seating. Older coaches converted with

A westbound Erie train behind an Alco PA carries several milk cars (including two flatcars with milk tanks) as head-end traffic in the mid-1940s. Trains magazine collection

additional seats were common through the 1950s; high-capacity double-deck ("gallery") cars became common in the 1960s and later. Modern operation is usually by a single diesel in push-pull style, with an operator's bay in the end of the rear passenger car (or a non-engined "power car") when the train is in "push" mode. Operation can be by an individual railroad, or by a railroad or Amtrak under the auspices of a local commuter authority.

Local trains hit all stops along a route. This Chicago Great Western local is leaving the Twin Cities with an F unit pulling an RPO, baggage car, and coach. TRAINS magazine collection

Mixed trains are freight trains that offer passenger accommodations, using a trailing combine or coach. This is Great Northern's Hutchinson, Minn., mixed train. William D. Middleton

Mail by rail

From the 1860s to the 1960s, the U.S. Postal Service contracted with railroads to carry mail. These contracts were lucrative, and mail was the highest-priority commodity carried by rail. This traffic fell into two categories: cars of stored mail transported between cities, which were carried in dedicated mail-express trains (in baggage-express cars) or as head-end traffic in passenger trains; and mail that was sorted en route in Railway Post Office (RPO) cars. On these cars, clerks (postal employees) sorted mail, picking up bags at stations on the fly by using hooks on the side of RPO cars and

A Chicago Metra commuter train eases into the 14th Street coach yard in 1992. Commuter trains carry passengers in and out of large metro areas on frequent schedules. Jeff Wilson

dropping off mail bags by tossing them onto platforms. The peak for mail operations was the late 1920s, when railroads hosted 1,500 RPO routes serving more than 200,000 miles of railroad. By the 1950s, as passenger train routes began dropping, many mail contracts were eliminated. The postal service transitioned to automated regional sorting centers in the early 1960s, with most storage mail moving to trucks. Although a couple of RPO routes on the East Coast hung on through the 1970s, virtually all rail mail traffic ended with the elimination of contracts in 1967. Railroads still carry a lot of mail and express traffic, but it is in truck trailers as piggyback movements in freight trains.

The Pullman Co.

The Pullman Palace Car Co., founded by George M. Pullman, began building sleeping cars in the 1860s. By 1900, after acquiring additional manufacturers and reorganizing as The Pullman Co., Pullman had a virtual monopoly on sleeper cars and operations in the U.S. Pullman built the cars and operated them as well, with railroads receiving payments for carrying the cars, many of which operated on routes crossing multiple railroads. This monopoly was ultimately found to be illegal: Pullman in 1944 was forced to divest itself of either the operating or carbuilding operation. The company chose to sell its operating division (the Pullman Co.) to a group of 57 railroads, and kept its carbuilding division (as Pullman-Standard, after acquiring Standard Steel Car Co. in 1929), which would survive, mainly building freight cars, until 1982). This freed other manufacturers to build sleeping cars, which they did; all sleeping cars were leased back to the new Pullman Co., which continued operating sleepers. The rapid downturn in passenger traffic that began in the late 1950s and continued through the 1960s caused railroads to begin dropping sleeping-car routes and service. The Pullman Co. ceased operations at the end of 1968, ending all car leases and liquidating its assets.

Amtrak

Amtrak—officially the National Rail Passenger Corporation—is a quasi-public agency that took over almost all intercity passenger service on May 1, 1971. Railroads had been losing passengers through the 1960s, and the elimination of mail contracts in that decade took away profitability. By that time, railroads all wanted to get out of the passenger business.

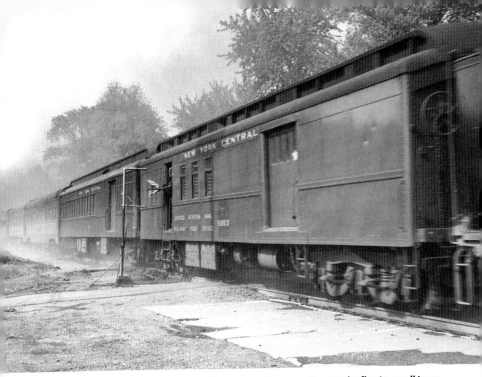

The catcher arm on a Railway Post Office car snatches a mailbag on the fly at a small town along the New York Central in the 1940s. A.C. Kalmbach

Railroads had to pay a fee to rid themselves of their passenger obligations and turn operations over to Amtrak; the Rio Grande, Rock Island, and Southern were all initially holdouts, choosing to continue operations rather than paying to discontinue trains. When Amtrak (Railpax until just before operations began) started, many routes were eliminated and others consolidated. Amtrak aquired used locomotives and passenger cars from previous owners, selecting the best equipment of what was available. Much of it, however, was old and had suffered from deferred maintenance.

Amtrak acquired much of its Northeast Corridor trackage (Washington, D.C., to Boston) in 1976, and now owns other stretches of track as well. Amtrak increased ridership, acquired new locomotives and freight cars, and upgraded facilities in the period since its formation, and continues operating while receiving government funding. Amtrak carried 15.8 million passengers in 1972 and a record 32.0 million passengers in 2019. As of 2022, the company owns more than 400 locomotives and about 2,100 passenger cars. Amtrak also operates commuter service in several cities in conjunction with state and regional agencies.

Several heavyweight Pullman cars trail a Chicago & North Western train in the 1940s. Pullman was the exclusive operator of sleeping cars into the 1960s. TRAINS magazine collection

Amtrak's eastbound *Pennsylvanian* is at Tipton, Pa., in 2008. The locomotive is P42B no. 75, with Amfleet cars trailing. Alex Mayes

Via Rail Canada

Via Rail Canada was formed in 1977, taking over Canadian National's intercity passenger operations. Via assumed Canadian Pacific's passenger operations the following year. It is a Crown corporation, dependent on funding from the Canadian government. As with Amtrak, Via cut and consolidated routes and acquired used equipment from its predecessor railroads. New locomotives and cars helped to increase ridership; Via carried 4.7 million passengers in 2018, and as of 2022 owned about 80 locomotives and 600 passenger cars.

Railway Express Agency

Express traffic comprises small package and parcel service as well as larger business shipments where expedited shipping time is desired. Through the 1960s, the Railway Express Agency (REA) provided this service for railroads. REA traced its roots to the American Railway Express Agency (AREA), which was formed during World War I when the government took over the

Via Rail Canada was formed in 1977. Here a train poses behind an FP9 shortly after Via's creation in the late 1970s. VIA Rail

country's seven existing express companies and combined their operations. In 1929, a group of 86 Class I railroads purchased the assets of AREA and formed a new company, Railway Express Agency, which became the sole provider of express services on American railroads.

Railroads provided space on passenger trains (in baggage and express cars), with trucks based at individual agencies (usually railroad stations) providing delivery and pickup services. By using passenger trains for shipments, several days could be cut from delivery times (five days cross country, compared to eight to ten for standard less-than-carload (LCL) service). Express prices were generally about double that of LCL rates.

The company provided services similar to today's UPS and FedEx, carrying small individual parcels as well as large business shipments, including carload and refrigerated shipments. REA was a large operation: in its heyday, it had 22,000 offices across the country and handled more than

230 million shipments per year. The downturn in passenger trains, coupled with restrictions requiring REA to use rail transportation on most routes (instead of more-efficient, more-flexible tractor-trailers) and the growth of private companies such as United Parcel Service, led to a big dropoff in REA's business by the 1960s. The company declared bankruptcy in 1975; operations were suspended and all assets liquidated later that year.

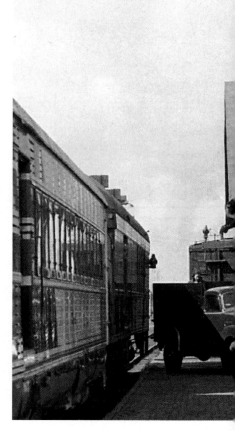

Dispatching: controlling train movements

Establishing rules for train movements became vital as soon as a railroad placed a second train in service. Getting trains over the line quickly and safely is paramount—there's no situation in railroading worse than accidentally giving two trains the authority to be on the same track at the same time. Railroads have used combinations of several methods for doing this, including timetables, signals, telegraph messages, train orders, and track warrants. All fall under control of the dispatcher, who has the responsibility for routing trains over a given portion of railroad.

Operating rules

Railroad operations are governed by a detailed set of rules, spelled out by number in a rulebook. Many railroads publish or published their own rules, but by the 1960s it was common for railroads to share rulebooks. Today, most western railroads follow the *General Code of Operating Rules* (GCOR), which superseded the *Consolidated Code of Operating Rules,* while eastern railroads follow the rulebook published by the Northeast Operating Rules Advisory Committee (NORAC). The goal is safe operation, with specific rules governing rights of trains; how train orders and warrants are to be used

A Railway Express Agency truck (right) and mail contractor pickup truck (left) transfer parcels and mail from a local passenger train at Oskaloosa, Iowa, in the 1950s. Robert Milner

and interpreted; whistle, horn, and bell usage; signal indications and meanings; and employee conduct rules. Railroad employees are required to know the rules and pass rules examinations; violating a rule can result in suspension or termination.

What makes a train a train? The rulebook definition is "an engine, with or without cars, displaying a marker." Rule books are specific about when markers can be added and removed, and what colors must be displayed (red to the rear). Oil lanterns on the back of a caboose served as markers through the early diesel era, with electric lights after that (and flags in the daytime), and since the 1980s, an end-of-train device (ETD) with light. Thus a helper locomotive returning by itself down a mountain is a train as long as it has a rear marker; a cut of 100 cars plus a caboose coupled to a locomotive in a yard isn't a train until the marker is in place on the rear car.

Centralized Traffic Control signals guard a junction on Canadian Pacific at Sturtevant, Wis. The three-headed signal displays red-over-red-over-red, meaning "stop." Jeff Wilson

Dispatching methods

Communication is key regardless of the dispatching method. Telegraph was used starting in the 1850s, with lines soon strung along most railroad routes. Telegraph would be used for dispatcher-to-operator communications into the 1940s, and on some lines into the 1960s. Railroads strung their own telephone lines in many areas starting in the early 1900s, and by the 1950s most communication was by phone—either railroads' own lines or commercial lines. Railroads began installing radio in some areas (in locomotives and cabooses) by the 1940s, but radio and microwave technology didn't become widespread until the 1960s as radio size and cost both dropped. By the 1980s, radio became the primary communication means between dispatchers and train crews.

Here are several ways railroads have controlled trains, and how they have evolved over the years. Chapter 4 includes additional information on the various signal systems.

Timetable and train-order (TT&TO) operation: The most common method of controlling train movements into the 1960s was by an employee timetable. The timetable lists all stations on a given route (usually by subdivision) with train schedules, including arrival and departure times as well as meeting points. The basis of the system was grouping trains into classes by superiority: first-class trains (passenger and express) were superior to second-class (priority freight) which were superior to third class (local freight). Additional ("extra") trains could be run; these were inferior to all other trains. In addition, trains of one direction (usually eastward or northward) were superior to trains of the same class in the other direction. A train may not leave a station prior to its scheduled departure time, and trains were required to clear the main line for all superior trains.

Dispatchers could modify the schedule to accommodate late trains, extra trains, and other situations by issuing train orders—written instructions transcribed by operators at local stations who then handed the orders to passing train crews (orders were tied to hoops that the operator held up; the engineer and conductor caught them with an arm). An example would be moving a meeting point to a siding at a different station.

Timetable and train-order operation worked well in the era when railroads had stations located every 10 to 20 miles. By the 1960s and later, railroads were closing many stations, eliminating operator positions. That and the growth of onboard radio communication led to the move to track warrants and other similar systems.

Some lines controlled by TT&TO were "dark," or unsignaled; many had lineside signals, either manual blocks or automatic block signals to provide an additional layer of safety.

Manual blocks. In a manual-block system, operators at stations set signal indications based on information from the dispatcher or neighboring block

SECOND CLASS	FIRST CLASS			Office Open Week Days	Signs	Distance from Ravenna	STATIONS	Sidings	Other Tracks	Office Open Sundays	FIRST CLASS		SECOND CLASS	
Daily Freight 75	Daily Freight 79	Daily Passenger 41	Daily Passenger 43								Daily Passenger 42	Daily Passenger 44	Daily Freight 80	Daily Freight 78
A.M. L 8.00	A.M. 12.30	P.M. L10.05	A.M. L 1.50	Continuous	B.O.K.R. T.W.Y&.	127.74	RAVENNA	Yard	Yard	Continuous	A.M. A 3.00	P.M. A 5.10	A.M. A 4.45	P.M. A10.45
				No Office.		133.41	SWEETWATER		9	No Office.	2.50	5.00	4.35	10.35
8.15	12.40	10.15	1.57	No Office.	F.	137.91	HAZARD	76	34	No Office.	2.42	4.49	4.25	10.25
8.30	12.50	10.25	2.02	7:00 a.m. to 3:00 p.m. 3:00 p.m. to 5:30 a.m.	W.	144.27	LITCHFIELD	138	35	12 mid. to 5:00 a.m. 9:00 p.m. to 12 mid.	2.34	4.38	4.15	10.00
8.45	1.00	10.38	2.10	7:00 a.m. to 4:00 p.m.		153.65	MASON	78	34	Closed.	2.21	4.24	3.55	9.37
9.05	1.13	10.52	2.21	7:00 a.m. to 4:00 p.m.		160.00	ANSLEY	125	42	Closed.	2.12	4.15	3.40	9.25
9.20	1.23	11.09	2.32	8:00 a.m. to 5:00 p.m.		167.55	BERWYN	104	32	Closed.	2.03	4.00	3.25	9.07
9.35	1.33	11.22	2.42	Continuous	C.W.Yd.	176.13	BROKEN BOW	Yard W76	Yard	Continuous	1.53	3.45	3.00	8.50
10.00	1.53	11.43	3.00	7:00 a.m. to 4:00 p.m.		184.72	MERNA	128	44	Closed.	1.41	3.27	2.35	8.25
10.20	2.35	11.59	3.12	11:30p.m. to 3:00 p.m.	W.	195.62	ANSELMO	138	44	12 mid. to 7:30 a.m. 11:30 p.m. to 3:30 p.m. 11:30 p.m. to 12 mid.	1.29	3.08	2.15	8.05
10.45	2.50	12.14	3.25	No Office.	F.	207.71	LINSCOTT	125	10	No Office.	1.15	2.50	1.58	7.45
11.15	3.10	12.33	3.39	7:00 a.m. to 4:00 p.m.	W.	215.47	DUNNING	76	43	1:00 p.m. to 4:00 p.m.	1.06	2.39	1.45	7.30
11.30	3.20	12.44	3.48	Continuous	C.W.	225.27	HALSEY	125	45	12 mid. to 7:00 a.m. 12 noon to 3:00 p.m. 11:00 p.m. to 12 mid.	12.55	2.27	1.30	7.15
11.50	3.35	12.55	3.59	No Office.	F.	235.18	NATICK	88	26	Closed.	12.43	2.10	1.10	7.00
12.10	3.50	1.10	4.11	6:00 a.m. to 3:00 a.m.		247.56	THEDFORD	136	20	Closed.	12.35	2.00	1.00	6.45

Ravenna and Seneca—Sub-division
ALLIANCE DIVISION. TIME TABLE No. 53. EFFECTIVE DEC. 7, 1947.
WESTWARD / EASTWARD — Capacity of Sidings / Other Tracks

This Burlington timetable from 1947 shows first- and second-class trains, the status of stations (times they are open), capacity of sidings and other tracks, milepost locations of stations, and distance between stations. **Bold times indicate meets.** Jeff Wilson collection

operator. The "block" was the stretch of track between signals (usually between stations), which could be 10 or more miles long. The signals were usually the station's train-order boards (more about signals in Chapter 4).

Although manual blocks worked well for lightly trafficked lines, operator error was always a possibility, especially as train speeds and the number of trains increased. Manual block systems were also limiting in terms of capacity because of the length of the blocks. Most busy lines shifted to other types of control by the 1900s. The manual block system, however, remained a practical option for lines with lower levels of traffic. Some secondary lines that saw just a few trains per day remained under manual block control into the 1950s.

Automatic block signals (ABS). Automatic signal systems offered several advantages over the manual block system. Blocks could be divided into smaller segments, allowing higher train capacity (1- to 2-mile blocks are common). Trackside signals convey the status of not just the upcoming block, but the two blocks ahead as well. By the 1890s, railroads had equipped many high-traffic main lines with ABS; its use would continue growing into the 1900s.

Absolute-permissive block signals (APB). A refinement of ABS in the early 1900s, absolute-permissive signals also respond to train direction, offering better protection for opposing movements. With APB, for example, a southbound train passing a signal at a passing siding would "tumble down" all opposing (northward) signals to red through the location of the next passing siding. Signals behind that train, however, would go to yellow and green as the train cleared, allowing a trailing southbound train to follow the first train at a safe distance. As train speeds increased, zones and levels of protection increased, indicating occupancy two or three blocks ahead instead of one. Many railroads added additional signal indications, usually with blinking green and yellow lights. Most main lines today are protected by some version of APB signaling.

With either ABS or APB, it's important to understand that the signals indicate occupancy, and don't imply permission to be on a specific track: That permission comes through timetables and train orders, track warrants, or other authority from the dispatcher via radio.

Centralized Traffic Control (CTC). Centralized Traffic Control allows a remote central dispatcher to guide train movements at a control panel by directly controlling turnouts and signals at passing sidings and junctions along a route. Intermediate signals between control points (sidings and junctions) are automatic (ABS or APB). No train orders, warrants, or orders are needed—trains just follow signal indications. The CTC controls are interlocked, preventing the dispatcher from setting up conflicting movements. The first system was installed in 1927—a 40-mile stretch on New York Central. The system proved popular, greatly increasing the capacity of single-track lines in particular (compared to TT&TO), and by the 1950s CTC had become the primary dispatching method for busy main lines, with one dispatcher able to efficiently control hundreds of miles of main line. Systems have evolved from mechanical switches and lights on control panels to microprocessor-controlled, screen-based systems.

Track warrant control, direct traffic control, occupancy control system. The widespread use of onboard radio systems (and their increased reliability), along with the elimination of most lineside railroad stations, led to control systems that allow direct communication between the dispatcher and train crews. Since the 1990s, most lines not controlled by CTC now use track warrant control (TWC) or a similar system. With TWC, dispatchers issue track warrants to train crews by radio, giving them authority to be in specific defined area until a specific time. Warrants are standardized forms; as dispatchers dictate them, they instruct crews to check certain boxes and enter station names or milepost numbers. Direct traffic control (DTC) is similar, but the railroad is divided into blocks, with warrants allowing trains to be in one or more (sequential) blocks. Canadian lines use a similar system, but call it OCS, or occupancy control system.

Interlockings: In 1870, the first U.S. rail junction with signals and turnouts that were "interlocked"—mechanically interconnected, ensuring that clearing one route through a crossing or diverging track would automatically lock out any other conflicting route—was installed. The interlocking system ensured that an operator couldn't accidentally align turnouts and signals against a route already cleared. Operators control interlockings at local structures. Most were towers, housing the operator and control panels and levers on the top floor and the mechanism on the bottom floor (single-story installations weren't as common, and were typically called "cabins"). The trackwork within the operator's control is known as the "interlocking plant." Operators worked in conjunction with dispatchers in prioritizing train movements through the plant.

An estimated 4,200 interlocking plants were in operation in the mid-

Through the 1960s, most major junctions were controlled locally by interlockings, with towers housing the operator and control equipment. Mark Vanderboom

1950s; after that time, the number began dwindling as many were transferred to control directly by dispatchers via CTC, or by automatic signal circuits at many simple crossings. By the 1990s only a few hundred interlocking plants remained in service; they are now virtually gone from the railroading scene.

Positive Train Control (PTC). Positive Train Control is a series of systems designed to track train locations and speeds and automatically apply brakes and stop trains if potential collisions or dangerous situations are detected. Examples are a train approaching another train on the same track, a train speeding in a restricted area, or a train approaching an open turnout. The goal is to reduce the chances of accidents caused by human error. The Federal Railroad Administration directed railroads to implement PTC as part of the Rail Safety Improvement Act of 2008, with an initial goal of having it operable by December 2015 (later extended). When it began operating in December 2020, PTC protected more than 57,000 miles of track. The FRA requires PTC on all lines carrying more than 5 million gross tons annually, as well as lines hosting passenger trains and those carrying specific hazardous materials. Like signals, PTC serves as a safety overlay for other dispatching systems such as track warrants and CTC.

1827 The Baltimore & Ohio Railroad is chartered; it broke ground the following year.

1830 23 miles of track are in operation in the U.S.

1836 First Canadian Railroad, the Champlain & St. Lawrence, opens.

1850 There are 9,021 miles of track in service in the U.S.

1857 Work begins on the first major Mexican railway: between Mexico City and Veracruz.

1863 Standard gauge of 4'-8½" is adopted.

This is a re-creation of the *Stourbridge Lion*, the first steam locomotive operated in the U.S. It was built in England and shipped to the U.S. in 1829. Delaware & Hudson

1865 Steel is first used for rail, replacing iron.

1869 The Golden Spike is driven, completing the first transcontinental railroad at Promontory Summit, Utah.

George Westinghouse introduces the straight air brake system.

1872 Westinghouse introduces the automatic air brake system.

1873 Eli Janney patents his design for a knuckle-style coupler.

1886 Remaining railroads in the South with 5-foot gauge convert to standard gauge.

1893 The Railroad Safety Appliance Act mandates automatic brakes and knuckle couplers.

1900 There are 192,556 route-miles of track in service in the U.S.

1907 Danger: 4,534 railroad employees are killed on duty, the all-time high.

1910 A total of 1,306 railroads are in operation in the U.S.

1916 Railroad mileage in U.S. peaks at 254,037 miles.

1917

The U.S. Government assumes control of the country's railroads during World War I through the United States Railroad Administration (USRA); control lasts into 1920.

Chicago, Burlington & Quincy's *Zephyr* was the first diesel-powered streamliner. It's shown here on its 1934 exhibition tour. Jeff Wilson collection

1920

U.S. railroad employment peaks at 2,076,000.

1929

Railway Express Agency (REA) is formed from the former American Railway Express.

1930

There are 2.28 million freight cars and 52,130 passenger cars in service.

1933

The first continuous welded rail (CWR) is laid in the U.S.

1934

The first streamliners hit the rails: Union Pacific's (distillate) M-10000 and Chicago, Burlington & Quincy's diesel-powered *Zephyr*.

The Association of American Railroads (AAR) is formed, replacing the American Railway Association (ARA) and several other groups.

The Electro-Motive Corp. FT was the first road freight diesel. It revolutionized railroading. It's shown here on the Rio Grande during its demonstration tour.
TRAINS magazine collection

1939 Electro-Motive's FT freight diesel embarks on its demonstration tour.

1950 U.S. railroads operate 26,680 steam, 15,396 diesel, and 827 electric locomotives.

The last reciprocating steam locomotive built in the U.S., Norfolk & Western 244, is turned out by the railroad's shops. Norfolk & Western

1952 Diesel locomotives outnumber steam locomotives for the first time.

1953 Last domestic steam locomotive is built, Norfolk & Western 0-8-0 no. 244.

1955 Trailer Train (later renamed TTX Co.) is founded, providing a pool of inter-modal equipment for members.

1957 The New York, Ontario & Western—a 541-mile line in New York—is the first major railroad to be abandoned.

1959 General Electric enters the road-diesel market with its Universal line of locomotives.

Trailer Train (later TTX) spurred intermodal operations by providing an equipment pool to its member railroads. This is one of its first 75-foot piggyback flats. J. David Ingles collection

The last EMD F units, electric/diesel-electric FL9s for New Haven, were built in 1960.
EMD

1960 EMD builds last F units, FL9s for New Haven.

1968 The New York Central and Pennsylvania railroads merge to form Penn Central. The new railroad declares bankruptcy in 1970.

1971 Amtrak is formed, taking control of most intercity passenger service in the U.S.

1975 REA Express (formerly Railway Express Agency) declares bankruptcy and is liquidated.

1976 Conrail is formed with the merger of several bankrupt Northeastern railroads.

1977 Via Rail Canada is formed, assuming control of Canadian intercity passenger trains.

A new ALC42 pulls an Amtrak train in 2022.
David Lassen

1980 Congress passes the Staggers Rail Act, effectively deregulating most aspects of the railroad industry.

CSX is formed with merger of Chessie System and Seaboard Coast Line/Family Lines.

1982 Norfolk Southern is formed with merger of Norfolk & Western and Southern Railway.

1992 Railroads begin using AEI (automatic equipment identification) tags and scanners.

1994 Last four-axle road locomotives are built (GP60s for Southern Pacific)

1995 BNSF Railway is formed with merger of Burlington Northern and Santa Fe.

Canadian National Railway is privatized.

1996 Mexican railroads are privatized.

2005 GM sells General Motors Locomotive Group (formerly Electro-Motive Division) to Greenbriar Equity Group and Berkshire Partners; the new company is Electro-Motive Diesel.

2010 U.S. companies operate 138,576 miles of railroad.

2012 The last DC-traction-motor diesel is built.

2019 General Electric sells its locomotive manufacturing division (GE Rail) to Wabtec; it becomes Wabtec's GE Transportation division.

2020 Positive Train Control (PTC) is activated on 57,000 miles of trackage.

Locomotives

■ Locomotives are the powered rail vehicles that pull trains. Since railroading's early years, they have grown in size, power, and complexity. They have been built with various power sources and driving mechanisms including steam, steam-turbine-electric, electric, diesel-electric, gas turbine-electric, and diesel-hydraulic. Modern locomotives are powerful, microprocessor-controlled, high-tech machines, but they trace their roots to the first simple steam locomotives of the 1830s.

Dieselization was nearing completion in 1955 as this fireman on a five-year-old Louisville & Nashville F unit looks at a recently retired steam locomotive. Since then, steam has vanished—as have cab units—and diesel technology has advanced significantly. William A. Akin

Modern diesels, like this SD70M, are high-tech marvels. They feature microprocessor control, high-efficiency engines, and most now have AC traction motors. Jeff Wilson

Reciprocating steam locomotives—which generate back-and-forth movement of pistons in cylinders which is then converted by rods to rotary motion at the wheels—were the primary locomotive type from the 1830s to the 1940s. Steam locomotives were powerful and worked well. They were not efficient in fuel usage—most of the heat generated was wasted—but that wasn't a major concern as coal was relatively inexpensive. Steam locomotives' downsides included their lack of adaptability, as different jobs and situations required locomotives of different sizes and designs, with varying wheel arrangements, driver sizes, locomotive weight, and other specifications. They were also major sources of pollution, which into the early 1900s wasn't a factor in the open countryside but was of increasing concern in urban areas. The main drawback for railroads was that steam locomotives were maintenance-intensive, requiring constant care and an army of workers to repair and feed them and keep them running.

Electric power came to railroads by the turn of the 20th century. "Traction" motors mounted to driving axles become common for streetcars in the 1890s, with power taken from overhead wires. This evolved to larger self-propelled inter-city passenger cars ("interurbans") as well as heavy electric (high-horsepower) locomotives that pulled trains rivaling those carried by steam locomotives by the 1910s. Electric locomotives are powerful and efficient, have high tractive effort at low speeds, and are adaptable to many situations including fast running or tough grades. Their main downside was the cost of building and maintaining the needed infrastructure, namely overhead wires (or third rails) and electric-supply substations.

The diesel-electric (usually simply called "diesel") takes advantage of the efficiency and flexibility of electric locomotives by bringing the power plant and generator on board. The diesel engine was developed in the 1890s and takes its name from its inventor, Rudolf Diesel. However, into the early 1900s diesel engines were large and slow—mainly suitable for stationary power plants. By the 1920s, technology had progressed to allow smaller engines that would fit on a locomotive platform. Diesel-electric locomotives grew in popularity for switching and passenger service in the 1930s and finally for freight trains in the 1940s. Diesel-electrics were efficient and proved to be adaptable to most uses. Although not as powerful as large steam locomotives initially, multiple diesel locomotives could be electrically connected and operated as a single locomotive, increasing their versatility.

Other types of locomotives were tried, but diesels prevailed for most situations, with electrics still in use in some areas, mainly for fast passenger service. Although most railroads saw the inevitable coming of diesels by the mid-1940s, a few railroads (especially coal haulers such as Norfolk & Western and Chesapeake & Ohio) clung to steam, with N&W building its last road steam locomotive in 1952 and the last reciprocating steam engine (an 0-8-0 switcher) in 1953.

Horsepower, tractive effort, and tonnage ratings

Tractive effort (or tractive force) is the force in pounds exerted by a locomotive, measured at the driving wheel. It is a theoretical figure: for steam, it is calculated by multiplying the boiler pressure times the square of the cylinder diameter times the piston stroke divided by driver diameter. Tractive effort isn't drawbar pull—it doesn't include operational factors—but it provides a baseline for comparison of locomotives. Horsepower is also largely theoretical for steam locomotives, meaning it's tough to directly compare power between steam and diesel. Baldwin developed a complex formula for calculating horsepower for steam locomotives that was widely used by railroads and other manufacturers. The results show as a curve, because horsepower increases as speed increases. A dynamometer car on a train can provide a good reading of drawbar horsepower for steam, but only for that specific train weight in that specific situation: a steam locomotive won't put out more horsepower than is required for a given situation.

For diesel locomotives, horsepower is determined by the power generated by the engine and the output voltage/amperage of the generator. Tractive effort is determined by a formula including the rated horsepower and locomotive speed.

Railroads test their new locomotives extensively to see how much they can pull (and how fast they can pull it) under various conditions and on specific operating districts. From this, they develop tonnage ratings for locomotive classes. This was typical for steam locomotives, where ratings could vary widely by type. For diesels, some railroads did the same thing by locomotive type, or published tables showing how much horsepower is required for a given amount of tonnage. From these charts and tables, railroads applied limits on train sizes and calculated ideal train speeds and scheduling.

STEAM LOCOMOTIVES

The first steam locomotives of the 1830s certainly don't resemble the steam locomotives of the early 1900s, but the basic elements of future locomotives are represented in early locomotives such as Stephenson's *Rocket*, the *Stourbridge Lion,* and the *DeWitt Clinton*: a horizontal boiler and cylinders with pistons that, through rods, turned driving wheels. Over the

Union Pacific 4-8-4 no. 814 is a modern steam locomotive. It's running its last miles in 1957 as it leads a westbound freight near Grand Island, Neb. John Krave

The *DeWitt Clinton* was the first train on the New York Central in 1831. The railroad built this replica in 1893. New York Central

next century locomotives grew, with four or more driving wheels and separate pilot wheels that initially supported the front of the boiler and later served primarily to guide locomotives into curves. Boiler size and pressure increased, from 150 pounds in the mid-1800s to 300-plus pounds by the 1930s. Firebox (grate) size also increased, as a larger fire was needed to supply more steam to provide more power; this resulted in trailing wheels that primarily served to support the firebox.

For steam, the words "engine" and "locomotive" are often used inter-

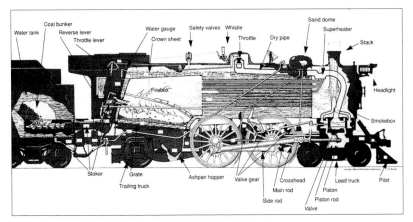

This cutaway drawing shows the key components of a typical steam locomotive, in this case a stoker-equipped, superheated 4-4-2. Kalmbach Media

changeably, and usually this doesn't present any issues in understanding. Just be aware that technically the engine is made up of the cylinders, rods, and driving wheels; together with the boiler and cab, the whole unit is a locomotive. Thus an articulated locomotive (singular) has a forward and rear engine under a single boiler.

How steam locomotives work

When water is heated to its boiling point and turns to steam, it expands to 1,700 times its original volume. When harnessed by a large boiler attached to pistons, rods, and other components, the resulting energy makes for a powerful locomotive.

You can get a basic idea of the workings of a steam locomotive from the drawing on page 95. The locomotive consists of a boiler atop running gear, with four or more drivers ("driving wheels") and—on road locomotives—lead and trailing trucks that help stabilize the ride and support the weight of the smokebox and firebox. A tender, connected to the locomotive with a drawbar, holds the fuel (coal or oil for modern locomotives) and water. A cab at the rear of the locomotive includes controls for the engineer and fireman.

Heat is provided by a fire in the firebox. Early locomotives were hand-fired—the fireman had to shovel the coal into the rear of the firebox. As boiler capacity increased, locomotives began using mechanical stokers (such as the horizontal and vertical augers shown in the drawing) to carry coal to the firebox. Oil-fired locomotives used adjustable jets to spray the fuel. A brick arch inside the firebox improves combustion.

Water in the boiler surrounds the firebox. The water level must stay above the crown sheet, at the top of the firebox, or the intense heat of the firebox will cause the sheet to weaken and fail, leading to a boiler explosion. A series of boiler tubes and flues run through the boiler, heating the water while carrying gases from the firebox to the smokebox.

Water is introduced into the boiler by the injector, which uses steam from the boiler to force water to the boiler. The water may first pass through a feedwater heater, a device located on or in the smokebox that preheats water before it is added to the boiler.

As the water boils, steam collects in the space at the top of the boiler. It is collected for use at the steam dome, where the throttle (controlled by a lever in the cab) opens to admit steam to the dry pipe. Steam passes through the dry pipe through the smokebox to a valve above each cylinder. In superheated locomotives, the steam first travels through superheater flues inside the boiler flues, raising the temperature of the steam. Some modern steam locomotives use a "front-end throttle," where the steam is regulated in the smokebox after it has passed through the superheater.

A safety valve atop the boiler releases if boiler pressure gets too high (operating pressure ranges from 150 psi for 1800s steam locomotives to 300 psi or higher for modern locomotives).

A cylinder forward of the drivers on each side includes a piston. When the valve above the cylinder opens to admit steam to the cylinder, the steam expands, forcing the piston into motion. The piston pushes or pulls the main rod, a heavy bar that's connected to the crankpin on the main driving wheel. The driving-wheel cranks on opposite sides of a two-cylinder locomotive are "quartered," meaning they're rotated 90 degrees to each other. This evens the forces of the cylinders on each side and keeps the rods from simultaneously "dead-centering," where no force is being transmitted. Side rods—the horizontal rods connecting the other drivers to the main driver—transfer the motion of the main rods to all drivers.

The valve gear is a linkage and series of rods and cranks that control the motion, operation, and timing of the valves, piston, and rods by regulating the cutoff (the amount of piston stroke where steam is admitted). Late or long cutoff, where steam is admitted for a longer period of the piston stroke, is used in starting and slow-speed operations where lots of power is needed (for instance, climbing a grade with a heavy train), raising the pressure. Short cutoff, where steam is admitted for only a short duration of the piston stroke, is used at higher speeds, which saves steam and conserves energy. Think of cutoff adjustments in a similar manner as using low or high gears in a truck. Valve gear follows many designs: Walschaerts is the most common; other valve gear include Baker, Stephenson, Southern, and Young.

Once the steam is done doing its job in the cylinders, it is "dead steam." It is then exhausted upward through the exhaust nozzle to the smokebox and out the exhaust stack. This pulls air through the boiler tubes and flues, creating the draft for the firebox. (In steam parlance, "live steam" is steam in the system that has yet to do its job; "dead steam" has done its job and is now waste to be ejected.)

On a two-cylinder locomotive, each rotation of the drivers equals four power strokes—the cylinder piston on each side pulls once and pushes once—providing four "chuffs" per driver revolution.

Steam locomotive types

Steam locomotives were built for very specific uses—often for certain operating districts or types of trains. Unlike diesels, steam locomotives could not simply be regeared for different speeds. Although steam locomotives could be operated together (double-headed) to power longer or heavier trains, it required a crew for each engine—as well as carefully coordinated operations between them.

Driver size is a good indicator of speed and power: the taller the drivers, the faster the maximum speed. Smaller (shorter) drivers means lower top speed but increased tractive effort. Driver size ranged from 50" diameter for switchers to 60"-70" for freight locomotives and 80" or larger for passenger engines. A rough rule of thumb is that a locomotive's top speed is its driver diameter in miles per hour.

There were several types of steam locomotives. A common descriptor is a locomotive's wheel arrangement (see "Wheel arrangements" on page 106), and although this was a good basic description of locomotive type, specifications varied widely among individual wheel arrangements. There are other key factors—here are the most common categories of steam locomotives:

Compound locomotives. Compound—also called "multiple-expansion"—locomotives differ from conventional ("simple") locomotives in that they use steam twice. Once steam has done its job in one cylinder (the high-pressure cylinder), instead of being discharged out the stack, it is

The most successful conventional compound locomotives were Baldwin's Vauclain compounds. They had two cylinders on each side (low-pressure above high-pressure) working in tandem. This is a Union Pacific 2-8-0. Fred Jukes

routed to a second cylinder (the low-pressure cylinder) and used again. The goal was to make the locomotive more efficient by using the steam twice. A number of methods were used to do this.

A cross-compound retained two cylinders like a conventional locomotive, with the high-pressure cylinder on one side and the low-pressure cylinder on the other. The low-pressure cylinder was noticeably larger than the high-pressure cylinder. This was required to provide the same power output, since a lot of the steam's energy had already been used by the first cylinder.

Four-cylinder compounds came in two types. Articulated compound locomotives (more on those in a bit) had the high-pressure cylinders at the rear engine and low-pressure cylinders on the front engine. Four-cylinder tandem compounds were conventional (non-articulated) designs, but had a pair of cylinders on each side—high- and low-pressure, working in tandem with each other. The most successful of these were Baldwin's Vauclain compounds, named for designer Samuel Vauclain.

Compound locomotives became popular in the 1880s, but fell out of favor by the 1910s. Compounds were more complex, could be difficult to balance, and required higher maintenance. By the early 1900s, builders found better ways to increase efficiency, including superheating, higher boiler pressure, and larger fireboxes.

Articulated locomotives. Articulated locomotives have two sets of drivers—two engines—under one boiler. The front engine pivots under the

Great Northern no. 2018 is a class N-3 2-8-8-0 articulated locomotive. It was built as a compound (Mallet) in 1912, but converted to simple in the 1920s. It's on an ore train in northern Minnesota in the 1930s. W.R. McGee

front of the boiler to negotiate curves. The extra driver set is indicated as an extra number in the Whyte classification (such as 2-8-8-2). Early articulateds were compound locomotives, and were known as "Mallets" (pronounced "malley") for Anatole Mallet's original design. Most were slow, powerful machines; some were lightweight, designed to go around sharper curves than a standard locomotive (many found service on logging railroads). Mallets were the most successful compound locomotives, with about 2,400 built, and many lasted until the end of the steam era.

Most later articulateds were simple (non-compound) locomotives built for speed as well as power. Among the best-known were Union Pacific's 4-6-6-4 Challenger and 4-8-8-4 Big Boy and Chesapeake & Ohio's 2-6-6-6 Allegheny designs.

Duplex locomotives have two driver sets in a rigid frame. This 4-4-6-4 was built in 1945; diesels, however, were well on their way to taking over mainline freight duties. Pennsylvania

Shay locomotives, like this Western Maryland three-truck design, are geared—they have vertical cylinders that turn a driveshaft along the right side of the locomotive. Lima

Duplex locomotives. Like an articulated design, a duplex locomotive has two sets of drivers under a single boiler. The duplex, however, has a rigid frame. By dividing the drivers into two groups, rods could be lighter, and the goal was a more-powerful, better-balanced locomotive for the same relative size as an equivalent conventional locomotive. The Pennsylvania was virtually the sole customer and (with Baldwin) developer of the concept. Overall the duplex design didn't work well—they were indeed powerful, but mechanically complex and prone to slipping. The most successful of the design were PRR's Q2 class, a 4-4-6-4 design built in 1945. By that time, however, diesels were well on their way to eliminating steam from service, making moot the duplex design's strengths and weaknesses.

Geared locomotives. Instead of traditional reciprocal rod motion and large driving wheels, geared steam locomotives transferred motion to a rotating driveshaft, which is then connected via gears to two or three driving trucks. They provided high tractive effort at low speeds and could traverse rough, undulating track. They were commonly used in logging and mining operations.

The three main types of geared locomotives were Shay, Climax, and Heisler. Shay locomotives had vertically oriented cylinders on the engi-

Tank locomotives lack tenders. The water supply is carried in a tank along or around the boiler, with a coal bunker behind the cab. This is a Lehigh Valley 0-6-0T. Noel Hiram Deeks

neer's side that turned a horizontal drive shaft running along the outside of the trucks on the right side of the locomotive. Climax locomotives had inclined cylinders on each side of the boiler that turned a transverse drive shaft; additional shafts and universal joints transferred power to the trucks. Heisler locomotives had cylinders inclined toward the body on each side (they formed a V if looking at the front of the locomotive), connecting to a drive shaft running under the boiler and connecting to the inner axle of each truck. Side rods transferred motion to the outer axle of each truck.

Tank locomotives. These steam locomotives don't pull a separate tender, instead carrying their water supply in tanks mounted to the sides of (or wrapping around) the boiler. They're typically small switching or industrial locomotives, but some larger ones were used for road freight and commuter service. These had extended frames with the trailing truck supporting the rear coal bunker. Two common designs for these were the Forney, which had a rigid frame, and the Mason Bogie, which had articulated drivers, allowing them to pivot under the boiler. Tank locomotives are indicated by adding a "T" to their Whyte classification (such as 2-4-4T).

Camelback locomotives. Anthracite, or hard coal, burns slowly, produces a lot of heat, and does so almost without smoke. These properties made anthracite the best coal for home heating, and for this it was cleaned and graded by size. The leftover pieces from this were called culm, which still had plenty of heat value, and it proved an ideal fuel for railroads that served the anthracite mines of eastern Pennsylvania. Anthracite's one

Camelback locomotives, like this Lehigh Valley 2-8-0, have the engineer's cab astride the boiler ahead of a wide rear firebox. The fireman rode a rear platform. John Locke

drawback was that it burned slowly, so it had to be burned in a wide, shallow fire. The narrow, deep fireboxes of 19th century locomotives wouldn't do. The solution was the Wootten firebox, developed by the Reading's John E. Wootten in the 1870s. It was as wide as the locomotive, with a grate area two to three times that of a standard firebox.

The disadvantage of the Wootten firebox was that it restricted the view forward and provided little room at the rear of the locomotive for a cab. The solution was to build a cab for the engineer straddling the boiler just ahead

The oil-fired Cab-Forward was Southern Pacific's solution to saving crews from smoke in tunnels. This is a class AC-10 4-8-8-4 built in 1942. Baldwin; collection of H.L. Broadbelt

of the firebox, while the fireman remained at the rear of the locomotive on a deck. The result was the distinctive design known as a camelback or Mother Hubbard. Contrary to popular myth, the design—despite its hazards and communication challenges between engineer and fireman—was never banned. By 1915 railroads had developed designs using conventional cabs on locomotives with Wootten fireboxes, and the last Camelbacks were built in 1927 for the Lehigh & New England.

Cab-Forward. Smoke in tunnels was a chronic problem for engine crews in the steam era, especially with slow, heavy trains. The Cab-Forward was Southern Pacific's method of combating the problem. Baldwin built several classes of these locomotives by flipping the locomotive around so the cab was in front, putting the smokestack well to the rear of the operating crew. All were articulateds and they were oil burners, which solved the problem of getting fuel to the firebox (which was also now at the front, just behind the cab). The first were compounds, but by the 1920s they were built as simple articulateds. The first (class MC-2 2-8-8-2s; MC for "Mallet compound") were delivered in 1909; the last (AC-12 4-8-8-2s) were built in 1943-1944.

Steam turbine locomotives. Locomotive designers long envied the designers of steamships and stationary power plants, as the available space and

Baldwin built this 6-8-6 steam turbine locomotive for Pennsylvania in 1944. It proved inefficient at slow speeds, and was soon scrapped. Pennsylvania Railroad

Baldwin/Westinghouse built three massive coal steam turbine locomotives for Chesapeake & Ohio in 1947-48. They were 154 feet long including tender. TRAINS magazine collection

conditions allowed using turbine engines instead of reciprocating engines. Locomotive builders did experiment with steam turbines in locomotives, although none proved successful.

In 1938 General Electric built a pair of 2500-hp steam-turbine-electric locomotives in an attempt to equal Electro-Motive Corporation's passenger diesels. The units were painted and lettered for Union Pacific and looked like a cross between UP's *City of Denver* diesels and the streamlined electric locomotives GE built that same year for the New Haven. Each unit had a 2-C+C-2 wheel arrangement; internal workings included a 1,500-pound pressure boiler, generator, and condensing system—components that needed plenty of care and maintenance.

The UP ran the locomotives on a few test trips, sent them around the country on a publicity tour, and, after a few trips in revenue service, returned them to GE. In 1943 Great Northern used them briefly to handle a surge in freight traffic between Wenatchee and Spokane, Wash., then sent them back to GE, where they were scrapped.

The Pennsylvania Railroad noted the success of a 4-6-2 turbine locomotive built by the London, Midland & Scottish Railway in 1935 and worked with Baldwin to advance the concept. In 1944 Baldwin delivered a steam-turbine locomotive to the Pennsy, no. 6200, class S2. It had a new wheel arrangement, 6-8-6 (it was to have been a 4-8-4, but wartime restrictions on the use of lightweight materials required extra axles) and weighed 589,970 pounds, a little more than Pennsy's J1 2-10-4. Its power unit was an adaptation of a Westinghouse marine power plant. It used two turbines—a large one for forward movement and a small one for reverse—which were clutched and geared to the second and third driver axles. All four axles were connected with conventional side rods.

The Pennsy found the locomotive could outpull conventional locomotives of the same size, and above 40 mph it was the equivalent of a 6,000-hp diesel. However, below that speed it was inefficient, using inordinate amounts of steam and coal. It worked in passenger service between Chicago and Crestline, Ohio, for a short period, then was placed in storage and eventually scrapped.

The most spectacular steam turbines were three built by Baldwin for Chesapeake & Ohio (also in collaboration with Westinghouse) in 1947-1948 (nos. 500-502). Each 856,000-pound locomotive was 106 feet long—plus a 48-foot tender—and rated at 6,000 hp. They proved inefficient and unreliable, and were scrapped in 1950. In 1954, Baldwin-Lima-Hamilton and Babcock & Wilcox teamed to build a similar locomotive for the Norfolk & Western. Number 2300, named *Jawn Henry,* weighed 818,000 pounds and rode on two pairs of six-wheel trucks with all axles powered, but the basic configuration—coal bunker up front, boiler behind the cab with firebox forward, turbines and electrical equipment at the rear—duplicated the C&O engines. It was scrapped in 1957.

A steam turbine in a stationary power plant or a ship runs at a near-constant speed in a clean, stable environment—and it isn't likely to encounter either condition in a locomotive. Turbines are delicate where reciprocating engines are robust, and the experimental, one-of-a-kind status of turbine locomotives put them at a disadvantage when it came to maintenance. The diesel engine was a much sturdier machine than the steam turbine and proved adaptable to railroad service.

Wheel arrangements (Whyte classifications)

Steam locomotives are classified by their number of leading (pilot) wheels, drivers, and trailing wheels using the Whyte system (named for Frederick M. Whyte, a New York Central mechanical engineer who came up with the system). It's easy to understand: if a locomotive has a two-wheel lead truck, eight driving wheels (four axles), and a two-wheel trailing truck, the locomotive is classified a 2-8-2. Articulated and duplex locomotives have an extra number for the additional set of drivers (a Union Pacific Big Boy, for example, is a 4-8-8-4). Most locomotives could be classified either as switchers (no pilot or trailing wheels), freight, or passenger locomotives, with some locomotive types used in both passenger and freight service. Characteristics of any given type—and their size—varied widely among railroads. Here's a summary of the most common wheel arrangements, their nicknames, and their typical uses, starting with locomotives lacking pilot trucks, then with two- and four-wheel lead trucks:

0-4-0, 0-6-0, 0-8-0: Switching. Switching locomotives had to operate well in either direction while pushing or pulling heavy cuts of cars, often through tight curves and complex trackwork. Switchers operated at slow speeds, negating the need for lead or trailing trucks for stability. This also maximized pulling power, as all of a switching locomotive's weight was on its driving wheels. Slow speeds allowed the use of small-diameter drivers (51" was typical; many later switchers had 57"), which increased tractive effort.

Switchers typically had small tenders, as fuel and water consumption were lower than road locomotives—they were constantly starting and stopping,

Switching locomotives lack pilot and trailing trucks. This is a Pennsylvania 0-6-0 with a slope-back tender. Trains magazine collection

This Northern Pacific 2-6-0 Mogul was built in the 1890s. Note the lightweight rods and small tender. Brian Solomon collection

not operating for long periods at high speed—and fuel and water sources were nearby in the yards in which they worked. Tenders for switchers were lower in profile or slope-backed to allow rearward visibility, critical for bidirectional operation. Switching locomotives also typically had smaller boilers and fireboxes compared to road locomotives. Other common switcher details included headlights and footboards on the rear of tenders, footboards instead of a pilot at the locomotive front, and often an additional sandbox, needed for bi-directional operation. Few 0-4-0s were built after 1900; by then railroads were opting for heavier 0-6-0s and then 0-8-0s to handle the increasing car and train sizes of the time.

0-8-8-0: Pusher/helper. The 0-8-8-0, first developed in 1907, could pull more than the couplers and freight car frames of its era could stand. Because the cars could withstand compression better than tension, additional power to get heavy trains up a grade was applied at the rear (usually ahead of the caboose). Later 0-8-8-0s were built as extra-heavy switchers for hump-yard duty. They were almost exclusively used in the East in mountainous territory.

2-4-2: Columbia. Passenger. In 1893 Baldwin Locomotive Works introduced the 2-4-2, the Columbia type. It had high drivers and a wide firebox supported by a rigid trailing axle; it was intended for fast passenger service despite its two-wheel lead truck, but was quickly superceded by the 4-4-2. The wheel arrangement became common for tank locomotives (as the 2-4-2T).

Chicago, Burlington & Quincy 2-6-2 (Prairie) no. 2152 was built in 1906. It's at Eola, Ill., in 1936. Prairies were developed as fast freight locomotives. A.H. Christiansen

2-6-0: Mogul. Freight. The 2-6-0 first appeared about 1852. It was a heavy freight locomotive at that time, offering about 50 percent more tractive effort than a contemporary 4-4-0. The Mogul proved to be a popular wheel arrangement through the 1800s, and with the coming of heavier, longer locomotives by the 1900s it had found its niche as a light freight locomotive. Although few were built after 1920, many remained in branchline and in other light-duty service until the end of the steam era.

2-6-2: Prairie. Freight and passenger. The Prairie was developed by the Chicago, Burlington & Quincy in 1900 to combine the pulling power of the 2-6-0 with the steaming capacity of a wide firebox, made possible by the addition of a trailing truck. The new type developed in two forms: a fast freight locomotive with drivers between 63" and 69", and a passenger

Lehigh & New England no. 19 is a 2-8-0 built by Baldwin in 1905. The Consolidation was the most common wheel arrangement built. Lehigh & New England

locomotive with 80" drivers. It was most popular among several Western railroads as a fast freight locomotive for use across the prairies between the Great Lakes and the Rockies. After 1910 the 2-6-2 was built primarily as an industrial and logging locomotive. Although more than 1,200 were built, issues with balancing led to the move to other wheel arrangements.

2-8-0: Consolidation. Freight. More Consolidations were built than any other wheel arrangement—about 21,000 from 1866 through the 1920s (and some even later). Its eight drivers offered more adhesion than previous six-coupled engines. In fairly simple form the 2-8-0 became almost the universal type for freight service between 1900 and 1910. After that the type began to develop in two directions. There was still a demand for light, simple 2-8-0s, and builders continued to produce such locomotives through the 1920s. Consolidations also began to accrue technological improvements like superheaters, mechanical stokers, and feedwater heaters.

On several railroads, notably Eastern coal-haulers, the type began to grow in girth and rear overhang—bigger boilers and wider, longer fireboxes. The object was to put as much weight as possible on the drivers and not worry much about speed.

The majority of 2-8-0s became second-rank locomotives when railroads turned to freight locomotives with trailing trucks. From the 1910s to the end of steam, Consolidations did all the jobs that weren't done by Mikados, Berkshires, and Northerns—and sometimes did those too, or pinch-hit for Pacifics, or stood in for switchers.

The 2-8-2 Mikado became the most popular freight locomotive of the early 1900s. This Chicago & North Western locomotive was built in the mid-1910s. Chicago & North Western

The Berkshire was a modern fast-freight locomotive. Nickel Plate 776 was among the last road steam locomotives built, in 1949 by Lima. Lima

2-8-2: Mikado. Freight. The 2-8-2 first appeared in the early 1890s, and the Mikado name dates to 1897 when Baldwin built a group of 2-8-2s for the Nippon Railway of Japan. The word means "emperor of Japan," and it had come into currency in 1885 with the opening of Gilbert and Sullivan's opera *The Mikado*. Railroads were initially slow to adopt the type in preference to the 2-8-0. The reason was that even 63" drivers, the largest used on 2-8-0s, were low enough to permit a wide firebox over the rear drivers. The switch to 2-8-2s was usually the result of a desire to increase freight train speed, which required not just a wide firebox but also a larger boiler. Like Pacifics, Mikados embodied a good balance between boiler size, grate area, and running gear.

In the 1910s, Mikados grew in popularity and became *the* standard freight locomotives. The USRA's 625 light 2-8-2s outnumbered all other USRA road engines combined—and there were also 233 heavy Mikes. Mikado construction eventually tapered off as railroads turned to larger power for freight trains, but some were built as late as late as 1949.

2-8-4: Berkshire. Fast freight. By the 1920s, railroads were looking to

Pennsylvania's I1 was an example of a heavy, high-tractive-effort 2-10-0. They were nicknamed "Hippos." Don Wood

The Chicago, Minneapolis, St. Paul & Omaha (Omaha Road) J1 class 2-10-2s, built in 1917, were designed for helper service near Hudson, Wis. Trains magazine collection

increase freight train speed as well as increase train size (tonnage capacity). The challenge was answered by the 2-8-4, which used a larger firebox (supported by a four-wheel trailing truck) and boiler, along with higher boiler pressure, to create more steam (see "Super-Power" on page 127). The first was built by Lima in 1924, and more than 600 would be built through 1949. The Berkshire (also called the Lima on Boston & Maine and Illinois Central and Kanawha on Chesapeake & Ohio) performed well, and proved to be an excellent fast freight locomotive on several railroads through the end of the steam era.

2-10-0: Decapod. Freight. The first 2-10-0s appeared in the 1860s. They fell into two categories: light locomotives designed to spread locomotive weight across five axles, decreasing the axle loading for light rail; or heavy, aiming for high tractive effort (such as the Pennsylvania I1s "Hippo"). The light versions were popular on secondary lines; the large ones were slow but carried high tonnage on heavy main lines. A notable subset of the class was a group of lightweight 2-10-0s purchased during World War I by the Russian government from American locomotive builders. After 857 locomotives had been shipped, the Russian revolution forced cancellation of the remainder of the order in 1917. The 200 completed Decapods not yet shipped were distributed to U.S. railroads by the USRA.

2-10-2: Santa Fe; 2-10-4: Texas. Freight. The Atchison, Topeka & Santa Fe developed the 2-10-2 just after 1900, adding a trailing truck to a 2-10-0 design to better enable them to operate in reverse when returning downgrade from pusher service. The type eventually became popular as a heavy freight locomotive among several railroads, with about 2,200 built through the 1920s. The 2-10-4 was a further development allowing a larger firebox, which permitted higher speeds.

Chesapeake & Ohio's 2-6-6-6 Allegheny locomotives, built in the 1940s, were modern articulateds that could carry heavy tonnage at speed. Lima

Norfolk & Western no. 2026 is a compound (Mallet) 2-8-8-2. They were designed for power, not speed. It was built in 1919. Trains magazine collection

2-6-6-2. Freight. The articulated 2-6-6-2 was more flexible than the 2-10-2 Santa Fe, albeit slightly more complex. Just over 900 were built from 1906 to 1949. Around 1910 the first 2-6-6-2 appeared with a firebox behind the drivers and supported by a trailing truck, and most subsequent 2-6-6-2s followed that pattern. The 2-6-6-2 remained a low-speed locomotive, far more likely to be seen bringing hopper cars down from the coal mines than handling mainline freight. The 2-6-6-2 also found employment in the logging industry in the western United States, often as a tank engine. Nearly all 2-6-6-2s were built as compounds, and a few were later converted to single-expansion locomotives.

2-6-6-4: Fast freight. The 2-6-6-4, first built by Baldwin in 1934, was among the first articulated locomotives designed to be both powerful and fast. They were designed to do the same work as a pair of light 2-8-2s, and led to development of larger, faster locomotives.

The Triplex design was unsuccessful, as the boiler could not produce steam fast enough to supply six cylinders. This Erie 2-8-8-8-2 was built in 1914. Erie

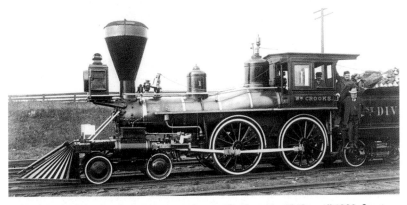

The 4-4-0 American was the most common locomotive from the 1840s until 1900. Great Northern's *Wm. Crooks* was built in 1868 is shown in 1908 after restoration. Library of Congress

2-6-6-6: Allegheny. Freight. The 2-6-6-6 was a modern, heavy freight locomotive that could also operate at speed. Lima built 60 for the Chesapeake & Ohio and eight near copies for Virginian from 1941 to 1948. They were regarded—with Union Pacific's Big Boys—as the largest locomotives built, and the ultimate in large, fast, modern steam power.

2-8-8-2; 2-10-10-2: Freight. The first 2-8-8-2s in North America were two experimental Mallets built by Baldwin in 1909 for Southern Pacific. Except for one single-expansion locomotive obtained by the Pennsylvania in 1911, 2-8-8-2 development followed typical patterns, with engines progressively larger and heavier. These were lumbering beasts with immense pulling power but little capability for speeds over 20 mph; they became popular as slow-speed mountain locomotives. The first fleet of simple 2-8-8-2s was begun in 1924 when Chesapeake & Ohio received the first of its H-7 class; by 1931 several roads had simple 2-8-8-2s. Norfolk & Western built the last

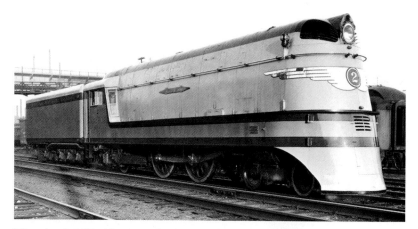

Milwaukee Road no. 2 is a streamlined, oil-burning 4-4-2 (Atlantic) built in 1935 for the railroad's lightweight high-speed *Hiawatha* trains. Milwaukee Road

in 1952. Few 2-10-10-2s were built; Santa Fe built 10 unsuccessful versions (from 2-10-2s) in 1911, but Alco built 10 for Virginian in 1918 that served through the 1950s. They were heavy, powerful, slow locomotives.

2-8-8-8-2, 2-8-8-8-4: Triplex. Helper. Built from 1914 to 1916, these designs were an effort to get more power than a two-engine articulated on one locomotive; the third engine was under the cab and tender. They were unsuccessful, as they were unable to produce steam fast enough to efficiently power all the cylinders. Erie had the three 2-8-8-8-2s, which survived as helpers into the 1920s; the lone 2-8-8-8-4, for Virginian, never made a successful revenue trip.

4-4-0: American. Freight and passenger. The 4-4-0 was introduced in 1836, and for almost six decades the 4-4-0 was *the* standard American locomotive. It was well balanced—it had three-point suspension: the center pin of the lead truck and the fulcrums of the equalizers between the drivers. The first 4-4-0s had deep, narrow fireboxes between the frames and the driver axles; later, larger Americans had fireboxes above the frames. Few Americans were built after 1900, but some remained in service into the 1940s and even the 1950s, having been bumped to secondary and branch lines. Most railroads had some services for which an American was entirely adequate; some branch lines had track and bridges that could support nothing heavier than a 4-4-0.

4-4-2: Atlantic. Passenger. In 1894 Baldwin designed a 4-4-2 for

The 4-6-0 Ten-Wheeler was a common fast passenger locomotive from the late 1800s into the 1900s. Union Pacific no. 1586 was built by Baldwin in 1910. Arthur Petersen

Atlantic Coast Line and named it for the railroad. The four-wheel lead truck provided stability at speed and allowed a longer, better-steaming boiler than the 2-4-2. The Atlantic quickly achieved widespread popularity for fast passenger trains. With the coming of steel passenger cars, train weights soon outgrew the Atlantic, and the type was relegated to short, light trains. The Pennsylvania (class E6) and Milwaukee Road (class A) notably built larger, more-modern versions for short, fast trains.

4-4-4: Jubilee. Passenger. Only 30 were built; the first four, for Reading in 1915, were unsuccessful. The Baltimore & Ohio built one (which proved slippery) and Canadian Pacific had 20, built 1936-1938 to modest success.

The Pacific 4-6-2 became the most common passenger locomotive of the 1900s. Missouri-Kansas-Texas no. 378 was built by Alco in 1915. Trains magazine collection

The Hudson (4-6-4) was more powerful than the Pacific, but was soon replaced in popularity by the 4-8-4. New York Central no. 5405 was built in 1937. New York Central

Mountain 4-8-2s, such as Norfolk & Western no. 137, became popular as fast dual-service locomotives. This one was built by Baldwin in 1923. Norfolk & Western

4-6-0: Ten-Wheeler. Passenger and freight. This arrangement first appeared in the late 1850s, and within a couple of decades became the second-most popular design behind the American. The 4-6-0 was the standard fast passenger locomotive into the 1900s. The design allowed a larger boiler than the 4-4-0, and the four-wheel pilot truck was stable at high speed. Some remained in service on secondary lines through the steam era.

4-6-2: Pacific. Passenger. The first true Pacifics were built in 1902, and by the 1910s the Pacific was on its way to becoming the most common passenger locomotive of the 1900s (about 6,800 total; the Pennsylvania alone had 696 of them). Pacifics varied widely by railroad in design, size, weight, and power. They offered greater steaming capacity than the Ten-Wheeler, more pulling power than the Atlantic, and greater stability at speed than the Prairie. By 1930 the type had been superseded by the Hudson and the Northern, but some were built after that date, and many served well into the 1950s, especially on secondary passenger trains.

4-6-4: Hudson. Passenger. Adding a four-wheel trailing truck to the Pacific created the 4-6-4, allowing a larger firebox and greater steaming

The 4-8-4 became the most popular locomotive of the late-steam era, serving in fast freight and passenger service. Rock Island no. 5000 was built in 1929. Rock Island

The 4-12-2 was a three-cylinder locomotive unique to the Union Pacific. It was the longest rigid-wheelbase locomotive built. Alco

capability for fast passenger trains. The first was built in 1927, and they were popular into the 1930s. However, they were soon superseded by 4-8-4s and diesels, with many scrapped in the 1940s as they weren't suited to other types of work.

4-8-0: Twelve-Wheeler. Freight. Although first built in the 1860s, the type didn't become common until the late 1880s, when it gained popularity as a road freight engine. Its four-wheel lead truck offered more stability than the Consolidation. Twelve-Wheelers offered more boiler capacity than contemporary 2-8-0s; in addition to extra length the boilers were usually greater in diameter. Few were built after 1900.

4-8-2: Mountain. Freight and passenger. In 1911 Alco built a pair of 4-8-2s for Chesapeake & Ohio, combining the eight drivers of the Mikado with the four-wheel lead truck of the Pacific. The Mountain type ultimately developed into a fast dual-service locomotive. Western railroads such as Southern Pacific, Union Pacific, and Santa Fe used the 4-8-2 as a long-distance heavy passenger locomotive; Eastern roads such as New York Central (which called it a Mohawk), Pennsylvania, and Baltimore & Ohio considered it primarily a fast freight engine. It proved popular, with more than 2,200 built through the late 1940s.

4-8-4: Northern (also Dixie, Niagara, Greenbrier, and others). Fast freight and passenger. The 4-8-4 was the ultimate development of non-articulated steam power, and the design became the standard modern American steam locomotive. Northerns varied widely in size and driver diameter depending upon service, and were popular for fast freight as well as heavy passenger service. A total of 1,115 were built from 1926 to 1950, and they remained front-line power until the end of the steam era.

4-10-2: Southern Pacific. Freight and passenger. The 4-10-2 was a three-cylinder design from Alco, with a total of 60 built from 1925 to 1927. Their long wheelbase limited the territory they could traverse. They were good fast freight and passenger engines, but the 4-8-4 proved more practical.

A Union Pacific Challenger (4-6-6-4) heads a freight in 1947. The wheel arrangement was well balanced and built for speed as well as power. Stan Kistler, Jr.

4-12-2: Union Pacific. Fast freight. Unique to Union Pacific, the three-cylinder 4-12-2 was the largest locomotive built with a rigid wheel-base. The third cylinder was at the front, and powered the lead driving axle. Alco built 88 of them from 1926 to 1930. The 4-12-2 was powerful and rode well at speed. They initially worked UP's main line across Wyoming, and after they were displaced by Challengers and Big Boys they moved to Kansas and Nebraska, where curves were broad.

Union Pacific's 4-8-8-4 Big Boy is generally regarded as the largest steam locomotive. Alco built 25 of them in 1941 and 1944. Trains magazine collection

4-4-4-4, 4-6-4-4, 4-4-6-4, 6-4-4-6 (see "Duplex locomotives" on page 101).

4-6-6-4: Challenger. Fast freight and passenger. Union Pacific introduced the 4-6-6-4 in 1936, with Northern Pacific and Spokane, Portland & Seattle following shortly. They were powerful, fast engines (69" or 70" drivers). The articulation of later 4-6-6-4s allowed only horizontal movement of the front engine. Vertical curves in the track were taken up entirely by the spring rigging, resulting in better weight distribution between the front and rear engines and greater stability than other articulateds. The UP used them regularly in passenger service.

4-8-8-4: Big Boy. Freight. The Big Boy was exclusive to the Union Pacific, and although certain specs were exceeded by other locomotives, the

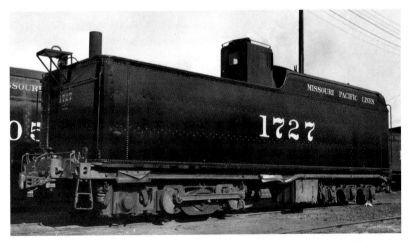

The rear truck of this Missouri Pacific tender is equipped with a booster engine. Also note the brakeman's shelter ("doghouse") on the deck. Louis A. Marre collection

4-8-8-4 is regarded as being the largest steam locomotive built. The Challenger design was expanded, with larger cylinders and an extra driving axle on each engine. The resulting locomotives were powerful and could move freight trains at speed on tough grades. The UP bought 25 from Alco (20 in 1941 and five in 1944); the coming of diesels precluded any more being built. They ran through the 1950s, mainly serving UP's main line across Sherman Hill (near Laramie, Wyo.).

The dynamo (center) is a small steam-powered generator. The whistle and safety valve are at left; the steam dome is at right, with the throttle link at the side. Trains magazine collection

This Chesapeake & Ohio 2-8-8-2 has two cross-compound air compressors on the smokebox front. The headlight is mounted low on the pilot deck, with class lights on either side of the Elesco feedwater heater (at top) and a bell directly below it.

Richard E. Prince

Ancillary details and components

Boosters. Although it takes far more tractive force to start a train than to keep it moving, paradoxically it requires less steam. A steam locomotive that could generate enough steam to haul a load at 40 or 50 mph had plenty of extra steam available at low speeds. The booster engine was devised to convert some of that steam to additional tractive force for starting a train.

The booster was a small two-cylinder steam engine usually mounted on the locomotive trailing truck, geared to one axle through an idler gear that could be moved in and out of mesh. It was a low-speed device, usable up to about 15 mph. The booster could also be located on an axle of a tender truck as in the photo on the previous page; power was transmitted to the other axle through side rods.

Dynamo (turbo-generator). The dynamo was a small, steam-powered generator in a boxy cylindrical housing, usually located atop the boiler just in front of the cab. A valve in the cab turned the steam on and off to activate the dynamo. They supplied 32 volts for headlights, marker lights, and cab lights, and emitted a distinctive high-pitched whine when on.

Headlights, class lights. The first steam locomotive headlights were oil lamps, placed at the front of the locomotive in a box with reflectors to increase the brightness. They were only illuminated at night, and were barely sufficient for the slow speeds of 1800s trains. Electric lamps became standard by the turn of the 20th century, providing more light. Styles and placement varied widely, with most railroads adopting standards. Backup lights were located on the rear wall of the tender. Classification lamps were located at the top corners of the smokebox front, with white indicating an extra movement and green indicating a following section of the same train.

The injector pulls water from the tender and combines it with steam to force the water into the boiler under pressure. Milwaukee Road

Bell, whistle. Bells and whistles were both used on steam locomotives from the 1830s onward, with rules covering their use (usually at stations, when trains start in motion, and grade crossings). Placement varied. Bells were often atop the boiler near the cab, with a cable running back to the cab for manual operation. By the 1900s, automatic (air-actuated) bells became common, with placement often moved forward to the front of the smokebox. Steam whistles have a distinctive sound notably different than an air horn. Whistles were generally located on the steam dome atop the boiler. Their system of short and long blasts has different meanings in the rulebook (see page 43 in Chapter 1).

Feedwater heaters and injectors. Introducing water to a boiler under high pressure is a challenge. Injectors use steam pressure to force water from the tender into the boiler. They were located on either side of the boiler or sometimes under the cab. To make locomotives more efficient, the feedwater heater was developed (the three main manufacturers were Coffin, Elesco, and Worthington; they were sometimes visible at the top front of the smokebox; see the photo on page 120). This device preheats water using steam and heat from the smokebox, raising the temperature of feed water significantly and making the boiler more efficient. All locomotives required two sources of feed water—either two injectors or an injector and a feedwater heater.

Air compressors and reservoirs. Air compressors (air pumps) provide air for the brake system and other accessories, with air stored in one or more horizontal cylindrical tanks called reservoirs. Compressors on steam locomotives (unlike diesels) were in the open, and visible either on the side of the locomotive above the drivers on the left side or at the front, mounted to the smokebox front or on a platform above the pilot. As train size increased, locomotives after about 1900 were equipped with a pair of compressors. Piping (which often ran back-and-forth to cool the just-compressed air) connected the compressors to the reservoirs, which were usually located under the running boards on the sides.

Sandbox. The sandbox (sometimes called "sand dome") is located atop the boiler, distinguished from the steam dome by having a series of pipes traveling from it downward to a point just in front of one or more driving wheels. Dry sand is used for traction, especially when starting or when rails are wet. A hatch on top allows filling. The sanders are actuated by a valve on the engineer's side of the cab, with air forcing the sand through the pipes.

Valve gear. The combination of levers, cranks, and small rods between the cylinders and drivers is the valve gear. It is controlled by the reverse lever in the cab. Moving the lever can both change the direction of travel and adjust the amount of time steam is admitted to the cylinder (called "cutoff"): short time for moving at speed; long time for starting and slow speed where maximum power is needed. Various valve gears were named for their inventors or dominant railroads—the most common were Walschaerts, Stephenson, Baker, Southern, and Young.

Stoker. Early locomotives were all hand-fired—the fireman shoveled coal from the tender into the firebox. By the early 1900s, steam locomotives were growing in size, and firemen were unable to keep up with the amount of coal required by larger fireboxes and boilers. Most larger locomotives in the 1900s were equipped with stokers, which carried coal via a screw-type auger from the bottom of the tender bunker to just below the firebox. Another auger brought the coal upward to the firebox, where steam jets blew the coal to distribute it evenly.

Tenders

By the 1850s the tender had developed into a U-shaped water tank surrounding the fuel bunker and resting on what was essentially a flatcar. Water was put into the tank through a covered hatch or manhole in the top (tender deck); a gate at the front of the fuel bunker helped contain the wood or coal. The rear wall of the coal bunker had a slope to move coal forward. Locomotives that burned oil had a tank in place of a coal bunker. As the photos throughout this chapter show, tender size and design varied widely.

Tender size depended on locomotive size: the larger the engine, the more fuel and water it used. The ratio between the fuel and water capacities was usually based on two water stops per fuel stop, as water is easier to obtain and store than coal or oil. A pound of coal, on the average, could turn 6 pounds (0.7 gallons) of water to steam, yielding an approximate ratio of 10,000 gallons of water to 14 tons of coal. In practice the proportion might be different. Tender size was also limited by turntable length. Many roads bought large locomotives with small tenders, then replaced the tenders with larger ones when longer turntables were installed.

In the late 1930s the cast-bed frame or pedestal ("centipede") tender appeared. The water-bottom frame was a single casting with pedestals for five axles supporting the middle and rear and a swiveling four-wheel truck supporting the front. The five rigid axles (which could move laterally) provided extra stability.

Vanderbilt tender. A round tank holds more than a rectangular tank with the same surface area, and a cylinder is stronger than a box. In 1901, Cornelius Vanderbilt (grandson of the Commodore) received a patent for a tender with a cylindrical water tank. It was lighter than a rectangular tender of the same capacity because of the inherent strength of its construction;

Vanderbilt tenders have cylindrical water tanks, with the coal bunker at the front. This is a **Union Pacific 4-4-2.** Trains magazine collection

rectangular tanks required a great deal of internal bracing. Some railroads used them widely, including Baltimore & Ohio, Great Northern, Southern Pacific, and Union Pacific (see pages 117 and 123).

Doghouse (brakeman's shelter). Freight-train operation often called for a brakeman on the head end. There wasn't much room for the brakeman in the cab on many early locomotives, but railroads were required to provide adequate space. A shelter on the tender deck—often called a doghouse—was sometimes the solution (see page 119). Specific design and use varied by railroad and locomotive type.

Fuel

Wood. Most locomotives through the Civil War era burned wood, as it was inexpensive and easily obtained in most regions. Although then cheap, wood was bulky for the amount of heat it contained. It took 5,000 pounds of wood to equal the heat value of 2,000 pounds of coal, and even then it was not as good a fuel. Burning embers and sparks were common, requiring tall smokestacks with internal spark arrestors (hence the wide "balloon" stacks of early steam locomotives). Wood was also labor-intensive to cut, store, transport, and load. As railroads increased in number and mileage and wood became valued for other purposes, it became more expensive, leading to a shift to coal by the 1870s.

Coal. Anthracite was the only type of coal mined in any quantity before 1840, and it wasn't ideal for locomotives as it burns slowly. Culm, the material left over from the grading process, eventually found use as a locomotive fuel, but it required the wide Wootten firebox (see "Camelback locomotives" on page 102). Bituminous, or soft coal, eventually fueled the majority of modern North American steam locomotives because its deposits were widespread; it became economically viable by the 1860s. Lignite, or brown coal, is a low-grade coal. Although lignite required special fireboxes, it was inexpensive and some railroads used it if there was an on-line source.

The phrase "burned what they hauled" is often used to explain why coal-carrying railroads were late converts to the diesel locomotive. "Burned what was nearby" is a more accurate way of putting it. Part of the cost of fuel is the cost of transportation. Railroads that had to bring in coal from a distance—those in New England, for example—were among the first to dieselize.

Oil. Crude oil came under consideration as a locomotive fuel in the 1880s.

A Santa Fe hostler opens the valve on a trackside standpipe to add oil to the tender of a 4-6-2. Steam locomotives used Bunker C, a heavy fuel oil. Santa Fe

Steam locomotive require frequent water stops. It can come from standpipes or directly from trackside water tanks. Trains magazine collection

It left no ashes, it was easy to handle, and it had a higher heat content per pound than coal. The problem was burning it in a firebox. Developing an effective atomizer and combustion chamber took some experimentation, and in 1894 Baldwin equipped a demonstrator locomotive, a Vauclain compound 4-6-0, to burn oil. By the 1900s, oil-fired locomotives were becoming more common, especially in the Southwest, where the oil fields were. It was occasionally used elsewhere to avoid the danger of sparks from coal (in forested country, for example) or for convenience (passenger trains).

Steam engines burned a thick, heavy type of oil then known as "Bunker C," now classified as no. 6 fuel oil. It required heating to flow smoothly. Bunker C's main benefit through the 1940s was that it was cheap. However, its price went up as refining techniques improved and it became the prime feedstock material for the growing plastics industry after that period, eliminating its main advantage as a fuel.

Water

Steam locomotives require a tremendous amount of water to make steam, with a large locomotive using as much as 6,000 gallons of water per hour. Tanks and water spouts were located frequently along lines, often every 20 miles or even closer. Water was easy to find in many places, but *good* water was a scarcer commodity. Most water—in rivers, lakes, and wells—contains minerals, which in locomotives created problems such as water foaming as it boiled and scale formations on the outside of the flues. In the Southwest,

Number 2500 was the first USRA locomotive: a light Mikado (2-8-2) built by Baldwin in July 1918 and assigned to Baltimore & Ohio. Trains magazine collection

railroads had problems simply supplying water at all. Railroads had to bring in good water to these areas by the trainload in tank cars, which was an expensive proposition. The lack of water was a key reason the Santa Fe and other railroads that crossed arid and desert areas were among the first to switch to diesels.

USRA steam locomotives

When the United States Railroad Administration (USRA) took over control of U.S. railroads in 1917 (see page 29 in Chapter 1), railroads' existing locomotive fleets were largely old and underpowered for the longer, heavier trains carrying wartime traffic. Among the USRA's first actions was designing and purchasing a fleet of standard locomotives of various wheel arrangements, then distributing them to various railroads as needed. The idea was that standard, modern designs that could be produced by any builder would permit a tremendous increase in locomotive production and would provide a fluid reserve of power that could be moved from railroad to railroad as needed.

An engineering committee made up of representatives from the three principal locomotive builders (Alco, Baldwin, and Lima) plus several railroads developed 12 standard locomotive designs in eight wheel arrangements: 0-6-0, 0-8-0, 2-8-2, 2-10-2, 2-6-6-2, 2-8-8-2, 4-6-2, and 4-8-2, with light and heavy versions of the 2-8-2, 2-10-2, 4-6-2, and 4-8-2. Specifications were published in April 1918. They were all designed as coal-burning, superheated locomotives. The USRA immediately placed orders for 555 locomotives with Alco and 470 with Baldwin (Lima was already working at capacity).

Among the roads receiving large numbers of USRA locomotives were Baltimore & Ohio (100 light Mikados), New York Central (95 light Mikados), Milwaukee Road (50 light Mikados; later changed to heavy Mikados), Erie (50 heavy Mikados—only 15 were delivered—20 heavy Pacifics, and 25 heavy Santa Fes), and Southern (50 light Santa Fes). All five heavy Mountains were for Chesapeake & Ohio. The first to emerge, on July 1, 1918, was Baldwin-built Baltimore & Ohio light Mikado 4500.

The USRA designs were good, witnessed by the fact that thousands of locomotives were built to the designs after USRA control ended in 1920. As an example, the 0-8-0 design—with just 175 built under USRA control—would see another 1,200 copies built, making it the all-time most-common steam locomotive design.

Super-Power

The ultimate culmination in steam locomotive development became known as the Super-Power era, with design fundamentals pioneered by William E. Woodward of Lima Locomotive Works in the mid-1920s. Until that time, steam locomotives were designed for specific jobs. Road locomotives were either meant to haul a lot of tonnage slowly or haul light trains at high speeds. Woodward's concept was to create larger, more-efficient locomotives that could do both: haul heavy trains fast.

The key to this was steam: A lot of it was needed to move heavy trains at speed. To provide this, designers took the efficiencies gained with superheaters and feedwater heaters, added larger fireboxes (100-square-foot and larger grates, along with more volume, or "furnace area"), increased boiler pressure (to 250 and eventually 300 psi), and large drivers. Higher pressure also allowed smaller cylinders, which meant less reciprocating weight.

This evolution came with a price: boilers had to be stronger; rods, wheels, and other components had to be lighter, stronger, and better balanced (often using lightweight alloys); lubricants had to be improved to deal with increased friction and higher temperatures; and many other components had to be refined and upgraded as well.

The result of this development was a series of outstanding locomotives that lived up to the Super-Power name. (Although other builders didn't use the "Super-Power" term, all began using the fundamental ideas Lima introduced.) Some of the best-known modern locomotives that followed these concepts were Nickel Plate Road's 2-8-4 Berkshires; 4-8-4s from New

York Central, Union Pacific, and others; and Chesapeake & Ohio's Allegheny 2-6-6-6 and UP's 4-8-8-4 Big Boy, both simple articulateds that could move tonnage up heavy grades and at speed.

DIESEL-ELECTRIC LOCOMOTIVES

Diesel-electrics began making inroads as switching locomotives in the 1920s, with early boxcabs from Alco/General Electric/Ingersoll-Rand. Railroads liked them because they required less daily maintenance than steam, and they kept city smoke inspectors at bay in urban areas. The Canadian Locomotive Company introduced a road passenger diesel on Canadian National in 1929, but it was the Chicago, Burlington & Quincy's diesel-powered

Santa Fe F3s—descendants of Electro-Motive's pioneering FT—in warbonnet red and silver lead passenger trains at Albuquerque, N.M., in 1964. J. David Ingles

Baltimore & Ohio boxcab switcher no. 1 was among the first diesel-electric locomotives. The 300-hp locomotive was built by Alco-GE-Ingersoll-Rand in 1925. General Electric

Zephyr of 1934 that showed that diesels were a practical option for high-speed trains. The *Zephyr* was a lightweight, streamlined, three-car articulated train built by Budd featuring fluted stainless-steel construction and an Electro-Motive Corp. (Winton) diesel engine. (Union Pacific's M-10000 streamliner of the same year used a distillate engine.) More diesel streamliners followed, and by 1940 both EMC and Alco were building stand-alone diesel locomotives for high-speed passenger service.

The diesel that revolutionized railroading—and ensured steam's demise—was the Electro-Motive FT, which embarked on its demonstration tour in late 1939. Railroads had accepted diesels for switching and fast passenger service, but were unconvinced that they were suitable for heavy freight trains. The FT proved that a diesel-electric could not only do the task, but that it could do it more efficiently and with far less maintenance and daily upkeep (no ashpans to dump, no flues to clean, no frequent water or coal stops to make — just a fueling stop every few hundred miles). By the end of World War II, hundreds of FTs were in service, and as Electro-Motive turned to newer models (and other builders entered the market), it became obvious to more and more people that diesels were the way of the future.

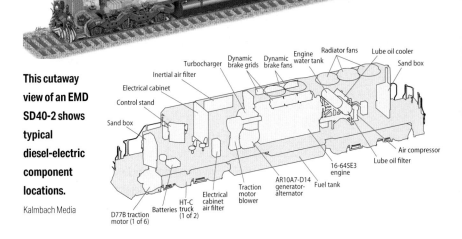

This cutaway view of an EMD SD40-2 shows typical diesel-electric component locations.

Kalmbach Media

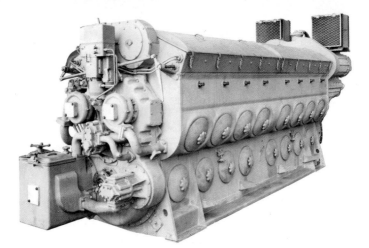

Electro-Motive's 567 diesel engine (this is a 16-cylinder 567C in 1954) was reliable and helped the builder dominate the early diesel-electric market. EMD

Diesel technology continued to evolve, with progressively larger, more-powerful, and more-efficient locomotives, leading to today's microprocessor-controlled 4,400-hp locomotives from EMD, GE, and others.

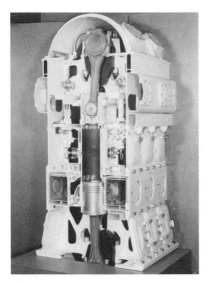

Fairbanks-Morse was known for its opposed-piston (OP) engine, which had two pistons in each cylinder and an upper and lower crankshaft. Fairbanks-Morse

How diesels work

Diesel-electric locomotives are essentially electric locomotives that carry their own generating plant. A diesel engine turns a generator or alternator to make electricity. The engineer controls the speed of the engine to regulate the amount of power. The electricity produced is routed to electric motors (called "traction motors") that power the wheels. Here's how it works:

The diesel engine itself (the "prime mover") is the heart of the locomotive. Locomotive engines have been built to many designs and sizes—typically six to 20 cylinders—but the principle is the same. Unlike a gasoline engine, which uses a spark to ignite the fuel in

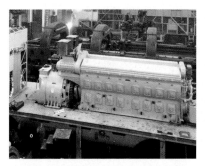

The frame of this under-construction EMD F unit shows the engine at right, the generator at the end of the engine at left, and the electrical cabinet at far left. EMD

Specific layouts vary, but locomotive controls are standardized. Brake handles are at left; throttle and dynamic brake in middle. Linn Westcott

each cylinder, a diesel engine fires by compression. This is done by compressing the intake air in each cylinder to 500 psi or higher, whereupon it reaches a temperature of about 1,000 degrees F. An atomized spray of diesel fuel is then injected and burns, propelling the piston.

Most diesel engines used in locomotives are V-style, with paired banks of cylinders. Some early (and some smaller) engines used a straight (in-line) design, with all cylinders positioned vertically in a line over the crankshaft. Baldwin's early VO and 600-series engines and Alco's 539 are examples.

Fairbanks-Morse locomotives were noted for that company's unique opposed-piston (OP) two-cycle diesel engines. In an OP engine, two pistons share a common vertical cylinder, so there's no cylinder head. Each bank of cylinders (one on top, one bottom), drives a crankshaft.

The crankshaft turns either a generator (DC transmission) or alternator (AC transmission). Generators were used into the 1960s, but the growing power of locomotives required ever-larger generators, and manufacturers were having a difficult time fitting them into locomotives. The solution was substituting an alternator, which is smaller and lighter than a generator for a given power output. The resulting AC power is sent through rectifiers, which convert it to DC. For DC-traction-motor locomotives (all locomotives through the 1980s), the DC then passes through the control system and to the traction motors.

The throttle is a sliding lever that on most road locomotives has eight notches, or control settings, plus idle. Idle is the position farthest away: pulling the throttle lever toward you increases the throttle. Some switchers

Each powered axle is driven by a traction motor mounted on the axle and truck frame. When installed, the small gear on the motor turns the large gear on the axle. William A. Akin

have "swipe" throttles without notches, allowing engineers quicker response and more-precise control; early GE road diesels had 16 control notches. The throttle position is indicated by the notch setting: for example, full throttle is "run 8" or "notch 8."

The throttle is linked electrically (pneumatically in some early diesels) with the engine governor. Increasing the throttle increases the fuel flow and thus engine speed, which increases the power from the generator or alternator, supplying more current to the traction motors.

A reverser lever on the control stand has forward, neutral, and reverse settings; removing the lever locks it in neutral. Unlike an automobile or truck, a diesel locomotive has no forward or reverse gears. It doesn't matter which direction a locomotive is pointing. Instead, the reverser changes the direction of current flow in the field windings of the traction motors. (It's a different process on modern AC traction-motor diesels.)

Each powered axle is driven by a traction motor, which is supported by both the axle and the truck frame. A small pinion gear on the traction motor armature turns a larger gear mounted on the axle. The number of teeth on each gear determines the gear ratio, which varies depending upon the locomotive service. Each manufacturer offered its locomotives with a range of gear ratios. A low-speed freight or switching locomotive will have a high gear ratio, such as 65:12, while a high-speed passenger locomotive would be equipped with a low gear ratio, such as 58:25. This allows the freight locomotive greater torque and tractive effort at low speeds, but limits its top speed; the passenger locomotive can cruise easily at high speed, but doesn't have as much pulling power at low speeds.

The coming of the AC traction motor was a radical innovation in diesel locomotive technology, made possible by microprocessor control. After years of testing, AC motors appeared in 1991 in EMD's SD60MAC, which served as a test-bed for the SD70MAC, which began production in 1993. That year GE also began producing an AC-motor locomotive, the AC4400CW. An AC traction motor offers several advantages over a DC motor. The AC motor is simpler, as it doesn't have the brushes and commutators needed in DC motors. This makes them much tougher, virtually eliminating the risk of damage from overheating under a heavy load. All DC motors have "short-time ratings"—the time a motor can withstand a specific high current load before overheating and damage occurs. The higher the amperage, the shorter the time allowed for the motor to operate at that level. The better torque of AC traction motors improves wheel-to-rail adhesion, with AC motors achieving adhesion above 35 percent, compared to about 30 percent for a DC motor.

As with a DC locomotive, the diesel engine on an AC diesel turns an alternator. However, the AC power directly from the alternator cannot be used by the traction motors. Rectifiers convert the AC to DC, which is then converted back to AC by a series of inverters that "chop" the current for use by the traction motors, a process that involves turning the power on and off rapidly (up to 500 times per second).

With few exceptions, locomotive trucks have four or six wheels. Four-wheel (two-axle) trucks have both axles powered. Most six-wheel (three-axle) trucks have three powered axles, but early passenger diesels and some early (and some more recent) freight locomotives have the center axle unpowered, using it as an idler to better spread the weight of the locomotive.

Diesel locomotives are known by wheel arrangements, just as steam locomotives. Powered axles on each truck are indicated by letters: "A" for one powered axle, "B" for two, "C" for three, and "D" for four. Numbers indicate unpowered (idler) axles. Thus a six-axle diesel with all axles powered is a C-C; a six-axle diesel with the center axle of each truck unpowered is an A1A-A1A.

Trucks

The locomotive sits on the bolster of each truck, which is supported on each side by a sideframe. A combination of coil and leaf springs, drop hangers, struts, and other components distribute weight and provide a

FOUR-CYCLE DIESEL

EXHAUST	INTAKE	COMPRESSION	POWER

EXHAUST

Exhaust

First upstroke

Crankshaft center line

Exhaust valve lifts and piston pushes out spent gases

INTAKE

Air

First downstroke

Air valve lifts and air is sucked and blown in

COMPRESSION

Second upstroke

Valves are closed, air is heated by compression

POWER

Fuel

Second downstroke

Fuel is injected and burned, driving piston downward

TWO-CYCLE DIESEL

SCAVENGING AND CHARGING CYLINDER

Exhaust

Upstroke

Exhaust and intake are effected while power stroke is coming to bottom

COMPRESSION

Air is heated by compression

INJECTION

Fuel

Downstroke

Fuel is injected and burned, driving piston downward

POWER

Exhaust valve begins to open near bottom of power stroke

smooth ride. Modern six-axle diesels (since the early 1990s) from EMD and GE feature radial or "self-steering" trucks. Older trucks have all three axles parallel with each other, meaning that when a three-axle truck is in a curve, only the middle axle follows the actual radius of the curve. The leading and trailing axles can't align properly, which causes wheel and rail wear, lowers adhesion, and can cause a rough ride. The axles on self-steering trucks pivot independently, reducing wear while increasing adhesion and ride quality.

Two- and four-cycle diesels

Diesel engines are either four- or two-cycle designs. A four-cycle engine completes four piston strokes (two up, two down, producing two driveshaft revolutions) to get one power stroke (see the illustration at left). The process starts with the intake stroke (the piston descends and clean air is drawn into the chamber), followed by the compression stroke (the piston moves upward and compresses the air), power stroke (fuel is admitted and burns from the high temperature gained by compression, forcing the piston downward), and exhaust stroke (the burned gases are discharged as the piston moves upward). Four-cycle engines are made practical by turbocharging, which we'll discuss in a bit.

A two-cycle engine accomplishes the same tasks with just two strokes and one revolution of the crankshaft, requiring the above steps to be accomplished in much less time. To do this, the cylinder simultaneously takes in clean air and expels exhaust gas on the piston downstroke, so that on the upstroke the new air is being compressed and is ready for ignition when the piston reaches the top of the cylinder.

Turbocharging

Turbocharging is a method of increasing an engine's power output without increasing its size. This is done by forcing more air into each cylinder, which allows more fuel to be injected and burned, resulting in more power. The turbocharger is powered by a turbine driven by expelled exhaust gases. The turbine, turning at 10,000 rpm (or higher), drives an impeller, which forces air at high pressure into the engine.

Electro-Motive did not turbocharge its two-cycle 567 engine until the late 1950s, instead using a Roots blower, a less-complex (non-turbine) device powered by the crankshaft. The blower forces air into the combustion chamber at a lower pressure than a turbo. Starting with its GP20 and SD24 models through its Dash-2 locomotives of the 1980s, EMD offered both turbocharged and non-turbocharged (Roots-blown) versions of most of its locomotives. Most other manufacturers turbocharged their four-cycle engines, with the exception of some switchers and other low-power locomotives.

The advantages of turbocharging, especially on early diesels, were often reduced by higher maintenance costs, which is why several railroads continued to opt for non-turbocharged locomotives into the 1980s.

Modern prime movers from GE (the GEVO) and EMD (model 1010) are microprocessor-controlled four-cycle engines that use multi-stage turbochargers, advanced cooling systems, and exhaust recirculating systems to meet stringent (EPA Tier 4) pollution limit requirements.

Dynamic brake grids

Radiator sections

Flow control valve

Storage tank

General Electric U-series diesels have their dynamic brake grids behind screen-covered openings at the rear. The radiator is atop the rear above the engine. General Electric

Dynamic braking

Dynamic brakes are an optional feature, but are found on almost all modern road locomotives. Dynamic brakes use the locomotive's traction motors as generators to provide resistance to a rolling train. Dynamics are employed mainly to keep a train's speed in check on downhill grades, as opposed to bringing a train to a complete stop.

To apply the dynamic brakes, the engineer moves the throttle to idle and sets the dynamic brake lever to "setup." This energizes the traction motor fields, which turns the traction motors into generators. Energizing the motor fields provides a great deal of turning resistance on the axles. The engineer then adjusts the amount of braking force by increasing the notches on the dynamic brake lever. (Specific controls vary by model and era.)

Dynamics provide significant rolling resistance, and dynamic brakes alone are sufficient to hold train speed in check in many downgrade braking situations. This saves a great deal of wear on brake shoes and provides a measure of safety beyond the train air brakes. On locomotives built into the 1970s, dynamics were typically effective from about 18 to 25 miles per hour. In the 1970s extended-range dynamics became an option, allowing effective braking down to 8 mph; the dynamic brakes on many of today's AC traction-motor locomotives are effective down to 1 mph.

The electricity generated by the traction motors is dissipated as heat in large banks or grids of resistors—much like a giant toaster—with fans to cool them. The resistor grids are located in various locations depending upon locomotive type. Older EMD hood diesels had a flared blister (housing) atop the middle of the long hood. Older GE diesels had grids in the screened radiator intake opening at the rear of each side (opposite page), while tall-hood Alco road diesels had dynamics mounted in the long hood at roof level, with screened openings on each side. Modern GE and EMD locomotives have the dynamics directly behind the cab or at the extreme rear of the hood, respectively.

Diesel ancillary details and components

Many additional systems and components work to keep a diesel-electric locomotive running, or to provide crew comfort or safety features. The design and location of many of these items also serve as spotting features in identifying the manufacturer or specific model.

Radiator. Diesel engines are liquid-cooled, using 250 to 350 gallons of water. The radiator is usually located at roof level at the rear of the loco-motive. Cooling air is pulled in through grilles or screens on the sides by thermostatically controlled fans located on the roof (sometimes mounted below a protective grille or screen). The fans draw air through the radiator and expel the hot air upward. Antifreeze is generally not used in locomotives because of the cost, the risk of contaminating lubricating oil, and the risk of long-term damage to metal surfaces in the engine. Older locomotives were generally allowed to idle to stay warm. Some modern engines do indeed use antifreeze; others have automatic start/stop features that sense when a stopped engine needs to be running.

Oil. A modern diesel can require up to 400 gallons of lube oil. An oil pan under the engine holds the oil, which is piped throughout the en-gine's moving parts for both lubrica-tion and cooling. Oil is generally not changed, as with a vehicle, but is kept

The roof overhang covers the radiator and rooftop fan housings on this GE U33B. Headlights, number boards, and class lights are on both ends. Trains magazine collection

Steam generators provided heat for passenger trains through the 1960s. This EMD E unit has two steam generators, marked by the two stacks and two vents on the roof. EMD

topped off, with filters keeping the oil clean.

Fuel. The fuel tank on most diesels is suspended from the underframe between the trucks. Some early diesels had a fuel tank under the cab or in the short hood. The tank on a modern road locomotive holds 3,000 to 5,000 gallons of No. 2 diesel fuel, and the engine will burn between 1 and 5 gallons of fuel per mile depending upon throttle setting and load.

Louvers and grilles. Diesel engines require a great deal of air, both for combustion and cooling. The louvers on the sides of early diesels covered oil-bath filters used for cleaning combustion air. Later engines often used paper filters (usually marked by a housing on the roof behind the cab). Inertial filters are used on locomotives with pressurized engine compartments. This is an active filter, essentially a small rotating cyclone, that suspends dust and particles from intake air and then expels them from the system. Grilles of various designs often cover air intakes.

Steam generators. Passenger diesels—and many dual-purpose freight diesels—through the 1960s were equipped with steam generators to provide heat for passenger cars. These were located at the rear of the locomotive for cab units and either in the tall nose, directly behind the cab, or at the rear of the carbody of hood units. A steam generator consists of a diesel-fired boiler with a vent, stack, and safety valve above it on the roof. The water tank for the steam generator could be located inside the body (common for cab units) or located next to the fuel tank under the frame.

Head-end power (HEP). In the 1970s, head-end-power (HEP) units became common, supplying electricity to cars for air conditioning, lighting, and heat. Some locomotives use a separate small diesel engine and generator housed in the rear of the locomotive body. Other passenger diesels use power from the main generator for supplying train power.

The heavy multiple-connector MU cable above the couplers connects the two locomotives electrically. The air hoses below connect the train line and relay brake information. Keith R. Tygum

Air reservoirs. Long, narrow tanks with rounded ends store compressed air for the brake system and other accessories, such as the bell, horn, and sanders. The reservoirs can be located below the frame, either lengthwise under the running board or transversely next to the fuel tank, or atop the roof, with air compressors located out of sight within the body.

Batteries. Diesel locomotives require a lot of battery power—actually a set of batteries—compared to an automobile or truck. A set of locomotive batteries can weigh up to 3,000 pounds. The batteries can be located in cabinets atop the running boards next to the cab (hood units) or under the frame (hood or cab units).

Horn and bell. The horn is located on the roof either atop the cab or on

Switchers are end-cab diesels, with most following similar designs. This is an 800-hp EMD SW8 built in 1950 for Rock Island. EMD

the long hood, or sometimes astride the hood. Horns have from one to five "bells," and are tuned to a specific chord. Their sounds are distinct by manufacturer and type; Leslie and Nathan are the most common. Bells can be traditional or "gong" style, and are sometimes visible on the nose or roof, but are often located out of sight behind the pilot or behind the lead truck.

Handrails and grab irons. Railings, hand grabs, and steps are required safety features at many locations, specified by regulations. They can be in many styles. The railings at the corner steps on switchers and road switchers are painted a contrasting color to the body for visibility.

Multiple-unit (MU) connections. Most diesels are equipped to allow MU operation, allowing two or more locomotives to be controlled by the engineer in the lead locomotive. Connections include a heavy multi-connector electrical cable that plugs into a socket on each adjoining locomotive. Several air hoses are also connected, including the main brake line (train line) and three to five smaller hoses on either side of the coupler that regulate air brake responses.

Types of diesel locomotives

Diesels are divided into three main categories: switching, freight, and passenger locomotives. Freight and passenger locomotives together are known as road locomotives, and are further defined by body style into carbody (cab unit), road-switcher, and cowl variations.

Switchers

Switching locomotives were the first common diesel-electrics, and began appearing in large numbers in the mid-1930s. Diesels were well-suited for yard, terminal, transfer, and other switching duties that require low speeds and high tractive effort. Diesels could run constantly and required no breaks for water, coal, or dumping ashes—just periodic refueling. Also appealing to railroads was that diesel switchers eliminated smoke citations in cities, a big concern with steam locomotives.

The first successful commercial diesel-electric switchers were boxcab locomotives. A 300-hp design built by an Alco-GE-Ingersoll-Rand partnership in 1925 is credited as the first successful diesel-electric switcher. The mid-1930s saw more-powerful locomotives (600 to 1,000 hp), and a move to what would become the common body style for switchers: a cab at one end, a hood enclosing the engine and electrical components, and walkways (run-

Cab units are streamlined diesels that have side trusses to help support the frame. This is an Electro-Motive E3 passenger diesel. Trains magazine collection

Alco's FA-2 was a streamlined freight cab unit rated at 1,600 hp. Alco cab units had a distinctive nose style compared to EMD E and F units. J. David Ingles

ning boards) on either side and at the front of the hood. Most manufacturers offered multiple horsepower options, ranging from 600 to 1,200 and finally (in the 1960s) 1,500 hp. Switchers typically have long service lives compared to road diesels, and many switchers built in the 1930s and '40s (even from minority builders) were still going strong in the 1970s and later.

Several features distinguish a switcher from a road locomotive. Most switchers have smaller engines and lower horsepower, since speed isn't a

The side truss framing is readily visible on this under-construction EMD F unit in 1950. The cab-unit/carbody design allowed a thinner, lighter frame. EMD

critical factor (most have maximum speeds of 30 to 35 mph). Because of this, trucks on most switchers have a shorter wheelbase and less shock-absorption qualities compared to road diesels. Switchers usually have swipe throttles or additional speed "notches" compared to the usual eight notches on a road locomotive, allowing greater control when switching cars. The end-cab design allows lots of window and windshield area, allowing crew members good visibility in all directions. Switchers typically don't have classification lights or additional headlights like their railroads' road locomotives. Most switchers don't have multiple-unit connections, dynamic brakes, or steam generators.

Basic switcher designs remained relatively unchanged through the 1960s, when the number of classification yards began dropping and railroads wanted more flexibility from switching locomotives. The answer was switchers with road trucks and higher horsepower, such as EMD's SW1500 and MP15. By the 1980s, railroads were adapting older four-axle (and later six-axle) road switchers (often with slugs) as yard units. Sales of new switchers dwindled, with the last of them (EMD MP15Ts) rolling out in 1987.

Cab unit freight and passenger diesels

When diesels began powering passenger trains in the 1930s, railroads wanted the power units in streamlined bodies to match their new, sleek

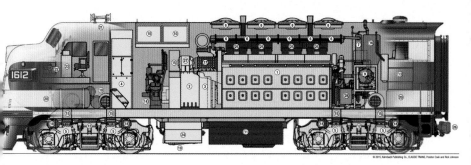

This drawing shows the components of an EMD F unit. Kalmbach Media

1. Engine
2. Main generator
3. Companion alternator
4. Electrical cabinet
5. Traction motors
6. Radiator
7. Lube oil filter
8. Radiator fans
9. Lube oil filter tank
10. Dynamic brake
11. Fuel tank
12. Trucks
13. Steam generator
14. Air compressor
15. Motor blowers
16. Coolant tank
17. Roots blower
18. Brake cylinders
19. Air reservoirs
20. Sand boxes
21. Horns
22. Cab heater
23. Operator's controls
24. Batteries
25. Exhaust manifolds
26. Couplers
27. Auxiliary generator
28. Lube oil strainers

trains. The first ones—Burlington's first *Zephyrs,* Union Pacific's M-10000, Illinois Central's *Green Diamond,* and others—were articulated with their train sets. By the late 1930s, railroads were finding that the benefits of articulation (mainly lighter weight) were outweighed by a lack of flexibility: If a single car or the power unit had a problem or needed repairs, the whole train had to be removed from service.

Separate locomotives became the norm by the late 1930s. A few were built to match specific trains, but interchangeable locomotives appeared with Electro-Motive's first E units in 1937, establishing the basic styling for passenger cab diesels for the next 25 years. This streamlined body style was known as a "cab unit" or "carbody" diesel. The E had two engines and rode on a pair of three-axle trucks with the center axle unpowered. Other manufacturers followed suit, with each having distinctive nose and cab stylings that made them fairly easy to identify. These included Alco with its DL and later PA (single-engine) models, Fairbanks-Morse with its opposed-piston-engined Erie-Built, and Baldwin with its "baby-face" and later "sharknose" models.

The cab-unit design carried over to the first road freight diesels as well, as Electro-Motive's revolutionary FT of 1939 followed the same basic design as the manufacturer's sleek E units, albeit shorter (single engined, on four-wheel trucks) with a less-slanted nose. Other manufacturers followed with freight cabs, including Alco's FAs, F-M's C-Liners, and Baldwin's DR-4-4-15 and RF-16. Over the years this style became known as cab, carbody, or covered-wagon diesels.

Cab diesels were designed so the truss framing of the body sides worked with the underframe to provide structural strength—similar to the design of a truss bridge. This is unlike switchers and hood-type diesels, which have much heavier underframes that are solely responsible for strength. Carbody diesels with cabs including throttles and control equipment are known as

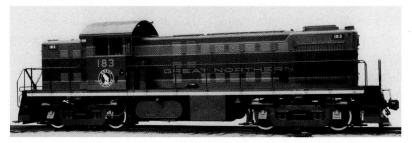

The Alco RS-1, introduced in 1941, is credited as being the first road-switcher. It's a stretched version of Alco's 1,000-hp S2 switcher on road trucks. Alco

"A units" and cabless locomotives are "B units" or boosters. For any given model, A and B units are mechanically identical except for the lack of an operating cab on B units. The purpose of this was the building-block concept, with the idea that railroads would have an A unit leading, followed by one or more B units, with an A unit trailing the consist (known as an A-B-A or A-B-B-A consist). Matched sets looked good, and having an A unit at each end avoided the need to turn locomotives at the end of a run.

Although aesthetically attractive, the carbody design made many maintenance chores difficult, with no easy side access to the engine, batteries, and other major components. This became more critical as locomotives aged. Switching maneuvers were difficult with cab units because of the lack of rear visibility. By the 1950s, railroads increasingly moved to road-switcher designs. The last freight cabs (F9s) rolled out in 1956, and a few passenger cabs came after that—the last one, Union Pacific E9A No. 914, was delivered in January 1964.

The cab design saw a renaissance beginning in the 1990s, as Amtrak received new streamlined Genesis-series passenger locomotives from GE, and

Electro-Motive's BL2 was a semi-streamlined design that offered few of the advantages of a true road switcher. It sold poorly, but gained a cult-like following among railfans. EMD

EMD's GP7 popularized the road-switcher; more than 2,700 were built from 1949-1954. They were easier to maintain and offered better visibility than cab units. Robert Milner

other locomotive designs followed, through the 2022 delivery of Siemens ALC-42 locomotives. Although the new locomotives look radically different compared to traditional cab units, the bodies feature a monocoque design that provides structural strength, so a traditional heavy underframe isn't needed.

Hood units (road switchers)

Once the first successful road freight diesels (EMC's FTs) hit the road in the early 1940s, it didn't take long to figure out that crews on mainline freight trains had different needs than those working in passenger service. En route switching with cab units could be challenging due to poor rearward visibility, with the engineer often having to lean out of the window to see signals from brakemen. This wasn't good under normal circumstances, and could be downright miserable and dangerous in darkness or bad weather.

Alco's RS-1, first built in March 1941, gets credit for being the first true road switcher. Alco took its popular 1,000-hp S-2 switcher, placed it on a longer frame, added AAR type B road trucks in place of the short-wheelbase type A switcher trucks, and added a short hood on the other end of the cab. The result was the road switcher, also called a "hood unit."

The key design difference compared to a cab unit is that a hood unit relies on a heavy frame to support the engine, generator, and other components. Unlike a cab unit, the hood is there just to shelter components, not to provide structural support for the frame. Doors along each side of the hood provide easy access to engine components compared to cabs, and the entire hood can be readily removed if necessary.

The RS-1 wasn't quite powerful enough for heavy mainline freight service. Alco's solution in 1946 was the RS-2, which upped the horsepower to 1,500—which rivaled contemporary cab diesels in freight service. By 1946 and 1947, Baldwin and Fairbanks-Morse were also offering road switchers.

Electro-Motive was slow to develop a road switcher. It offered beefier versions of its switchers (as the NW3, NW4, and NW5) with road trucks as

EMD's SD40 and later SD40-2 (shown here) popularized six-axle diesels as fast freight locomotives. Iowa, Chicago & Eastern 6424 is a former Union Pacific engine. Jeff Wilson

transfer, terminal, and branchline freight locomotives, but didn't aggressively market them. It wasn't until the introduction of the BL2 in 1948 that EMD had anything resembling a true road switcher—albeit a light-duty one (the "BL" stood for "branch line"). It sold poorly; it was semi-streamlined, offering slightly better visibility, but it was difficult and expensive to fabricate and offered no improvement on engine access compared to a cab unit.

It wasn't until 1949 that EMD finally built a true road switcher, the 1,500-hp GP7. Even then, EMD didn't think of it as a mainline locomotive until railroads started treating it as such—and began buying them in droves. Although it appeared much later than other road switchers, the GP7 gets credit for popularizing the design concept, and more than 2,700 were sold. The GP7 featured the same proven 567 engine and mechanical and electrical equipment of its cab-unit sister, the popular F7.

Railroads soon became sold on the road switcher because of cost, operational benefits, and ease of maintenance. Six-axle road switchers began appearing in the mid-1940s. These were originally designed to spread the weight of a locomotive over two more axles, making them suitable for lightweight rail, and most early versions (such as Alco's RSC-2) had center idler (unpowered) axles. Railroads soon found unpowered axles ill-suited for freight locomotives where high tractive effort (as opposed to high speed, as on passenger units) was needed.

Great Northern 434 is an EMD F45 built in 1969. It's a cowl locomotive (basically an enclosed SD45), as the exterior shell does not contribute to frame support. EMD

Wide-nose ("safety cab") designs became standard by the 1990s. This BNSF (former Santa Fe) GP60M was among the last four-axle road diesels built. Jeff Wilson

Cab interior designs changed in the 1990s, with console-style controls and computer screens. This is a Union Pacific SD9043MAC in 1996. Union Pacific

Alco built a six-powered-axle version of the RS-1 (the RSD-1) in 1946, but only turned out six examples. However, others soon followed, by Baldwin (DRS-6-6-15, 1948), Alco (RSD-4, 1950), Fairbanks-Morse (H-16-66, 1950), and EMD (SD7, 1951). Through the 1950s, six-axle diesel sales increased, and they began finding their niche in heavy-duty drag service, especially at low speeds where high tractive effort was needed. Four-axle diesels were the speedsters on priority freight trains.

That began to change in the late 1960s, as EMD's SD40 and SD45 (and later Dash-2 versions) proved themselves capable of hauling high-speed freight trains as well as lugging drag freights. By the mid-1970s, six-axle diesels were outselling four-axle diesels, and by the 1990s, EMD and GE no longer built four-axle road switchers.

Alco's PA passenger diesels, built 1946-1953, are an example of first-generation diesels—those built to replace steam. Alco

Cowl units and wide noses

Cowl units began appearing in the 1960s. They have streamlined sides and noses, but—although lacking side running boards—are classified

General Electric entered the road-diesel market with its 2,500-hp U25B in 1959. They are second-generation diesels, as they were replacements for early diesels. General Electric

as road switchers. Although primarily passenger or dual-service locomotives, some freight-only cowl locomotives were also built. Unlike a cab unit, the sheathing on a cowl locomotive provides no additional structural support to the frame, and internally and mechanically they are essentially identical to a hood unit. Examples include EMD's F45, FP45, SDP40F, F40PH, and SD40-2F and GE's U30CG and P30CH. The cowl provides a streamlined look (important to some passenger operators) and provides more protection to crew members having to move between units on moving trains.

An element from the cowl designs that became common on later conventional road switchers was the wide, full-body-width nose, sometimes called a

General Electric's Dash 9-44CW, built 1993-2004, is an example of a third-generation diesel, with advanced engine design and microprocessor controls. Jeff Wilson

"safety cab." It first appeared on a non-cowl-body locomotive with the EMD DDA40X in 1969, and by the 1980s both GE and EMD offered their locomotives with versions of the wide nose. The EMD SD60M also debuted a new cab layout, with desk console controls replacing conventional control stands.

First- through fourth-generation diesels

Diesels have, on average, long lifespans, with about 15 to 20 years in heavy service as intended. This is usually followed by another 15 to 25 years in

This GE ET44AC is a fourth-generation diesel, with AC traction motors and a Tier 4-compliant GEVO engine. It debuted in 2012 and remains in production as of 2022. Cody Grivno

secondary or reduced service (sometimes even longer, with rebuilding of the engine and other major components). Distinguishing diesels built during various periods is often referred to by "generation," as in first, second, third, and fourth. There's a bit of overlap in the times that define them, but here's a general summary:

First-generation diesels are the early locomotives that directly replaced steam locomotives. This covers the first diesels of the 1920s up to those built through the late 1950s, including all carbody diesels, early road switchers (through EMD's GP9/SD9 and Alco's RS line), and all locomotives built by minority builders Baldwin, Lima, and Fairbanks-Morse.

Second-generation diesels are those that railroads purchased to replace early diesels (as opposed to replacing steam). They are marked by increased horsepower; the usual dividing mark is GE's pioneering 2,500-hp U25B of 1959; EMD's first turbocharged road diesels, the 2,400-hp SD24 (1958) and

2,000-hp GP20 (1960); and Alco's Century line, introduced in 1963. Through this period, horsepower kept increasing, with 3,000-hp models (EMD GP40 and SD40 series; GE U30B and U30C) to 3,600-hp (EMD SD45 and SD45-2; GE U36C) common into the 1970s.

Third-generation diesels are marked by the introduction of microprocessor controls, which improved engine and fuel efficiency, traction, and wheel-slip control, and also allowed the eventual advent of AC traction motors. EMD's SD60 line and GE's Dash 8 series of locomotives were the first. Both major manufacturers also developed new, larger diesel engines, with horsepower eventually moving to 4,000 to 4,400 hp for most models. Further developments were EMD's SD70 line and GE's Dash 9 and AC4400 models. Both manufacturers tried higher-horsepower locomotives, but they were not successful.

Fourth-generation diesels, the latest evolution in locomotive design, are largely the result of increasingly stringent EPA emissions regulations, beginning with Tier 0 in 2000 and advancing to Tier 4 in 2015. Existing locomotives met Tier 1 specs in the early 2000s, but tougher Tier 2 regulations, which took effect Jan. 1, 2005, forced both GE and EMD to redesign locomotives to be both more fuel efficient and cleaner to operate. The results (GE's Evolution-series GEVO locomotives and EMD's SD70ACe and SD70M-2) feature advanced electronic engine controls, diagnostics, automatic shutdown and startup, and even more advanced microprocessor systems. Tier 4 required a major revision of locomotive designs, including the engine itself, increased cooling capacity, and multi-stage turbochargers. GE met the regulations with its ET44AC and ET44C4, and EMD with its SD70ACe-T4.

Spotting features

To identify a locomotive, start with the basic shape of the cab, nose, and hood to determine the builder, then the wheel arrangement to determine the class. Figuring out the specific model is a matter of looking at details such as grille, window, porthole, and

EMD's 6,600-hp DDA40X, built for Union Pacific, was the most successful of the double-engine diesels. Trains magazine collection

louver style and locations; the number and location of hood doors; type of trucks (and number of axles); and the number and style of exhaust stacks and rooftop fans. See *Guide to North American Diesel Locomotives*, by Jeff Wilson (Kalmbach, 2017) for detailed information on individual locomotive models.

Locomotives are often modified over time, with their appearance changed. Grab irons are added and moved; louvers and grilles are added, removed, or modified; and side panels can be changed or swapped among locomotives. Locomotives are sometimes given new engines or are completely rebuilt, which can drastically change their appearance. (Because of this, the photos and notes throughout this book apply mainly to locomotives as built.)

Twin-engine diesels

The 1960s saw a flurry of super-sized, twin-engine locomotives from the three remaining builders (Alco, EMD, GE). Designed and built mainly at the

A Seaboard Coast Line SW9 is with a slug built from an old Baldwin diesel in 1976. Slugs have traction motors but no engine, getting power from a neighboring locomotive. Mike Small

request of the Union Pacific and Southern Pacific, these locomotives amounted to two standard locomotives joined together on a longer frame. These included EMD's DD35 and DDA40X, GE's U50 and U50C, and Alco's C-855 (although only three Alcos were built). Twin-engine hood diesels actually date back to the late 1940s, such as Baldwin's 2,000-hp DT-6-6-20, but those were for low-speed operation and sold as transfer locomotives. The new, big diesels of the 1960s were intended for high-speed freight service.

Genset locomotives have multiple paired engine/generator sets. This 2,000-hp RailPower RP20BD has three gensets; the model has been produced since 2008. RailPower Technologies

The loss in flexibility of these high-horsepower units (two were often too much power and one not enough) and the unique maintenance issues they presented (and when in the shop, it was the equivalent of having two locomotives out of service) doomed most of them to short careers, although the 6,600-hp DDA40X "Centennial" proved quite successful on the UP and enjoyed a normal diesel-electric life span. Most were out of service by 1980.

Slugs

A slug (or "slug unit" or "mate") is a locomotive that has traction motors but lacks its own diesel engine. It receives electricity from a neighboring locomotive (sometimes called a "mother") via a cable. The idea is that at low speeds and high engine RPMs, a diesel locomotive produces more current

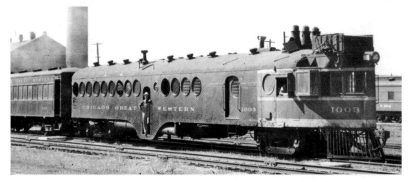

McKean was the first to build a successful gas-electric motor car, turning out 152 of them from 1905-1917. Chicago Great Western 1003 is at Oelwein, Iowa, in 1950. W.L. Heitter

Electro-Motive built Burlington no. 9735 (body by Pullman-Standard) in 1929 with a gasoline engine. It was later rebuilt with a 400-hp diesel. J. David Ingles collection

Budd's Rail Diesel Car (RDC), built from 1949-1962, used a pair of 275-hp diesel engines and featured the company's fluted stainless-steel body design. Budd

than its own traction motors can use. It's therefore efficient to route this power to a slug to provide additional tractive effort. Many railroads converted slugs from older locomotives, often cutting down the hood, removing the cab, and adding ballast to increase weight. Slugs are typically used in heavy low-speed service, such as yards, hump service, or as pusher locomotives.

Genset and battery-powered locomotives

A genset locomotive uses two to four smaller diesel engine/generator sets instead of one large prime mover. Only as many sets as needed operate at any given time based on the power required. The goals are fuel savings, reduced emissions, and less wear on components, along with the ability to remove individual engine/generator sets for maintenance. However, after an initial surge in orders starting just after 2000, railroads found that their higher initial cost wasn't offset by savings, with higher maintenance costs and lower reliability than expected. Many have been retired. Experiments are continuing with battery-powered locomotives, which rely exclusively on banks of batteries for power; Union Pacific ordered 20 battery-powered yard locomotives from Wabtec and Progress Rail in 2022.

Motor cars, railcars, Rail Diesel Cars

The first successful internal-combustion rail vehicles were self-powered gas-electric passenger cars, called motor cars, railcars, or "doodlebugs." McKean was the first to build a successful one, in 1905. The company would build 152 of the distinctive prow-nosed railcars through 1917. They were 55 or 70 feet long and used 100- to 300-hp gas engines mounted to the front

This Krauss-Maffei ML4000 diesel-hydraulic was purchased by Rio Grande in 1961 but sold to Southern Pacific in 1964. All of SP's K-M hydraulics were retired by 1968. J.W. Swanberg

truck, which powered the wheels mechanically through a drive train. They proved popular and economical for local and branchline passenger service, although mechanical issues plagued the pioneering McKean design.

Other companies also built them. The most successful was Electro-Motive Corp., which built more than 400 from 1924 through the early 1930s using

Winton gasoline engines (175-hp and larger) to drive a small generator, which powered traction motors on the lead truck. Later, more-powerful versions used distillate or diesel enignes up to 600 hp. Bodies were built by outside contractors including St. Louis Car Co. and Pullman. The Depression caused sales to dry up in the early 1930s.

By the late 1940s, railroads were again looking for economical options for secondary runs, and the Budd Company came through with a modernized version of the railcar, which it called the Budd Rail Diesel Car (RDC). They

This view of a 4,000-hp New Haven EP-4 electric in New York shows the extensive wiring, catenary, and infrastructure required for heavy electric operation. J.J. Farwell

The AEM-7 is a dual-cab, 7,000-hp electric locomotive used by Amtrak in the Northeast Corridor. The locomotives were built by EMD/ASEA from 1978-1988. EMD

were built in several configurations from 73 to 85 feet long, with Budd's familiar fluted stainless construction. The RDC uses a pair of 275-hp Detroit Diesel engines, each of which directly drives an axle via a hydraulic torque converter. Budd built 398 of them from 1949 to 1962. Many remained in commuter service through the 1980s, and some remained in service in Canada as of 2020.

Diesel-hydraulic locomotives

The 1960s saw experimentation with direct (hydraulic) drives in place of traction motors on diesel locomotives. Southern Pacific from 1961-1964 bought 18 diesel-hydraulic locomotives from German manufacturer Krauss-Maffei. The 3,600-hp ML4000 had a pair of V-16 Maybach diesel engines with Voith hydraulic transmissions (Rio Grande also bought three, but sold them to SP soon after). The SP also bought three C-DH643 diesel-hydraulics from Alco, which were also a twin-engine design (4,200 hp) using Voith transmissions. The locomotives didn't perform on grades as the railroad had hoped, and although they performed reasonably well in other service, they were maintenance intensive, didn't offer any savings over conventional diesel-electrics, and the K-M units' Maybach diesel engines were oddballs on the railroad. The coming of high-horsepower conventional locomotives (such as EMD's 3,600-hp SD45 and GE's 3,600-hp U36C) doomed the diesel-hydraulics, and all of were out of service by 1968.

ELECTRIC AND TURBINE LOCOMOTIVES

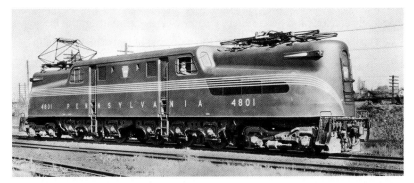

Pennsylvania's GG1 is perhaps the best-known electric locomotive. From 1934-1943, 139 were built, and some served into the 1980s. General Electric

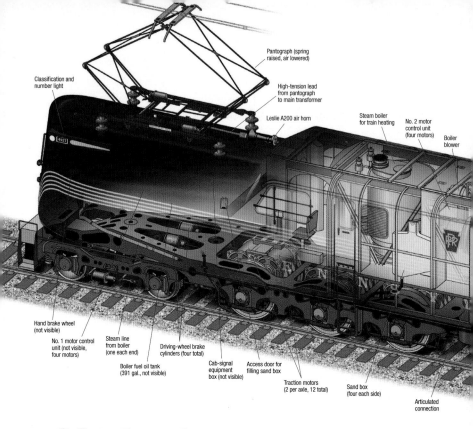

Pantograph (spring raised, air lowered)

Classification and number light

High-tension lead from pantograph to main transformer

Leslie A200 air horn

Steam boiler for train heating

No. 2 motor control unit (four motors)

Boiler blower

Hand brake wheel (not visible)

No. 1 motor control unit (not visible, four motors)

Steam line from boiler (one each end)

Driving-wheel brake cylinders (four total)

Boiler fuel oil tank (391 gal., not visible)

Cab-signal equipment box (not visible)

Access door for filling sand box

Traction motors (2 per axle, 12 total)

Sand box (four each side)

Articulated connection

GG1 electric cutaway

Electric locomotives receive their power from an external source, either an overhead wire or a powered third rail next to the running rails. They are extremely efficient and powerful, but heavy electric railroads in the U.S. have historically been quite limited due to the high cost of installing and maintaining the overhead wire or third rail. Streetcars and interurban lines by the 1890s were taking advantage of the technology, along with elevated and underground commuter lines using MU cars (self-propelled passenger cars that could be coupled together electrically). The construction of these early interurban lines was light—with smaller rail, tighter curves, and steeper grades compared to steam railroads—and most were out of service by the 1930s and 1940s.

"Heavy electrics"—with large locomotives rivaling the power of contemporary steam locomotives, and pulling trains on Class I railroads—first

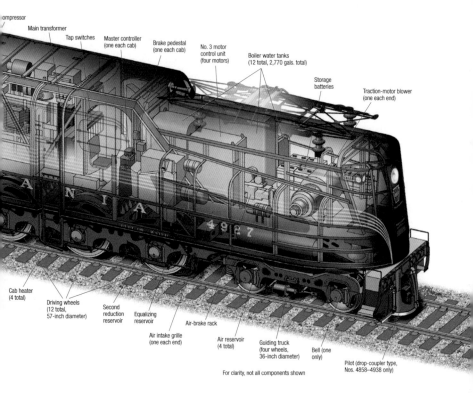

Compressor

Main transformer

Tap switches

Master controller (one each cab)

Brake pedestal (one each cab)

No. 3 motor control unit (four motors)

Boiler water tanks (12 total, 2,770 gals. total)

Storage batteries

Traction-motor blower (one each end)

Cab heater (4 total)

Driving wheels (12 total, 57-inch diameter)

Second reduction reservoir

Equalizing reservoir

Air-brake rack

Air intake grille (one each end)

Air reservoir (4 total)

Guiding truck (four wheels, 36-inch diameter)

Bell (one only)

Pilot (drop-coupler type, Nos. 4858–4938 only)

For clarity, not all components shown

appeared in the 1910s. Electrified zones on Class I railroads have been relatively rare in North America: the Milwaukee Road and Great Northern had electrified zones in mountainous territory in the west, and in the east Pennsylvania, New York Central, and New Haven (much of which still exists as Amtrak's Northeast Corridor), plus the Virginian, along with a couple of industrial railroads around the country.

Heavy electric locomotives look much like diesel-electrics, but instead of an engine, their bodies hold transformers and rectifiers for converting and controlling electricity for their traction motors. Some of the best-known electric locomotives were Pennsylvania's GG1, Milwaukee Road's Bi-Polar E-2, Virginian's EL-C rectifiers, and the streamlined Little Joes of Milwaukee Road and the Chicago South Shore & South Bend.

Early heavy electric locomotives paved the way for later diesel electrics. Most early electrics featured boxcab designs, with wheel arrangements resembling steam design (lead and trailing trucks, with driving wheels in the middle). Wheel arrangements were specified as with diesels, with unpowered axles numbered and powered axles lettered. Thus the Pennsylvania GG1 (page 158), which has two-axle leading and trailing trucks and two sets of three driving axles was a 2+C-C+2. Later electrics became streamlined, then styled more like contemporary road switchers, and by the 1950s were receiving conventional trucks in the style of diesel-electric locomotives.

Gas-turbine locomotives

Gas-turbine-electric locomotives (GTELs) enjoyed more success than the earlier experimental coal-turbine locomotives. The principle of a turbine engine is very simple: burning fuel creates heat; hot air expands and the resulting pressure/air flow then turns a fan-type blade attached to a shaft. The rotating shaft then powers a generator/alternator to create electricity. The engineering, however, is much more difficult, especially on a moving platform. Turbines operate at high speeds and high temperatures, requiring precise balance in moving parts; high-grade, lightweight alloys in construction; and high-quality, high-temp lubricants.

The most successful GTELs were the 55 operated by Union Pacific, built by General Electric from 1952-1961. Although not fuel efficient, they used

Union Pacific operated the largest fleet of gas-turbine-electrics (GTELs): 55 locomotives built by General Electric from 1952 to 1961. Union Pacific

Bunker C (no. 6 fuel oil), a heavy oil that was significantly cheaper than diesel fuel through the early 1950s (and which, as discussed earlier, was also used by oil-burning steam locomotives). Early single-unit GTELs were 4,500 hp, and later two-unit turbines were rated at 8,500 hp. They received 24,000-gallon fuel tenders, giving them a very long, impressive appearance. They were used on fast freight trains, and found success on UP's high-traffic main line.

Improved refining methods and the boom in the plastics industry caused Bunker C prices to rise by the 1960s, eliminating any savings from the technology compared to conventional diesels. That, together with the GTELs' advancing age and increased maintenance costs, led to the turbines' retirements. All were off the UP roster by 1969.

Another brief use of turbine locomotives came in the late 1960s. Smaller turbine-powered locomotives from United Aircraft, Rohr, and the French firm ANF powered some passenger trains in Canada and the Northeastern U.S. (Amtrak) from 1968 into the 1990s. These used jet fuel ("aviation turbine fuel") for power.

Turbine engines were ultimately unsuccessful in railroading, as they are at their best when they can run at high speeds for long periods of time. They are ideal for stationary power plants, ship engines, and aircraft engines. The rapid acceleration/deceleration cycles required of train locomotives in most types of service simply don't match the strengths of the turbine design.

LOCOMOTIVE BUILDERS

A number of manufacturers have built steam, diesel, and electric locomotives from the 1800s through today. Here's a summary of the major builders that have turned out locomotives from 1900 to the present:

American Locomotive Company (Alco)

The country's second-largest steam locomotive builder, the American Locomotive Co. (Alco) was created in 1901, when eight companies merged in order to better compete with the ever-expanding Baldwin Locomotive Works. The components were Brooks Locomotive Works (Dunkirk, N.Y.; "Dunkirk Works" by the 1920s), the second-largest builder in the Alco group; Cooke Locomotive & Machine Works (Paterson, N.J.; ceased production in 1926); Dickson Manufacturing Company (Scranton, Pa.; ceased production in 1909); Manchester Locomotive Works (Manchester, N.H.; ceased production in 1913); Pittsburgh Locomotive & Car Works (ceased production in 1919); Rhode Island Locomotive Works (Providence; ceased production in 1908), Richmond Locomotive Works (Richmond, Va.); and Schenectady (N.Y.) Locomotive Works, the company's primary plant. Two additional firms joined Alco shortly after it was established: the Locomotive & Machine Company of Montreal (1902) and Rogers Locomotive Works (1905). In 1928, Alco consolidated all remaining U.S. locomotive production at Schenectady. Alco also had a Canadian subsidiary, Montreal Locomotive Works (MLW), which built locomotives in Montreal, Quebec. Alco outshopped its last steam locomotive in 1948.

Alco was an early builder of electric and internal-combustion locomotives. In the 1920s, Alco partnered with General Electric and Ingersoll-Rand in producing a line of 60- and 100-ton boxcab diesel-electric switchers. Alco began building conventional-design switchers on its own in the 1930s, and in 1940 entered a marketing and production partnership with GE that would last until 1953.

Although Alco was the second-largest diesel locomotive builder (and briefly led diesel sales in the mid-1930s), sales of Alco road diesels always trailed EMD, and its market share fell throughout the 1950s. The company officially became Alco Products in 1956. Former partner GE, which entered the domestic road-switcher market with its U25B in 1959, soon eclipsed Alco in sales. Alco left the locomotive business in 1969, although MLW acquired Alco's design patents and continued building its own locomotives. Bombardier acquired a major interest in MLW in 1975, eventually merging MLW. Bombardier continued building locomotives until 1985.

Baldwin Locomotive Works

Baldwin was the largest, longest-lived, and most-successful steam locomotive builder. It was started in Philadelphia in 1831 by Matthias W. Baldwin, and produced its first locomotive in 1832. By the late 1800s Baldwin was building almost 700 locomotives a year, accounting for 30 to 40 percent of the domestic market. In 1903 the company began building a new plant in Eddystone, Pa., about 12 miles southwest of Philadelphia; the move to Eddystone wasn't completed until June 1928.

During the Depression, Baldwin purchased several machinery firms, among them the Whitcomb Locomotive Works of Rochelle, Ill., and the Milwaukee Locomotive Manufacturing Company, both builders of small gasoline and diesel locomotives. The cost of diversification and the construction of the new plant at Eddystone combined to put Baldwin into bankruptcy in 1935. World War II brought a brief return to prosperity, but its decline resumed after the war. Baldwin built its last domestic steam locomotives in 1949, ten Chesapeake & Ohio 2-6-6-2s that were updated versions of a 1910 design.

Baldwin built heavy electric locomotives in partnership with Westinghouse starting in 1895 (Westinghouse would later supply electrical components for several diesel-electric builders). Baldwin had begun producing diesel switchers in the late 1930s and started building road diesels in 1945. With sales declining and rival EMD's market share increasing (Baldwin's diesel market share never exceeded 13 percent), Baldwin merged with Lima-Hamilton in 1950. Lima, the third-largest steam builder, didn't start building production-model diesel locomotives until 1949, two years after it had merged with diesel engine maker Hamilton. By that time the market simply couldn't support another diesel manufacturer.

Following the Baldwin-Lima-Hamilton merger, the Lima-Hamilton line of switchers and road switchers was discontinued, and the company focused its attention on Baldwin's models. The company's sales continued to fall, and Baldwin built its last diesel locomotive in 1956—just seven years after building its last steam locomotive.

Brookville

Brookville, established in 1918 as Brookville Locomotive Works, has a long history of building small industrial locomotives and heavy equipment (rail and non-rail) for the mining industry. The Brookville, Pa.-based company, which became Brookville Equipment Corporation in 1998, still builds small locomotives and also manufactures rapid-transit cars and, since the 2010s, builds and rebuilds heavy-duty diesel-electric freight and passenger locomotives. As of 2022, its new locomotive offerings include the BL36PH streamlined (semi-monocoque) passenger locomotive and dual-service BL20GH road-switcher.

Canadian Locomotive Company

The Canadian Locomotive Company (CLC) dates from 1850, when a predecessor machinery works was founded at Kingston, Ontario. It produced its first locomotive in 1856 and was the pre-eminent locomotive builder in Canada until 1900. That year it ceased production; a group of Kingston industrialists bought and reorganized it as Canadian Locomotive Company. Production resumed, and by 1905 CLC was producing 45 locomotives a year.

In 1923 CLC built Canadian National's first 4-8-2, and in 1924 it built the largest locomotives in the British Empire—five 2-10-2s for CN. In 1928 it constructed the first of CN's 4-8-4s and North America's first road diesel, CN 9000. In 1950 Fairbanks-Morse acquired CLC. The Kingston plant produced FM-design diesels until about 1956.

Electro-Motive Corporation, Electro-Motive Division, General Motors Locomotive Group; Electro-Motive Diesel

The Electro-Motive Corporation (EMC) got its start by contracting construction of gas-electric motor cars (doodlebugs) by other companies in the early 1920s, using GE electrical equipment, Winton engines, and carbodies built by St. Louis Car Co., Pullman, and others. General Motors purchased both EMC and the Winton Engine Co. in 1930, but kept them as separate entities. The companies helped develop power cars for several high-speed passenger trains, notably the Burlington Route's *Zephyr* and Union Pacific's M-10000 in 1934. Switch engines and stand-alone passenger locomotives followed. After having its first locomotives assembled by outside contractors, EMC completed its own plant in LaGrange, Ill., in 1936.

General Motors merged Winton and EMC in 1941, and EMC became the Electro-Motive Division of GM (EMD). By the end of World War II, EMD—led by its pioneering FT cab-unit road diesel (introduced in 1939)—had a huge lead in diesel market share. The company would maintain the top spot in North American locomotive sales into the 1980s.

In 1950, GM opened a locomotive plant in London, Ontario. General Motors Diesel, Ltd. (GMD; later General Motors Diesel Division, GMDD) built locomotives for Canadian railroads and other export buyers.

General Electric eclipsed EMD in sales in the mid-1980s. General Motors shifted all assembly operations to the London plant in 1988, although many locomotives were also built at other independent and railroad-owned shops on a contract basis. At the same time, EMD and GMDD officially became General Motors Locomotive Group (GMLG).

In 2005, GM sold GMLG to Greenbriar Equity Group and Berkshire Partners. The new owners created a new company, Electro-Motive Diesel. In 2010, the new EMD was sold to Progress Rail Services, a subsidiary of Caterpillar.

Electro-Motive Diesel now has its headquarters, as well as engineering and parts manufacturing facilities, at McCook, Ill., with locomotive assembly in Muncie, Ind.

Fairbanks-Morse

Fairbanks-Morse was a late entrant to diesel locomotive manufacturing. The company's unique opposed-piston (OP) diesel engine, which has two pistons in each cylinder with no cylinder head, was first used in naval vessels in the early 1930s. Looking for other applications for the design, F-M turned to railroads. In 1939, the company's OP engines were used in six railcars built by St. Louis Car Co. for the Southern Railway.

The company's first diesel switchers appeared in 1944, with cab units and road-switchers following shortly after World War II. Although the OP engine offered more power compared to a similar-size conventional diesel, maintenance problems and costs countered the OP engine's power and efficiency gains. The company's locomotive sales slowed during the 1950s, with the last F-M domestic diesel built in 1958 and the last export order completed in 1963.

Locomotives were built at F-M's plant in Beloit, Wis., except for the company's big six-axle Erie-Built cab units, which were built at (and named after) General Electric's Erie, Pa., plant. (They were built before GE introduced its own line of heavy locomotives.) Fairbanks-Morse-design locomotives were also built at F-M's Canadian licensee, Canadian Locomotive Co.

General Electric

General Electric was a pioneer in electric railway equipment, building traction motors, generators, and control equipment for streetcars and electric railways in the 1890s. The company began supplying electrical equipment to gas-electric manufacturers in the 1920s. GE was an early partner with locomotive builder Alco and diesel engine maker Ingersoll-Rand, building heavy electric locomotives with Alco and diesel-electric boxcab switchers with Alco/I-R in the 1920s, and providing equipment— and doing assembly—for Electro-Motive and others in the 1930s.

General Electric built several small- to medium-size switching and industrial diesel locomotives (notably its 44-ton and 70-ton models) beginning in the 1930s, and from 1940 to 1953 partnered with Alco to produce road freight and passenger locomotives.

The company entered the domestic heavy-duty locomotive market on its own in 1959 when it introduced the Universal (U) series of locomotives, starting with the 2,500-hp U25B. The first production models appeared in 1961, and within three years GE had bumped Alco from the No. 2 locomotive builder spot in the country. By 1968, GE's market share was 33 percent. Numerous improvements to GE's line led to increased sales, and by the mid-1980s, GE became North America's largest locomotive builder.

In 2019, Wabtec (successor to Westinghouse) merged GE's locomotive business (GE Transportation), with GE Transportation becoming a division of Wabtec. Locomotives are assembled at Erie, Pa., and Fort Worth, Texas, with engines manufactured at Grove City, Pa.

Knoxville Locomotive Works

Knoxville (KLW) was established in Knoxville, Tenn., in 1998, and its primary business is remanufacturing and rebuilding diesel-electric locomotives. It sells several B-B and C-C diesel-electric locomotives from 1,050 to 3,200 hp. It is affiliated with Gulf & Ohio Railways, a holding company that operates four U.S. shortline railroads as of 2022.

Lima Locomotive Works

In the 1870s a Michigan logger, Ephraim Shay, developed a geared locomotive; in 1878 Lima Machine Works (mainly a builder of agricultural and sawmill equipment) built a locomotive to Shay's design for one of Shay's neighbors. After building several other logging locomotives of conventional design, in the early 1880s, Lima began building and marketing Shay locomotives in earnest. In 1891 the company acquired the Lima plant of the Lafayette Car Works, moved its operations there, and reorganized as the Lima Locomotive & Machine Company.

In 1911 Lima built its first locomotives for Class I railroads, 23 0-6-0 switchers for the Southern Railway and Mobile & Ohio. The firm was reorganized in 1912 as the Lima Locomotive Corporation and began constructing new shop facilities. In 1914, the production of conventional locomotives exceeded that of Shays for the first time. In 1916 the company was sold to Joel Coffin, who owned several companies that built locomotive parts. The firm became the Lima Locomotive Works.

During the early 1920s, railroads began recognizing that speed was as important as locomotive efficiency in freight service. Lima's chief engineer, William E. Woodard, approached the matter from the standpoint of boiler capacity. Woodard saw that sustained power output depended not on boiler pressure, weight on drivers, and driver and cylinder dimensions, but on the capacity of the boiler to generate steam. Woodard's Super-Power concept (see page 127) became the basis for Lima's locomotive innovations that resulted in high-speed, powerful locomotives such as Chesapeake & Ohio's high-drivered 2-10-4s, the modern 2-8-4 Berkshires of such roads as the Nickel Plate and Pere Marquette, and the 2-6-6-6s of C&O and Virginian. Lima was the third-largest steam builder, but regarded as the most innovative; innovations, however, were not able to slow the move to diesels, and Lima built its last steam locomotive in 1949.

Lima was too late to the diesel market to capture much business. In 1947 Lima merged with General Machinery Corporation of Hamilton, Ohio, taking advantage of that company's diesel engine designs, to form the Lima-Hamilton Corporation. The merged company built just 175 diesel locomotives into 1951 when it merged with Baldwin Locomotive Works to form the Baldwin-Lima-Hamilton Corporation; the Lima-Hamilton line of diesels was discontinued.

MotivePower Inc. (MPI); Morrison-Knudsen

MPI, a wholly owned subsidiary of Wabtec, rebuilds and repowers locomotives and also offers its own line, led by the MPXpress series of passenger diesels (since 2003); the current iteration is the MP54AC passenger locomotive, a streamlined genset diesel-electric. The company traces its history to Morrison-Knudsen, which established its MK Rail subsidiary to build and rebuild diesel-electrics in Boise, Idaho, starting in 1972. In 1996, the company became MotivePower Industries' Boise Locomotive division. The company merged with Westinghouse Air Brake in 1999, becoming the company's MotivePower, Inc., division The MPI Boise plant closed in 2020 with Wabco's merger with GE Transportation, with MPI production moving to the former GE plant in Erie, Pa.

Siemens Mobility

Siemens Mobility is the locomotive-building company of Siemens, with a manufacturing plant in Sacramento, Calif. (corporate headquarters is in Munich, Germany). The parent company has been involved in electric railroad technology and development internationally since the 1800s, and Siemens was an innovator in developing AC traction-motor technology in the 1970s and 1980s. The company began producing its own line of locomotives in the 2000s, with the latest the Siemens Charger line of streamlined passenger diesels produced since 2016.

1814 English inventor George Stephenson builds the first of several steam locomotives.

1829 Delaware & Hudson's *Stourbridge Lion* becomes the first commercial steam locomotive operated in America.

1831 Baldwin Locomotive Works is founded in Philadelphia by Matthias W. Baldwin.

1878 Ephraim Shay introduces the first practical geared steam locomotive.

George Stephenson's early designs featured geared drive trains, but a horizontal boiler.
Library of Congress

1901 The American Locomotive Co. (Alco) is formed with the merger of eight locomotive builders.

1901 The first domestic 2-8-2 (Mikado) is built by Baldwin; the wheel type would become the standard freight locomotive into the 1930s.

1904 First Mallet in U.S.—an 0-6-6-0—is built by Alco for Baltimore & Ohio.

Lima's 2-8-2 for New York Central featured higher pressure, larger firebox, and other modern features. Lima

1905 First experimental diesel locomotive built, by International Power Co., using Corliss engines, GE electrical equipment, and an Alco carbody.

1910 Baldwin builds its first Cab-Forward 2-8-8-2 for Southern Pacific.

1918 The USRA (United States Railroad Administration) issues standard designs for several steam locomotive types.

1922 Lima builds experimental 2-8-2 for New York Central, debuting many of its Super-Power concepts.

1922 Electro-Motive begins marketing gas-electric railcars.

1924 Alco-GE-Ingersoll-Rand builds several boxcab diesel-electrics.

1926 Alco builds the first 4-8-4, for Northern Pacific. More than 1,100 would be built, making it the most popular "modern" wheel arrangement.

1929 First North American road diesel, Canadian National no. 9000 (Westinghouse-Beardmore), powers the *International Limited*.

1932 Winton develops its model 201 diesel engine

1934 First diesel streamliner: Burlington's *Zephyr*

1937 EMC builds first passenger E unit diesels.

1939 Electro-Motive freight FT begins demonstration tour

1941 Alco builds the first 4-8-8-4 Big Boy for Union Pacific.

Alco introduces its RS-1, the first road switcher.

1944 Fairbanks-Morse introduces a line of diesel switchers.

The FT ensured the demise of steam. EMC

1947 Steam builder Lima merges with diesel builder Hamilton.

1948 Alco builds its last steam locomotive.

1949 Lima builds its last steam locomotive.

The GP7 wasn't the first road switcher, but it sold the concept to railroads across the country. EMD

EMD introduces its first true road-switcher, the GP7.

1950 Baldwin merges with Lima-Hamilton.

LOCOMOTIVE TIMELINE

1950 Norfolk & Western builds three J-class 4-8-4s, the last passenger steam locomotives built.

1953 Norfolk & Western turns out the last reciprocating steam locomotive built in the U.S. (0-8-0 no. 244).

Norfolk & Western's streamlined 4-8-4s were truly modern steam locomotives.
Norfolk & Western

1955 Steam stalwart Norfolk & Western orders its first diesels.

1956 Baldwin-Lima-Hamilton ceases operation.

1958 Fairbanks-Morse ceases domestic locomotive production.

1959 General Electric introduces its Universal line of road diesel locomotives.

1960 Regular steam operation ends on Class I railroads.

1969 Alco exits locomotive business.

1988 EMD and GMDD officially become GMLG (General Motors Locomotive Group); all production moved to London, Ontario.

1991 The AC-motor GMLG SD60MAC begins testing; the production SD70MAC would appear in 1993.

1994 The last four-axle road freight locomotives (GP60s for Southern Pacific) are delivered.

2005 GM sells GMLG to Greenbriar Equity Group and Berkshire Partners; new company is Electro-Motive Diesel.

2010 EMD is sold to Caterpillar subsidiary Progress Rail Services.

2012 Last DC-motor diesel-electric locomotive is built.

2015 Tier 4 emissions standards take effect for new locomotives.

2022 Amtrak places its first Siemens Charger ALC42 diesels in service

The SD60MAC's AC traction motors would eventually become standard. GMLG

Rolling stock

■ The term "rolling stock" is broad, meaning all cars that roll on the rails. This includes freight cars, passenger cars, and non-revenue equipment such as cabooses and cars in maintenance-of-way service. The first rolling stock of the 1830s was small—essentially stagecoaches and freight wagons equipped with rail wheels on two axles (four wheels per car). Designs soon shifted to larger, stronger cars for both passenger and freight equipment, with wood-bodied cars riding atop pairs of four-wheel trucks. The use of trucks provided a smoother ride than four-wheel cars, and allowed larger cars with higher capacity.

Freight equipment includes a broad range of car types. This view of an early 1960s yard includes a variety of 40-foot boxcars—still the standard car type of the era—plus a new New York Central cylindrical covered hopper, an older Wabash two-bay covered hopper, and a couple of gondolas. John Ingles; J. David Ingles collection

Most cars featured all-wood body construction into the early 1900s. This 30-ton wood refrigerator car was built in 1892. It rides on archbar trucks. Trains magazine collection

All-wood construction was standard through the 1800s, including the body as well as the floor and frame. Trucks were typically archbar design, comprising multiple iron (later steel) components bolted together with side springs and holding iron wheels, but often had wood beams for frames. Capacity of wood freight cars was typically 20 to 25 tons by 1900. Although wood cars were relatively inexpensive to both build and repair, they were not durable and were subject to extensive damage in derailments. For passenger cars, this also included high risk of fire, with oil lamps, coal stoves (for heat), and wood construction a bad combination—especially as train speeds and car sizes began increasing.

Pennsylvania Railroad's X-29 was the first common all-steel boxcar. The railroad built more than 30,000 cars to this design from the 1920s into the 1930s. John Ingles; J. David Ingles collection

Modern cars feature all-steel construction and (typically) 110-ton capacity. This 5,660-cf, five-bay, pressure-differential covered hopper was built in 2004. Jeff Wilson

Steel-bodied freight cars began appearing in the 1890s, first with hopper cars and tank cars. Passenger cars began receiving steel frames shortly thereafter, with the first all-steel passenger cars appearing in 1907 (ushering in what became known as the "heavyweight era"). Boxcars retained wood bodies (often with steel body framework on steel underframes) into the 1920s, and refrigerator cars retained wood bodies for another two decades, but most freight cars were all-steel by the 1930s. Further refinements included cast-steel trucks by the 1910s, welded construction beginning in the 1950s, and continued increases in capacity (both weight and interior space) through today.

Car ownership

Railroads were responsible for providing cars to their online shippers for freight and to provide passenger service, and individual railroads historically have owned most of the rolling stock for doing this. For passenger service, cars were owned by the railroads with the exception of sleeping cars (see "Pullman Company" in Chapter 1), and for the most part passenger cars stayed on their home rails.

For freight service, railroads owned fleets of various car types. These are interchanged with other railroads as needed, with rules covering rates and reloading (see "Freight car use rules" on page 197), so freight trains typically carry cars bearing a variety of road names from across the country.

Privately owned freight cars have increased significantly in number since the 1970s. Historically, railroads have loved multi-purpose cars, which is

This 6,000-gallon pressure (300 psi) tank car was built in 1961 to carry tetraethyl lead. It's owned by UTLX and leased to Houston Chemical Corp. John Ingles; J. David Ingles collection

why the common boxcar was used for everything from boxed goods to lumber to bulk grain into the 1960s. Railroads have long tried to avoid buying cars devoted to carrying seasonal goods or single commodities (stock cars, refrigerator cars, tank cars, covered hoppers), leading to private companies owning most of these car types. This can be a shipper (such as a grain company), a car leasing company (such as Union Tank Car; many car builders have their own leasing companies), or a subsidiary company formed by a railroad or group of railroads (such as Pacific Fruit Express, long owned by Union Pacific and Southern Pacific for operating refrigerator cars).

The increase in specialty cars has led to an increase in privately owned cars. In 1977, railroads owned 1.3 million freight cars (about 80 percent of the total North American fleet), but by 2015 this had dropped to 420,000 cars (29 percent).

FREIGHT CARS
Gross rail load (GRL) and car capacity

Freight car size had been increasing throughout the late steam and early diesel eras, but the 1960s saw a dramatic increase in "jumbo" cars of various types to take advantage of new rules on rates. Car size is rated by—and regulated according to—both overall dimensions and weight. In terms of capacity, cars are known by their nominal carrying capacity in tons: typically 110 tons, 100 tons, and 70 tons for modern cars, up from the 40- and 50-ton cars that were most common during the steam and early diesel eras. This is important both in terms of how much cargo can be loaded in a car and in

Lettering on this boxcar includes capacity info, builder's insignia (Pullman-Standard), Plate C clearance designation, ownership (Brae), and car class (XP). Trains magazine collection

what routes can handle cars of various weights.

However, although these descriptions are commonly used, they are just rough estimates of a car's load limit. The actual capacity of any given car varies by the car's unloaded ("light" or "tare") weight. The key number is the gross rail load, or GRL. This is the total weight allowed on the rails for a car, and is calculated by adding car's light weight plus the weight of the load.

Look at the stenciling on any freight car and you'll see the light weight and load limit in pounds, rounded to the nearest 100 (as seen in the photo above, there used to be a line for "capacity" but it was an estimation—its use was eliminated in 1989). Adding the light weight and load limit gives you the GRL.

Over the years the AAR has set GRL limits for unrestricted interchange along with higher limits for restricted interchange. In the early 1900s, this was for 30-ton (103,000-pound GRL) and 40-ton (136,000-pound) cars. By the 1920s, most routes allowed 50-ton cars (then a GRL of 169,000 pounds), making them the standard for unrestricted interchange anywhere on the rail system. By the 1950s, there were also plenty of 70-ton (210,000-pound GRL) and 100-ton (251,000-pound GRL) cars in service, but they were allowed only on certain routes.

Railroads wanted the increased capacity of larger cars, and provided for this by improving bridges and using heavier rail—first on main routes, then on secondary lines and, in some cases, branch lines. In 1963 the AAR increased the weight limits for each weight class: to 263,000 pounds for

This 286K (110-ton), 3,770-cf four-bay aluminum coal hopper was built by Johnstown America in 1999. Coal cars are built to maximize the weight of the load. The painted end at right marks the rotary-coupler end. Jeff Wilson

100-ton cars, 220,000 for 70-ton cars, and 177,000 for 50-ton cars. This marked the true start of the 100-ton car as standard, although many 70-ton cars would continue to be built.

Effective in January 1995, the AAR approved the use of 110-ton cars with a GRL of 286,000 pounds (AAR standard S-259, issued in November 1994)—commonly listed as 286K—including specifications for car and truck/journal design to handle the increased weight. Some railroads had been using such cars since 1991 by bilateral agreements, based on track and bridge strengths on specific routes, and use can still be limited on some routes.

Many in the industry predict the coming of even heavier cars, with a GRL of 315,000 pounds (125-ton cars). Railroads have been upgrading their main routes to handle such cars, but widespread approval is still in the future. These cars require 7" x 12" journals and 38" wheels (compared to 6½" x 12" journals and 36" wheels for 286K cars). Some railcar manufacturers are offering cars that can be converted to fit the new, larger trucks.

It's important to note that many cars still fall well under the maximum GRLs, depending upon the products they carry. Unit-train coal gondolas, for example, are designed to carry as much coal by weight as possible, and will almost always max out their load limits. On the other hand, many of the huge 86-foot, high-cube auto parts boxcars built in the 1960s and '70s were 70-ton cars. The metal stampings these cars carried were bulky but not heavy, and a load that completely filled the car interior might only weigh about 20 tons. The higher weight limit was not needed.

This is why the various GRL limits are in place: It's still more cost-effective to build a lower-capacity car, because the components required will be lighter and less expensive. In the decade of the 2010s, 80 percent of cars added to the fleet were 286K (110-ton) cars. Many 263K cars have been upgraded to 286K as well. For most of these, it was a matter of upgrading the truck capacity, as the carbodies had been built to handle the higher weight.

Car size; Plate clearance diagrams

Along with weight, railcar size (exterior height, length, and width) is also regulated to make sure cars will fit under bridges, pass through tunnels, and safely pass next to other lineside obstructions and each other on parallel tracks.

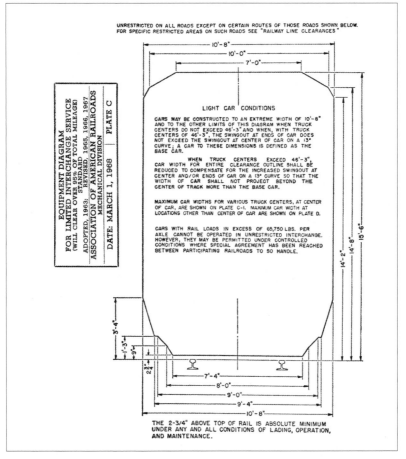

Plate diagrams specify width and height limits for various car lengths. This is the 1968 revision of the Plate C clearance diagram. AAR

"Plate" diagrams, indicated by letters, were developed by the AAR to provide a guideline for rolling stock clearance. For each Plate designation, a published diagram shows a car outline with maximum allowable dimensions at various car heights. Specifications call out various car lengths and truck-center spacing, limiting mid-car or end-car overhang on specific curves.

Plate B clearance, first adopted in 1948, means a car is unrestricted for interchange and can travel on any route. The basic outside dimensions include a maximum exterior height of 15'-1" (above railhead) and width of 10'-8" (the maximum for any Plate diagram).

Plate C clearance was adopted in 1963, and at the time provided clearance on 95 percent of routes. It allows a height of 15'-6". In 1974 came Plate E (15'-9") and Plate F (17'-0"), the latter for high-cube boxcars. Plate H (1994) was adopted for double-stack container cars, allowing a 20'-2" height. Specifically for 89-foot enclosed auto racks are Plate J (2005), allowing a 19'-0" height, and Plate K (2005) which allows a 20'-3" height but narrows the width to 10'-0".

Since the early 1970s, freight cars larger than Plate B have a stencil on the side indicating their clearance. If a car's dimensions exceed a particular Plate designation, it is marked as such (for example, "EXCEEDS PLATE C"). Plate diagrams are periodically reviewed and revised. You can find these diagrams published in *Official Railway Equipment Registers,* along with other information on car restrictions and use.

Freight car lettering

Lettering includes optional as well as required elements, all of which have evolved significantly since the steam era. Here are the basics of various lettering and marking details found on freight cars.

Road name and herald. These aren't required, but through the 1960s most railroads spelled out their road names on boxcars and other cars where space allowed, often with heralds or stylized initials. On older single-sheathed wood boxcars, with the bracing on the outside, this was often left off.

Slogans and brands. The steam-to-diesel transition era saw the introduction of many new streamlined passenger trains. Railroads wisely saw freight cars as rolling billboards for their new named trains, and splashed the train names and slogans on boxcars in particular. The better-known examples tended to be the railroads with the largest freight car fleets, which would be seen in trains across the country. Common examples include Santa Fe's *Chief* and *Super Chief,* Burlington's "Way of the *Zephyrs,*" Chicago & North Western's *400* Fleet, Seaboard's *Orange Blossom Special,* and Union Pacific's "Road of The Streamliners."

Privately owned and leased cars often carry the names and brands of their lessees. This was especially common for meat reefers (which were in dedicat-

This Northern Pacific 40-foot boxcar, built in 1958, shows a large version of the railroad's logo with a plug for its *North Coast Limited* passenger train. John Ingles, J. David Ingles collection

Lettering on this 1977-built IPD (incentive per-diem) boxcar includes the railroad name, a note that it has cushioning, dimensional data, and an ACF builder's logo. The lower black boxes are consolidated stencils; the top plate is an ACI bar-code panel. J. David Ingles collection

ed service to specific packing companies), as well as tank cars and covered hoppers owned or leased by petroleum, chemical, and grain companies. A 1930s ruling prohibits the use of car-side advertising for products not produced by the lessees (the so-called ban against "billboard reefers," colorful cars that through the 1920s often carried elaborate graphics for various products that often had no connection to what the cars carried).

Reporting marks and number. The reporting marks are the unique set of initials assigned to every railroad and private car owner for identification. Private (non-railroad) owners have reporting marks ending in "X." Each car's number is unique to that set of reporting marks. The reporting marks and number must also be placed on car ends. With mergers, the new company sometimes continues using old reporting marks from predecessor railroads.

Capacity. This is the car's nominal capacity in pounds (see Gross Rail Load on page 178). Most transition-era cars were 40-ton (80,000-pound), 50-ton (100,000-pound), or 70-ton (140,000-pound) cars; by the 1960s many cars were 100-ton (200,000). This capacity was largely determined by the trucks used. This line was eliminated in 1989, and many older cars have this line painted out.

Load limit. This is the maximum weight limit for the load itself. A star next to the load limit indicates that the limit is based on the car's construction and underframe, not the truck's journals and spring package. This number wouldn't be changed if a car's light weight changes. The load limit is based upon the car's weight when empty, which leads us to ...

This Pennsylvania car is assigned to auto-parts service (class XAP). The "155" is the pool it's assigned to; the stencil directs its return to Cleveland when empty. J. David Ingles collection

Light weight. This is the car's actual weight when empty. The light weight and load limit when added will equal the car's Gross Rail Load (GRL). The word "NEW" to the right of the light weight, with a date, indicates the weight was taken when the car was built. Cars are periodically reweighed, and reweighed after repairs or rebuilding. If the reweighing shows a difference (generally 300 pounds or more), the new weight is stenciled in place, and the date and shop initials where this is done are added in place of the "NEW" stencil. Tank cars didn't require reweighing, because shipping charges are by gallons.

Dimensional data. For boxcars and refrigerator cars, this includes internal and external height, length, and width. Covered hoppers, hoppers, and many boxcars and reefers include cubic-foot capacity, and tank cars include capacity in gallons (usually stenciled on the car end). This is generally found on the right side.

Bearing repack date. The journal boxes of solid-bearing trucks had bearing pads or cotton waste that held oil to lubricate the bearings. The date these were replaced were marked, along with the railroad or shop initials. This was usually on the side sill just above the truck.

AAR classification. Cars' AAR mechanical classifications (for example, XM for a general-purpose boxcar, XAP for an auto-parts car) began appearing on cars in the 1950s. This is usually found near the capacity data.

Built date. The month and year of construction appeared near the dimensional data for cars built into the 1970s; after that, this information was placed in the consolidated stencils. A car that is rebuilt will have both the built and rebuilt date stenciled.

Builder's insignia. Car manufacturers often stencil their initials, insignia, or logo on each car side. Cars built by railroads' own shops may include this information.

Routing and loading information. Cars in dedicated service for a specific customer are stenciled with information on where the car should be sent when empty, and/or what route to use. This information is now included in a car's Umler (electronic data) information. Cars used for a specific lading (especially tank cars and covered hoppers in dedicated service) are lettered with that information.

Special equipment. Specially equipped cars—such as those with loading racks, cushioned underframes, or special lining—have lettering or logos to indicate this. Through the 1960s, automobile boxcars (with loading racks)

Modern tank cars include a matrix with test requirements and dates. The "1987" hazmat placard indicates a load of ethanol in this 2006-built DOT 111A100W1 car. Jeff Wilson

had a 3"-wide, horizontal white stripe on the door (right-hand door on double-door cars) with the car's inside center height stenciled on the stripe and the rack type stenciled below the stripe.

Test information. Tank cars include the date and location where the tank, safety valves, steam lines, and other equipment were tested, with the relevant data. Tank cars also include the ICC or DOT specification class for the car. In the 1990s, this began appearing as a grid (matrix) on the car side.

Hazmat placards. Cars carrying hazardous materials require placards identifying the product being carried. Into the 1970s, this was simply a diamond-shaped card (on each side and end) with a generic warning such as "dangerous" or "inflammable." In the late 1970s, following the Hazardous Materials Transportation Act of 1975, placards became product-specific, listing characteristics of the products being carried along with their four-digit identifying code. Among the most common on railcars are 1075 for LPG, 1203 for gasoline, and 1170 for ethanol. These are mainly found on tank cars, but can be seen on covered hoppers, boxcars, and other car types as well.

Consolidated stencils. These are the black panels on the lower right side of freight cars; they began appearing in 1972. They carry the car's built date and inspection and maintenance information, including COTS (clean, oil, test, and stencil), IDT (in-date test for brake inspection), and LUB

Every modern freight car carries an Automatic Equipment Identification (AEI) tag on each side. The box houses an electronic transponder read by trackside scanners. Jeff Wilson

(lubrication date for roller bearings) or RPKD (for repacking journal boxes). All cars were to have these panels by 1979. Cars initially had single or double (separate) panels, then a combined double panel, and now a three-panel design, with the narrow bottom panel for built/rebuilt dates.

Wheel-inspection dots. These marks—a small black square with a yellow or white circle—began appearing in March 1978. All North American cars had to be inspected for a certain type of defective wheel; cars not having the wheels received white dots; cars with the defective wheels received a yellow dot, and these had to have their wheels replaced (and yellow dot changed to white) by December 1978. Cars built or repainted after this time will not have this mark.

ACI labels. Railroads' initial attempt at automated identification was ACI (Automatic Car Identification), introduced in 1967 (marketed by GTE as KarTrak) and mandated for all interchange cars by 1970 (see Chapter 4). This was an optical system that used trackside scanners to read bar-code plates—vertical black plates with colored horizontal bands—on cars. The system didn't work well, as grime made reading panels unreliable, and the system was abandoned in 1977. Many cars could still be found with old ACI plates into the 2000s.

AEI tag. Since 1994, each freight car must carry an Automatic Equipment Identification (AEI) tag. This is a small box located on each side of a car that houses a radio transponder that responds to trackside readers to communicate car identity and other information as cars roll by.

Chalk marks. Through the 1960s it was common for car agents and others to add chalk mark notations on cars to indicate routing, train numbers, track numbers, and other special information. This would usually be found in the lower corners of the sides, and sometimes next to the doors.

Reflective striping. Reflective strips have been required on new rolling stock since 2005, and all freight cars were to be equipped by 2015. Strips can be vertical or horizontal, and placement varies by car type, with a minimum of 3.5 square feet of reflective material on each side. Many older cars had this striping as well, but it was at the car owner's option.

Other lettering indicates the type of wheels, couplers, brake pads, and other equipment, along with specific loading restrictions or instructions, as well as door (or valve, hatch, or outlet gate) operating instructions.

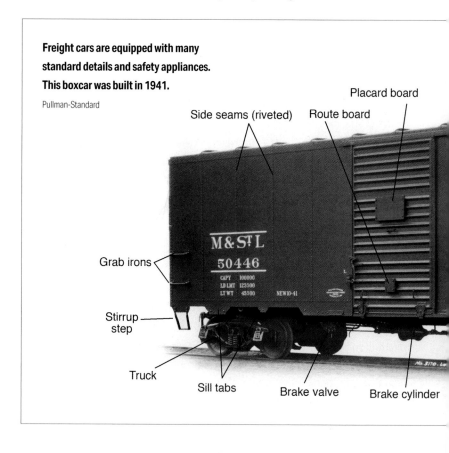

Freight cars are equipped with many standard details and safety appliances. This boxcar was built in 1941.

Pullman-Standard

Side seams (riveted)

Route board

Placard board

Grab irons

Stirrup step

Truck

Sill tabs

Brake valve

Brake cylinder

M&StL
50446

CAPY 100000
LD LMT 123500
LT WT 45300   NEW 10-41

Components and safety appliances

Freight cars are required to have a variety of safety gear, and a lot of components are common among all cars (although specific locations can vary). Stirrup-style steps are found at all four corners, with grab irons and/or ladders. Running boards (the proper term for "roofwalks") were used on boxcars and other house cars into the 1960s. They were eliminated on new equipment starting in 1966, and were removed from existing cars as they were shopped. This led to the lowering of the brakewheel on the ends as well. On each end is a coupler, with (as you look at the end) the uncoupling lever at the left and the air hose to the right.

Brake gear (brake systems were described in Chapter 1) is located under most cars, and is often visible. Components on tank and hopper cars are often located on the end platforms or under the end hopper slope sheets. The brake wheel is located on the "B" end of a car (the opposite end is the "A"

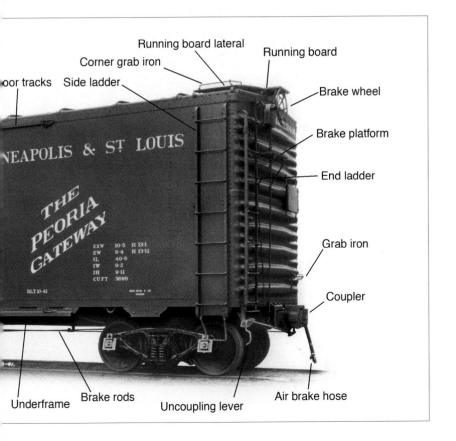

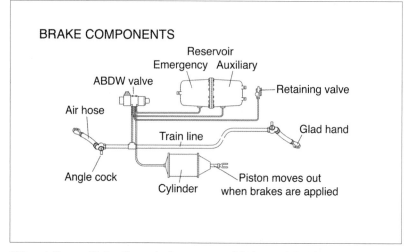

BRAKE COMPONENTS

Although the specific location varies by car type and design, each freight and passenger car has a full set of brake gear that's connected to the main air (train) line. Kalmbach Media

Brake components are most visible on hopper cars, where gear is typically located on the ends under the slope sheet. This view also shows the uncoupling lever. Trains magazine collection

end). These were originally at roof-height level, but were moved down when running boards were eliminated.

Freight car trucks

Most freight-car trucks have four wheels: two axles with a wheel on each end, mounted on a frame. This assembly—sideframes and bolster, along with springs, brake beams, and other components—is known as a truck. Each truck weighs four to five tons. Each car has a bolster at each end—a trans-

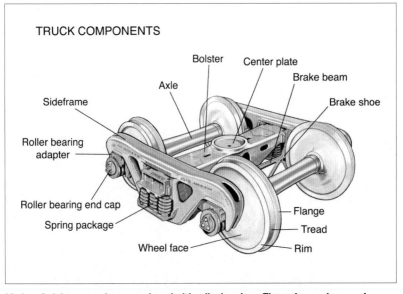

TRUCK COMPONENTS

Bolster
Center plate
Brake beam
Axle
Sideframe
Brake shoe
Roller bearing adapter
Roller bearing end cap
Flange
Spring package
Tread
Wheel face
Rim

Modern freight car trucks are equipped with roller bearings. The spring package varies based on the weight capacity. This is ASF's Ride Control design. ASF Industries

verse member across the bottom of the car frame, inset from the end of the body. A kingpin centered on the car's bolster rests in a hole in the center plate at the middle of the truck bolster. The weight of the car body is all that's needed to keep a car on its trucks.

Each end of the truck bolster rests in a notch in the center of the sideframe atop a group of springs (called a "spring package"). The bolster isn't solidly attached to the sideframe—it's allowed to float up and down on the spring package. The number and type of springs are based on the weight capacity of the car. Each package usually has 7 to 9 main coil springs, and each of these springs may have an additional internal spring or hard-rubber or hydraulic snubber. The springs cushion the load and stabilize the ride; snubbers and wedges act like shock absorbers by controlling spring motion, avoiding bouncing and rocking.

Each end of the sideframe rests on the outboard end of an axle; a 5'-6" wheelbase (distance between axles) is standard. On all modern cars the axle end is a roller bearing, with a roller bearing adapter on the sideframe. The end caps of the axles rotate. Roller-bearing trucks have been required on all new and rebuilt 100-ton cars since 1963, on all new cars since 1968, and on all equipment in interchange service as of 1995.

The roller-bearing axle end is held above by the roller-bearing adapter, which is in turn held in jaws of the truck sideframe. Jeff Wilson

Earlier trucks were solid- or plain-bearing (often incorrectly referred to as "friction-bearing"). Solid-bearing trucks were maintenance intensive. They relied on brass bearings mounted in the truck sideframes resting atop the rotating smooth outer axle ends of each wheelset. These were covered by journal boxes, which contained pads or clumps of stranded cotton (called "waste") impregnated with oil to lubricate the bearing and axle surfaces. Journal boxes were checked frequently, because if a box or bearing ran dry—or if waste or a pad got hung up in the bearing—the result was a dry, overheated bearing, or "hotbox." At best, this meant having to set out the affected car and replace the bearing; if unnoticed, the resulting fire and heat could result in a failure of the axle, resulting in a wreck. These hazards were exacerbated with high speeds and heavy cars.

Roller bearings are sealed units that require little maintenance—they can go more than 500,000 miles without servicing. They also provide far less rolling resistance and drag compared to solid bearings.

Truck variations include three-axle (six-wheel) versions, used on some heavy-duty cars, and various spring packages. Specific truck designs vary by manufacturer.

Solid-bearing trucks rely on oil held in journal boxes for lubrication. The journal-box lid is open, showing the axle end seated on its "brass" or bearing above. Jeff Wilson

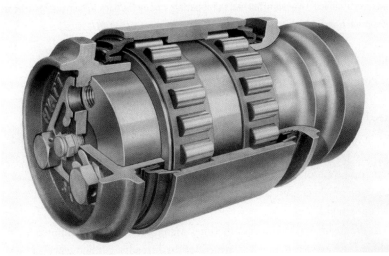

This cutaway view shows how roller bearings use a series of cylindrical rollers in a sealed package to transfer motion from the axle. Hyatt

Wheels

Freight car wheels are steel, shaped to a contour approved by the AAR. A flange on the inside edge of the tread keeps the tread on the railhead. Freight car wheels are made in four diameters: 28", 33", 36", and 38". Cars with 100- and 110-ton capacity ride on 36" wheels, while 70-ton cars ride on 33" wheels. Low-profile 70-ton piggyback and auto rack cars use 28" wheels, and

Cast-iron ("chilled") wheels often had spiral-pattern ribs on the back to help dissipate heat generated from braking. Iron wheels were banned on new cars in 1957. Jeff Wilson

the 125-ton trucks used on some intermodal cars use 38" wheels.

Steel wheels are either single- or two-wear. Single-wear wheels are lighter, with a thin (1¼") tread profile, and are scrapped when the tread (flange/tread profile) wears below a safe limit. Two-wear (or multi-wear) wheels are heavier and have a thicker (2") tread. They can be turned on a lathe and recut to restore the profile to the proper contour. Two-wear wheels are more expensive, but for heavy-duty or long-life cars they are more economical. The type of wheel used is usually stenciled on the car end (i.e. "1W WROT STEEL WHEELS").

In the steam era, railroads sometimes used cast-iron wheels (known as "chilled" wheels for the heat treatment of their treads). Chilled wheels often had ribs cast on the back, to better dissipate the heat generated during braking that could weaken the wheel. Steel wheels had become common by the 1920s, with chilled wheels fading from use by the 1940s. Chilled wheels couldn't be used on new cars after 1957, and they were banned from interchange service in 1970.

Car cushioning and load restraints

Damage to lading caused by hard coupling and slack action (running in and out while a train is in motion) has long been a concern for railroads.

Cushioning systems first appeared in the 1920s—the Duryea cushion underframe was the first popular solution, using springs and a moving center sill to absorb shock forces. Cushion devices were upgraded and became more popular in the 1950s. Freight-car cushioning systems fall into two types: End-of-car (EOC; also EOCC for end of car cushioning) or Center-of-Car (COC) units.

Early EOC cushioning was usually some form of rubber-pad draft gear. Hydraulic EOCs began appearing in the 1950s, and gained popularity rapidly, especially on long cars where a moving center sill wasn't practical. These have a hydraulic unit with piston behind the coupler, with a spring that returns the unit to position. They are made in many styles with varying return distances; 10" and 15" are the most popular.

The first modern hydraulic COC unit was the Hydra-Cushion in 1955. It uses a sliding center sill with friction plates and a hydraulic chamber in the middle to cushion slack action, with large springs that return the sill to a normal position. It uses a vertical hydraulic cylinder, which can often be seen below the sill under the middle of the car. Other COC systems followed, including Keystone (Shock Control), ACF Freight-Saver, and Pullman-Standard Hydroframe. These systems used horizontal hydraulic units that weren't visible from the side. A 20" travel distance is typical for these systems.

By the 2010s, cars with EOC systems far outnumbered COC systems

You can often spot cars with cushioning by their extended draft gear, which protrudes from the car end (at left). Also note the extended uncoupling lever. Jeff Wilson

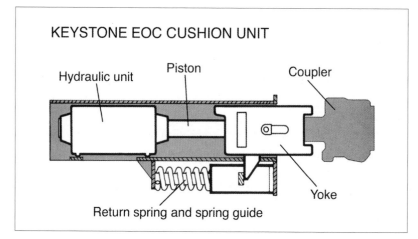

KEYSTONE EOC CUSHION UNIT

Hydraulic unit · Piston · Coupler · Yoke · Return spring and spring guide

End-of-car cushioning units combine hydraulic pistons to absorb the shock of slack or coupling, with a spring that returns the coupler to its original position. Keystone

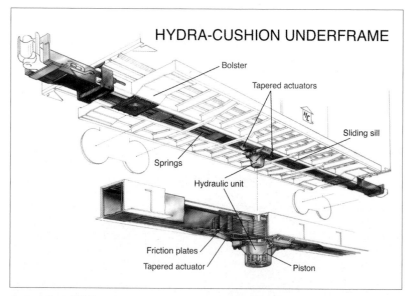

HYDRA-CUSHION UNDERFRAME

Bolster · Tapered actuators · Sliding sill · Springs · Hydraulic unit · Friction plates · Tapered actuator · Piston

Center-of-car (COC) cushioning devices use the car's center sill to absorb shocks. The Hydra-Cushion in 1955 was the first to use hydraulic devices. Southern Pacific

(about 255,000 to 38,000). The popularity of EOC systems increased dramatically as technology improved through the 1970s and later: EOC devices are lighter, less expensive, and easier to install than COC units.

Car lettering often touts the presence of cushioning, sometimes with

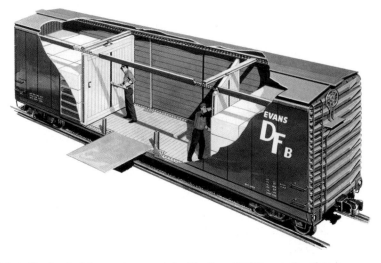

Internal load restraints come in many styles. The Evans DF ("Damage Free") design uses sliding partitions that can be positioned or locked against the wall. Evans Industries

generic "Cushion Car" lettering but often with specific system references. The presence of cushioning is also usually obvious in the coupler box, which extends out from the car end to allow travel.

The other method of combating potential slack action is with internal load restraints. The illustration above shows one design, sliding internal partitions that could be positioned against a load and locked in place. Other devices include belts or nets that attach to hooks in pockets along the wall and other styles of load dividers that latch along the walls. As with cushioning devices, the presence of load dividers is often indicated in lettering on the car.

Freight car use rules

How cars are chosen for loading and how they can be used varies by the car type and who owns them. The governing instructions for this are in the *Code of Car Service Rules,* published by the AAR (Circular OT-10, September 2018) and updated regularly.

Car use rules have evolved over time, in part because of the reduction in number of railroads. In the early 1960s there were more than 100 Class I railroads in North America; this number has dropped to seven. Historically, car rules have required that foreign-road cars should be used first for loading to off-line destinations, preferably to a destination on the owning road, via the home road, or at least toward the home road.

Most cars received a set per-diem (daily) fee paid to its owner by the railroad where they resided (with some privately owned cars this was a mileage charge) as of midnight each day. This has evolved significantly, and the current standard is a mileage charge plus an hourly fee, both of which are calculated based on the value and age of the freight car.

Car owners can program the Umler (Universal Machine Language Equipment Register, the North American database of all revenue-service cars) listing with various codes that instruct other railroads what to do with cars once they've been unloaded. This can include returning the car to its owner via the reverse route, or specifying whether the car may be given a new load without the owner's permission. It can specify that a new load may be unrestricted for destination, or that the load must be to or via the home railroad.

For cars assigned to a specific shipper or commodity pool, cars are returned to the shipper via the reverse route of the loaded movement (or per the owners' instructions).

Unassigned cars can be returned to the home railroad at any junction, or to the delivering road where the previous load was received.

USRA freight cars

The first major attempt at standard freight car designs came with the United States Railroad Association (USRA) temporary takeover of U.S. railroads in 1917. The USRA directed the design and construction of

This Chicago & North Western 40-foot, 50-ton car was built in 1925. It's a variation of the USRA single-sheathed boxcar design of World War I. Chicago & North Western

100,000 boxcars, hoppers, and gondolas to be distributed to a number of railroads. In addition, into the 1920s many railroads ordered additional cars built to USRA designs. They featured steel underframes and modern (for the era) safety appliances. Of the 50,000 USRA boxcars built, half featured single-sheathed wood bodies (horizontal wood sheathing inside of steel bracing) and half were double-sheathed, with smooth vertical wood sides over wood interior bracing. The single-sheathed designs were longer lasting; many of the double-sheathed cars were later rebuilt with steel bodies.

ARA, AAR standard freight cars

By the 1930s, committees made up of representatives from builders and railroads developed standard designs for many steel freight car types, including boxcars, hoppers, and gondolas. The designs were under the auspices of the American Railway Association (ARA) until 1932 and the Association of American Railroads (AAR) thereafter. Specific designs were generally referred to by the year they were introduced (i.e. "1932 ARA boxcar" and "1944 AAR boxcar"), and were built by many manufacturers and individual railroads. Cars built to the same standard design still varied widely in details, including door styles, end designs, roof designs, and truck styles. Manufacturers often developed their own designs as well. Upgrades included improved corner and roof construction, as well as increased interior height.

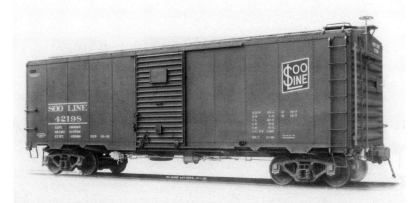

This Soo Line boxcar, built by Pullman-Standard in 1936, follows the 1932 ARA (American Railway Association) design for 40-foot steel cars. Its 9'-4" interior height is shorter than later AAR designs; other details also changed with newer designs. Pullman-Standard

FREIGHT CAR TYPES

Boxcars

Boxcars are the ultimate multi-purpose freight car. They were the most-common freight car type through the 1950s, and into the early diesel era they carried almost everything, including boxed, bagged, and crated goods, lumber, machinery, automobiles, auto parts, and bulk products like grain and coal. Railroads loved boxcars, because—unlike single-commodity cars—they were ready for another load as soon as they were unloaded.

Wood construction was typical into the 1920s, when steel cars began appearing. By World War I, the 40-foot car was standard, with some 50-foot cars also appearing. The 40-foot-long, 50-ton capacity steel car with six-foot-wide sliding side doors was *the* standard freight car of the 1940s and 1950s. The era of specialization and larger car sizes began in the 1950s and continues today, with 50-, 60-, and 86-foot boxcars from the 1960s onward. Many of these newer cars have wider doors (or double doors), and many have plug doors that provide a tighter seal than traditional sliding doors. Internal load restraint devices (belts or moveable bulkheads) became common, and the percentage of boxcars with cushion underframes also increased.

Boxcar numbers have declined steadily since the 1960s with the advent of other specialty cars, and as of 2020 they account for just 8 percent of the total freight car fleet. Much of what was once carried in boxcars now travels in containers. Most remaining boxcars (79 percent) are specialized, designed to carry specific lading, with general-purpose cars a small fraction of the total freight car fleet. Here are some common boxcars over the years:

The FBOX is a modern 50-foot, 286K, excess-height boxcar operated by TTX. This one has a 12-foot door opening. They're typically used for paper and paper products. Jeff Wilson

Ventilated boxcars had adjustable slats on the doors and ends to allow air flow through the car. They fell out of favor by the 1940s with the advent of ventilated reefers. Seaboard Air Line

Ventilated boxcars: These cars had built-in vents, usually openings with horizontal slats that could be opened or closed. They were used to carry produce (namely melons) that required cool temperatures but not refrigeration. Most disappeared by the 1930s, as refrigerator cars were by then built with ventilation capabilities.

Single-sheathed wood. Wood-bodied, steel-underframe boxcars from

Number of freight cars in service by type, 1941-2020						
	1941	**1955**	**1978**	**2010**	**2017**	**2020**
Boxcars	738,000	783,000	435,700	142,000	133,000	117,000
Covd Hpr	*—	47,000	246,100	479,000	585,000	568,000
Tank	150,000	150,000	174,000	306,000	432,000	439,000
Flat	66,000	60,000	146,400	198,000	155,000	208,000
Intermodal°	—	—	—	77,000	73,100	74,000
Hopper	*839,000	514,000	321,900	168,000	135,000	121,000
Gondola	*—	293,000	n/a	241,000	231,000	195,000
Reefer	147,000	125,000	20,900	15,500	13,400	12,400
Stock	59,000	39,000	1,000	—	—	—
Total**	2,014,000	2,051,000	1,678,000	1,596,000	1,632,000	1,631,000

Sources: AAR UMLER reports (revenue cars only), misc. AAR reports, *Official Railway Equipment Register,* various editions
* Through 1950, hopper car totals included gondolas and covered hoppers
° Intermodal cars are also included in flatcar totals
** Total also includes some miscellaneous revenue cars of other types

the World War I era onward were either single- or double-sheathed, with sheathing inside and/or outside of the side bracing. Single-sheathed cars, with visible truss-style steel framing, became the most common (40- and 50-foot versions)—see the USRA-copy car on page 198—as double-sheathed cars suffered from problems with sheathing rotting from moisture trapped between the walls.

40- and 50-foot AAR steel. Steel cars became common by the early 1930s, with the 40-foot, 50-ton car standard, with 50-foot versions common as auto-parts and automobile cars. Most were built to various iterations of ARA and AAR standard specifications, with variations in hardware (doors, ends, roofs, trucks). They were the most common car type through the 1950s; some survived in grain service into the 1980s.

50- and 60-foot auto parts. The early 1960s also saw the introduction of new styles of 50- and 60-foot cars designed to carry heavier, high-density auto parts. Similar single- and double-door cars were also used to carry wood products, paper, and canned goods and other food products. They could have smooth sides or exterior posts, and single or double standard or plug doors.

86-foot auto parts. The biggest boxcars were the 86-foot, excess-height ("high-cube") cars that appeared in the early 1960s. They were designed specifically to carry bulky, light-density auto parts in interchangeable racks

This Great Northern car, built in 1949, is typical of "modern" 40-foot steel boxcars. Most of these 40-foot cars had six-foot-wide sliding doors. John Ingles, J. David Ingles collection

This 60-foot Louisville & Nashville car was built in 1963. It was designed to carry auto parts and was assigned to a specific manufacturer/equipment pool. John Ingles; J. David Ingles collection

The largest common boxcars were the 86-foot, excess-height (high-cube) auto-parts cars designed to carry lightweight stampings and components. This Southern Ry. car was built by Pullman-Standard in 1966. John Ingles; J. David Ingles collection

designed to fit the car's interior dimensions. They served into the 1990s.

All-door boxcars. These cars were designed to carry finished lumber. The most common were the Thrall-Door car and the Evans Side Slider. They had four wide doors on each side, allowing half of the car to be open at a time for loading and unloading. They were built from the late 1960s to the 1970s. The doors proved to be maintenance headaches; center-beam cars soon took most lumber traffic.

Railbox and IPD (incentive-per-diem) boxcars. New 50-foot, 70-ton boxcar designs (mainly exterior-post cars with wide door openings) began appearing in the early 1970s. Railbox cars were developed and operated as a pool—they could be reloaded and sent anywhere, not bound by interchange rules. Also, per-diem rates (the daily fee paid for car use) were incentivized for new cars, and thousands of new 50-foot general-purpose cars were pur-

All-door boxcars have four wide sliding doors on each side. They were designed to carry lumber. This is an Evans Side Slider built in 1976. J. David Ingles collection

Incentive per-diem (IPD) 50-foot boxcars were purchased by dozens of small railroads and leasing companies in the 1970s. This one was built in 1977. R.J. Wilhelm; J. David Ingles collection

chased by investing corporations, most of which used shortline railroads to operate them. These were known as incentive per-diem (IPD) cars, and wore dozens of new, colorful paint schemes. They were also operated as pool cars, without movement restrictions.

FBOX, TBOX cars. The newest boxcars are the 110-ton TBOX (60-foot) and FBOX (50-foot) cars that began appearing in 2003 (see page 200). They are operated by TTX, and carry paper and other products.

Covered hoppers

Covered hoppers are enclosed cars for carrying dry bulk products such as grain, cement, sand, and plastic pellets. They have hatches along the roof for loading (either small individual hatches or long "trough" hatches), with discharge gates or hoppers on the underbody. They are generally classified by capacity in cubic feet, along with the number of internal compartments and outlet bays. The first production covered hoppers appeared in 1934, and they have evolved from being a rare specialty car in the 1930s to become the most-common car on the rails today. Covered hoppers account for about 26 percent of the total freight car fleet, with most (about three-quarters) privately owned.

Most early cars were two-bay designs to carry dry bulk cement, a heavy, dense product that had been carried in bags in boxcars. Longer three-bay

The Trinity 5,161-cf, three-bay, 110-ton covered hopper became the most-common grain car of the early 2000s. Other manufacturers offer similar cars. Jeff Wilson

Two-bay covered hoppers are used for dense, heavy products such as cement and sand. This 110-ton ARI-built car has a 3,272-cf capacity. Jeff Wilson

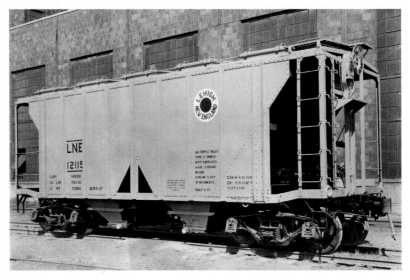

The first popular covered hopper was a 70-ton, two-bay, 1,790-cf car designed by American Car & Foundry for cement hauler Lehigh & New England. This one was built in 1937. AC&F

cars to carry lighter-density carbon black and phosphate were common by the 1950s. Powdered cement, lime, and sand are common commodities today, generally carried in two-bay cars with capacities to 3,300 cf. Grain—the most common lading for covered hoppers today—didn't travel much in covered hoppers until the 1960s, when a battle over rates (which went to the U.S. Supreme Court) was won by railroads. Since then, three-bay cars from 4,500- to 5,200-cubic-foot capacity have become the standard grain car. Plastic pellets are another common lading. Their light weight allows bigger cars, to 6,000-cf and larger capacity (with four to six bays).

Notable designs include Southern Railway's Big John aluminum car of the early 1960s, which was the first true grain car, and cylindrical (tank-style) covered hoppers from ACF and multiple Canadian builders from the 1960s to the 1980s.

Airslide. General American introduced its Airslide covered hopper in 1954. The car has outlet-bay walls lined with perforated fabric; air flowing through the fabric liquifies the lading, allowing it to empty fully. Multiple sizes with one or two longitudinal outlet bays were built into the 1980s. Airslide cars have a distinctive, boxy appearance with external vertical posts.

Pressure-differential cars use air pressure to aid unloading, with hoses or pipes connected to the outlet gates. These are often used for fine products

Canadian railroads favored cylindrical covered hopper designs. This government-owned car, built in 1981, was assigned to Canadian Pacific. Trains magazine collection

General American's Airslide covered hoppers have a boxy appearance. They have perforated-fabric-lined outlet bays. This one was built in 1974. Jeff Wilson collection

Pressure-differential cars, like this North American car, use air pressure to force lading out of the body. Note the air piping running along the sides of the outlet bays. Jeff Wilson

such as flour, sugar, and carbon black. Appearance varies by manufacturer: many look like standard covered hoppers, but with piping along the outlet bays; others, like the North American car on the previous page, have filled-in areas under the end bay slope sheets.

Tank cars

Tank cars are currently the second-most common freight car, with more than 400,000 in service as of 2020. All are privately owned, with the exception of railroad-owned cars in company service. Tank cars carry the widest range of lading of any freight car—more than 1,500 commodities—from hazardous and flammable products such as crude oil, ethanol, acids, and liquified petroleum gas (LPG) to edible goods such as vegetable oil and corn syrup to industrial products like clay slurry, molten sulfur, and tar.

Tank cars were among the first all-steel cars. Car size increased through the 1900s, with 8,000-gallon cars common by the 1930s and 10,000 to 12,000-gallon cars by the 1950s. The 1960s saw a dramatic increase in size, to 20,000 and 30,000 gallons, with some jumbo four-truck cars reaching 50,000 gallons late in the decade. Maximum capacity for new tank cars was capped at 34,500 gallons as of 1971.

The huge variety of products carried means there are more than 90 tank car specifications. Variations include size, which is based on the density of the lading they carry—a 17,000-gallon corn syrup car and 33,000-gallon LPG car carry about the same weight of lading. Cars can be insulated or uninsulated; unheated or heated (by steam coils located inside the tank or

This UTLX 30,000-gallon, 100-ton, non-insulated/non-pressure car was in ethanol service in this 2006 photo. You can see the car's shelf coupler at the right. Jeff Wilson

The largest (34,000-gallon) cars today carry LPG and (shown here) anhydrous ammonia. They're pressurized cars. This one is being unloaded in 2007. Jeff Wilson

This 16,000-gallon insulated, non-pressure car was built by ACF in 1981. It's carrying potassium hydroxide in this 2006 view. The thin jacket covering the insulation on the sides slightly overlaps the ends, creating distinctive rims. Jeff Wilson

between the tank and external jacketing; the steam coils are connected to an external source for unloading to aid dense products to flow), and non-pressure or pressurized (with 300- to 500-psi ratings) for products such as LPG, anhydrous ammonia, and chlorine. Most non-pressure cars have bottom outlet pipes (cars carrying acid do not)—the drawing on page 210 shows typical controls on a non-pressure car. Pressure cars have connections and controls in a covered hatch atop the car.

Early cars were riveted, with large expansion domes atop the tank, with welding used only for pressurized cars. By the 1950s most new tank cars fea-

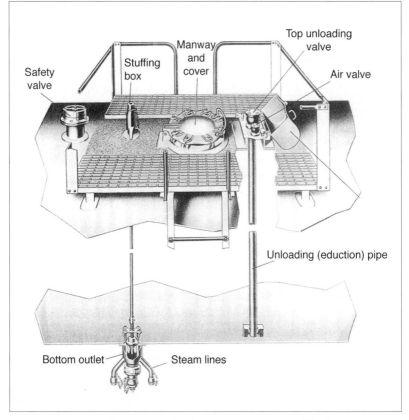

This drawing shows typical components of a non-pressure tank car with a bottom unloading outlet and steam lines. GATX Inc.

tured welded construction. Cars had separate frames through the 1950s, but since then the tank itself serves as the frame on most cars. Another change was the elimination of the expansion dome.

Gondolas

Gondolas are the pickup trucks of the railroad world, used for many types of bulky items, new steel products, steel scrap, and bulk loads of coal and aggregates. They are currently the third-most common car behind covered hoppers and tank cars. Historically, gondolas fell into two broad categories: Mill gons and general-service (GS) gons. Mill gondolas have shorter sides and ends, and are designed to carry both finished products of steel mills (including coiled steel, steel sheets and slabs, pipe, and beams) as well as

In the steam and early diesel eras, general-purpose tank cars were riveted, with separate frames and large expansion domes. This 10,000-gallon car was built in 1926. Library of Congress

Modern gondolas are 110-ton (286K GRL) cars. Most feature external vertical posts in a variety of patterns. They tend to get beaten up in service. Jeff Wilson

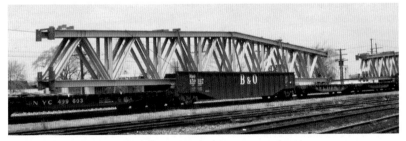

Some mill gondolas have end doors that fold down into the car, allowing them to carry longer loads. This car has idler flats on each end to provide clearance for its long truss load in this mid-1960s scene. John Ingles; J. David Ingles collection

This modern 4,480-cf, 286K bathtub-style coal gondola features aluminum construction. It was built by FreightCar America in 2004. Jeff Wilson

Purpose-built wood-chip gondolas began appearing in the early 1960s. This 65-foot, 100-ton car, built for Northern Pacific, was serving Burlington Northern in 1992. Jeff Wilson

inbound scrap. They are longer than GS gons, usually either 52 or 65 feet. Some mill gons have ends that fold down ("drop-end" cars), allowing them to carry items longer than the car itself. The typical GS gon through the early diesel era was 41 feet long; shorter in length but with taller sides than mill gons. Many had doors on the floor ("drop-bottom" gons), allowing them to carry bulk products—many Western railroads used GS gons for coal.

Coal gondolas: The first high-capacity coal gondolas (90- to 110-ton) actually appeared in the 1910s, on heavy-haul lines of the Norfolk & Western, Pennsylvania, and Virginian railroads. However, it was the coming of the unit coal train and large electric utilities in the early 1960s that led to the modern 100- and 110-ton coal gondolas with rotary couplers (the rotary end is marked with a contrasting color), with capacities of 3,700 to 4,700 cf (western sub-bituminous coal is less dense than eastern bituminous coal, so coal cars serving mines in the west are often larger). Many coal gons since the 1970s feature aluminum construction. Many styles have been built; those with floors extending downward between the trucks are known as "bathtub" gondolas.

Wood chip cars. Specialized purpose-built cars for carrying wood chips from lumber mills to paper mills began appearing in the early 1960s. Most were 100-ton cars measuring 65 feet long, excess height, with end doors and capacities of 6,000 to 6,800 cubic feet. Modern 110-ton versions are up to 75 feet long with an 8,200-cf capacity. Hopper versions of these large wood chip cars have also been built.

Hopper cars

Hopper cars are open-top cars with bottom outlets and slanted floors for carrying bulk products that don't require protection from the elements. Through the steam era, they were often simply called "coal cars," since that was their primary lading; they also carry aggregates of various types. Because of the abuse they receive, hoppers were among the earliest steel cars, with steel construction common by the 1910s. By World War I, the standard hopper car was a two-bay, 50 to 55-ton car (1,800 to 2,100 cf); this size would remain popular through the 1950s. Larger 70-ton three-bay cars became common by the 1950s, with capacity increasing to 100 and 110 tons (3,600 to 4,300 cf) from the 1960s through today. Variations include cars with more outlet gates (rapid-discharge cars). Through the 1950s most

Some utilities still prefer hopper cars for coal. This 286K, 4,300-cf aluminum Johnstown America car has five outlet bays and a rotary coupler (on the left end). Jeff Wilson

Two-bay 50-ton hoppers like this Monon car were the typical coal car through the 1950s. It features offset sides: interior posts with external top side stiffeners. Trains magazine collection

hoppers featured "offset-side" construction, with smooth sides on interior vertical posts (as on the Monon car above). Since that time, cars with external vertical posts have become most common.

In the 1960s, rotary dumpers became popular at electric utilities, leading to the adaptation of rotary couplers to allow cars to be dumped while coupled. These are indicated by painting the end panel of the car a contrasting color. The emergence of large-capacity gondolas cut down on the number of hopper cars in coal service, but some utilities still prefer bottom-dump cars. Rapid-discharge cars feature additional bottom outlet gates.

Ore cars. Iron ore and processed taconite (ore) pellets are very dense, heavy commodities that would max out the weight limit on a standard hop-

Ore cars are short, and most have a coupled length that matches the pocket spacing on Great Lakes ore docks. This is a Milwaukee Road car in 1965. John Ingles; J. David Ingles collection

Ballast cars are hopper cars with outlet gates that allow dumping either between or outside the rails. Union Pacific paints its maintenance-of-way cars green. Jeff Wilson

per well before the car is full. Individual ore car designs vary, but most are short—24 to 26 feet long (many are designed to match ore-pocket spacing on Great Lakes ore docks)—with lengthwise outlet gates. Raw ore and pellets are most often carried in solid trains.

Ballast cars. Ballast cars are hopper cars with longitudinal outlet gates that allow directional dumping, so ballast can be distributed either between the rails and outside the rails as needed.

Flatcars

Flatcars have been used since railroads' earliest days for carrying almost anything that can't fit in a boxcar. Steel construction was common by the

Many modern flatcars have built-in hooks, chains, and winches for securing heavy equipment and implement loads. This car is owned by TTX. Jeff Wilson

early 1900s, and 40-foot cars gave way to 46- and 53-foot cars by the 1940s, with 60-foot and longer cars common today. Many flats are equipped with end bulkheads to help secure loads. They carry machinery, pipe, steel products, vehicles (including early piggyback traffic), construction equipment, boilers, tanks, lumber, and many other products. Heavy-duty flatcars, many with depressed center sections, are used for oversize and overweight loads such as transformers, generators, and large tanks. These sometimes have multiple trucks and can be rated from 125 to 250 tons.

Flatcars became more specialized by the 1960s. Variations include intermodal cars (see the next section), cars for carrying automobile frames, and machinery cars, which have built-in hooks and winches on their decks for carrying construction equipment and farm machinery.

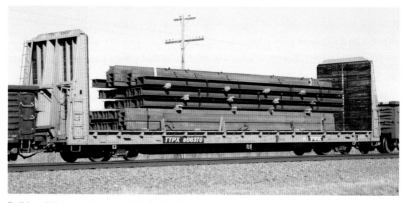

Bulkhead flats are often used for loads of metal beams and piping and lumber products. This TTX 286K car has a 62-foot length between bulkheads. Jeff Wilson

Coil cars. Coil cars are specialized flatcars (actually categorized as gondolas) with removable covers for carrying rolled steel coils. Evans built the first one in 1964, and they became common by the end of that decade. Coil cars have multiple V-shaped troughs, with one or two removable (lift-off) covers to protect the load (most modern versions have single covers).

Center-beam cars. First appearing in the late 1970s, center-beam cars are designed for carrying bundles of dimensional lumber or wrapped bundles of plywood and other sheet building materials. They are long (60 or 72 feet between bulkheads) cars with heavy center railings, with built-in cables that wrap from the center sill upward around the load and anchor to the top of the center beam.

Coil-steel cars have a longitudinal cradle for carrying rolled steel. Early cars typically had two removable hoods; most modern cars like this 286K Thrall design have one. Jeff Wilson

Center-beam flatcars began appearing in the late 1970s. They carry dimensional lumber and bundled sheet materials, and have built-in cables for securing loads. Jeff Wilson

Three- and two-deck auto racks mounted atop 89-foot flatcars saved the auto business for railroads in the 1960s. Most racks were open until the 1970s. John Ingles; J. David Ingles collection

Auto racks. Through the 1950s, autos were carried in racks in double-door 40- and 50-foot boxcars—four to a car—a very inefficient, labor-intensive method. The first open auto racks appeared in 1960, built atop long (85- and 89-foot) flatcars. They allowed carrying 15 autos per car, and were efficient to load and unload via end ramps. Bi- and tri-level open racks soon became common, with bi-levels for restricted-height routes and to carry pickup trucks, vans, SUVs and minivans. Vandalism and other damage led to enclosed racks with perforated metal side panels to shield the autos. These began appearing in large numbers in the 1970s.

Enclosed auto racks became standard in the 1980s. They are operated in pools; most flatcars are owned by TTX, with racks owned by individual railroads. Jeff Wilson

Intermodal equipment

Trailer-on-flatcar (TOFC, or "piggyback") loads grew from a trickle in the 1930s to a major traffic source in the 1950s. Trailers were initially carried on standard flatcars that had been converted to piggyback service by addition of fold-down end ramps, pedestals (to hold the trailer kingpin), and rub rails (to keep trailer wheels on the car when they were being backed on board on end-loading ramps). Most flatcars carried single trailers; some longer (53-foot) flatcars could carry two short trailers. The increase in trailer traffic in the 1950s—and longer trailers—led to the lock-down trailer hitch and longer specialized flatcars. The growth in container traffic in the 1970s and the move to lift-on/lift-off ramps led to specialized spine and well cars.

Piggyback flatcars. The first purpose-built flatcar for carrying trailers was

Well ("double-stack") cars carry two levels of containers—two 53-footers in this Trinity-built articulated car. This is the B end of a three-unit car. Jeff Wilson

The 89-foot flatcar was the most common intermodal car from the early 1960s into the 1980s. Here several are carrying UPS 40-foot trailers in 1992. Jeff Wilson

a 75-foot car (that could carry two 35-foot trailers) in 1955. As trailer size increased, piggyback flats grew as well: 85-foot cars by 1959 and 89-foot cars by 1960. These flatcars were the most common car in intermodal service into the 1980s (Trailer Train owned more than 47,000 in 1980, with railroads owning several thousand more). Most were retired by the early 2010s; a 1990s version was the "Long Runner," two drawbar-connected 89-foot cars that could carry three 53-foot trailers, with one spanning the joint between cars.

Articulated spine cars. Spine ("skeleton") cars began appearing in the 1970s in the effort to save fuel. The move to lift-on/lift-off facilities (instead of ramps) for piggyback and growing container traffic allowed the design,

Articulated spine cars gained in popularity in the 1980s, with all-purpose (container/trailer) designs becoming the most common design. Jeff Wilson

with a heavy center sill with a hitch at one end and wheel platforms at the other. Each car is articulated, with cars from three to 10 platforms long. Initial designs carried trailers only; later designs could carry either containers or trailers ("AP," for all-purpose spine car).

Double-stack (well) cars. As international container traffic grew rapidly through the 1970s, the double-stack (well) car emerged, with the first production cars in 1981. These cars have low wells suspended between their trucks, allowing two long containers to be carried one atop the other (or a long container atop two 20-footers). Cars are built in three- to five-platform articulated sets and as stand-alone cars. Modern cars have either 40- or 53-foot wells; 45- and 48-foot wells were built, but faded from use as container sizes standardized at 40 feet (international) and 53 feet (domestic). Since the early 2000s, all well cars with 45- and 48-foot platforms have been rebuilt with 40- or 53-foot wells. Well cars are now the main intermodal car type.

Trailers. Early piggyback traffic involved railroads carrying either common-carrier trucking trailers or their own trailers in less-than-carload (LCL) service. By the late 1950s, railroads began acquiring large fleets of trailers for trailer-load freight service. Trailer length grew from 32 feet in the 1940s to 35 feet by the early 1950s. The 40-foot trailer became legal nationwide in 1957 and was the standard until 1981, when the 45-foot trailer appeared. Size increased to 48 feet in 1985 and 53 feet in 1991.

Containers. Containers surpassed trailers in traffic volume in 1991, and currently account for more than 90 percent of rail intermodal traffic. Containers fall into two categories: international and domestic. International containers since 1965 have size standards adopted by ISO (the International

The top container is a 48-foot domestic (8'-6" wide) version; the bottom box is a 40-foot international (8'-0" wide) container. An IBC (inter-box connector) secures them at the castings; its lever can be seen protruding to the left of the castings. Jeff Wilson

Organization for Standardization) with standard connectors at the corner castings. The most common of these are 20- and 40-foot containers, 8'-0" wide and 8'-0" tall. The standard height increased to 8'-6" in the early 1970s, with an optional "high-cube" version 9'-6" tall, and 45-foot versions began

RoadRailers don't require railcars, instead riding on their own wheels (as here) or on special freight car trucks between trailers (most common since the early 1990s). Curt Tillotson, Jr.

appearing in 1982. Domestic containers are larger, matching the increased trailer lengths allowed on U.S. highways. In 1986, this meant a 48-foot container, 8'-6" wide and 9'-6" tall, followed by a 53-foot version in 1991 (now the standard for domestics). These longer containers all still have their connector castings spaced at 40 feet in length and 8'-0" wide to match ISO containers. Variations include tank, refrigerated, and open-top containers.

RoadRailers. RoadRailers are trailers that can be operated either on the highway or on rails. The first ones appeared in the late 1950s, and were short single-axle trailers with built-in rail wheels at the rear. They were built specifically to handle U.S. Mail at the ends of passenger trains. The concept reappeared in 1978 and has been in operation on limited routes since then. The modern design uses full-length trailers, initially with attached rail wheels, but by the 1990s this switched to a design with separate railroad bogies (trucks) added and removed at terminals.

Refrigerator cars

Also known as "reefers," these cars carry perishables—mainly meat, fruits, vegetables, and frozen foods. Most have been privately owned, either by shippers (meat cars) or by railroad subsidiary companies (such as Pacific Fruit Express). Through the 1940s, refrigerator cars were cooled by ice and known as ice-bunker cars: a bunker at each end of the car held chunk or crushed ice to cool their loads. Ice was loaded through a pair of rooftop

This modern 72-foot mechanical refrigerator car was built by Gunderson. Cryo-Trans operated many cryogenic cars in the 1990s, but all were eventually converted to mechanical cars by adding end-of-car refrigeration units. Jeff Wilson

Into the 1960s, most reefers were 36- to 40-foot cars cooled by ice in end bunkers. This is a Santa Fe class RR-29 car built in 1940, one of the first steel refrigerator cars. Santa Fe

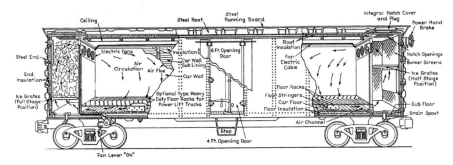

Ice was added to bunkers via roof hatches. Many cars had fans to aid air flow through the car. Slatted floor racks also aided air circulation. Preco, Inc.

hatches above each bunker. Cars are insulated between their inner and outer walls; most ice cars were 40-foot cars with swinging side doors through the 1950s and sliding plug doors thereafter. Ice car numbers dropped significantly through the 1960s, with a few surviving into the 1970s.

Mechanical reefers. Mechanical cars use a small diesel engine to power an on-board refrigeration unit. They first appeared in the 1940s, mainly for frozen foods. They grew in popularity in the 1960s for produce as well, and are now the only type in use. Modern refrigerator cars mainly carry frozen foods; some still carry fresh produce, but most of that traffic moved to trucks by the 1970s. Early mechanical cars were 40-footers, with 57-foot cars typical by the 1960s and many 60-foot and longer cars in service today.

Express reefers. Shippers were willing to pay express rates for some perishable traffic; this traffic traveled in express reefers as head-end traffic on

Pacific Fruit Express was long the largest operator of refrigerator cars. This 57-foot mechanical car was built by Pacific Car & Foundry in 1971. Jim Hediger

Express reefers were equipped with high-speed trucks and steam and signal lines, allowing them to be carried as head-end traffic on passenger trains. Most were wooden 50-foot cars; they were rare by the 1960s. TRAINS magazine collection

passenger trains (see Chapter 1) into the 1960s. Most were 50-foot wood or steel cars equipped with high-speed trucks as well as steam and signal lines.

Milk cars. Milk cars resembled express reefers, but although they were insulated cars, they did not have ice bunkers. They carried raw milk from rural areas to large-city bottling plants. "Can cars" had open interiors for carrying milk cans; bulk cars had pairs of insulated tanks (most of these were built

This bulk milk car was built by General American-Pfaudler in 1947. It's a non-refrigerated 50-foot steel car with a pair of internal insulated glass-lined tanks. General American

by General American with Pfaudler tanks). Most milk cars operated out of Boston and New York City. Truck traffic greatly diminished rail milk traffic by the 1950s, and railroad milk traffic was gone by the 1970s.

Cryogenic reefers. Refrigerator cars cooled by carbon dioxide (CO_2) became popular starting in 1990. These 76-foot, 110-ton cars used a charge of frozen CO_2, applied after the car was sealed. A 15-ton charge would keep the interior below zero for about two weeks. A sharp increase in CO_2 prices led to these cars' conversion to conventional mechanical cars by 2001.

Insulated boxcars (bunkerless refrigerator cars). The development of highly efficient insulating materials (polyurethane and polystyrene foam) by the late 1950s led to the "bunkerless refrigerator car." If the load and car were precooled, these cars could retain their internal temperatures for several days without additional refrigeration. Many were classified as reefers (RB,

Insulated boxcars feature plug doors and high-efficiency foam insulation. Several owners classified them as "bunkerless refrigerator" cars, class RB. John Ingles; J. David Ingles collection

for refrigerator, bunkerless), while others were classified as insulated boxcars (BI) depending on the owner. Many were owned by refrigerator car operating groups (such as Fruit Growers Express) as well as individual railroads, and they are typically 50 to 65 feet long. They are often used for beverages and canned and bottled food goods.

Stock cars. Livestock rode in enclosed cars with horizontally slatted sides to allow ventilation. Steers, pigs, and sheep were the most common riders. Stock cars were common from the 1800s through the 1950s, especially on "granger" railroads of the Midwest, West, and Southwest. Increased trucking and the relocation of packing plants nearer to feedlots greatly diminished railroad livestock traffic by the 1960s, with most stock cars retired by 1980. Most stock cars remained wood through the steam and early diesel eras. Cheap construction was desired, since the traffic was seasonal and one-way. Some railroads acquired steel cars in the 1950s and later, usually by rebuilding older boxcars as stock cars. Cars were single-deck (for cattle), double-deck (pigs and sheep), or convertible, with retractable upper decks. Most were 36- or 40-foot cars, although some 50-foot cars were rebuilt from older 40-footers. Also notable were 86-foot, double-deck steel stock cars built by Ortner in the mid-1960s; fewer than 100 were built, most for Northern Pacific and General American leasing.

Stock cars had slatted sides for ventilation. Most, like these Chicago & North Western cars, had wood bodies. Most were gone by the 1960s; this view is from 1943. Library of Congress

PASSENGER CARS
Wood, heavyweight, and lightweight cars

In the late 1800s, passenger cars were made of wood, with truss-rod underframes giving way to steel underframes by the first few years of the 1900s. They were short, usually 50 to 60 feet long, riding on four-wheel trucks. A typical late-1800s coach seated 60 passengers. Railroads' luxury trains had larger, nicer equipment, and Pullman's sleeping (and "Palace") cars provided luxury travel for first-class passengers, but all with wood-bodied cars. The advent of air brakes, automatic couplers, and more-powerful locomotives made safety a serious issue: wood bodies crushed easily—even

The *Lark* was a Southern Pacific all-Pullman overnight train between San Francisco and Los Angeles. The round-end observation car has a tailsign with the train name. Southern Pacific

The *Pioneer* was the first sleeping car put in service by Pullman, in 1865. Early passenger cars featured wood construction, with clerestory roofs and open end platforms. AAR

The Pennsylvania ushered in the heavyweight era in 1907 with its 80-foot steel class P70 coach. The railroad built and purchased more than 1,000 of them. Pennsylvania Railroad

in seemingly minor accidents—and burned readily.

The first all-steel passenger cars appeared in 1907, ushering in the era of "heavyweight" passenger cars. Size increased, with 70 feet typical for coaches and some cars 80 feet or longer. Heavyweights lived up to their names: all-steel cars were substantially heavier than earlier wood cars and contemporary freight cars, with 80-85 tons typical for a coach and sleepers and dining cars weighing even more. Roofs could be rounded, although some retained the clerestory roof style with a raised (lengthwise) center. Specific designs varied widely, but heavyweight construction remained standard for new passenger cars through the 1930s.

New equipment typically went to a railroad's fastest, most-prestigious trains, with older equipment bumped down to secondary trains and then locals and branch line trains. Old coaches were often assigned to commuter service. Many older wood cars remained in service beyond World War II: in 1942, about half of passenger cars in service were wood, with 33 percent all-steel and the remainder wood with steel underframes. Many heavyweight cars remained in service through the 1960s.

Railroads and car builders began experimenting with new lightweight materials (and new methods of propulsion) in the mid-1930s. Two new revolutionary streamlined, articulated, internal-combustion-powered passenger trains debuted in 1934. The first was Union Pacific's M-10000, built by Pullman-Standard. Its cars featured aluminum construction, and it was powered by a Winton (Electro-Motive Corp.) distillate engine. Shortly thereafter came Chicago, Burlington & Quincy's *Zephyr,* built by the Budd Co. The *Zephyr* was built using fluted stainless-steel construction and powered by a Winton/EMC diesel engine, making it the first diesel-powered streamliner. Many new

U.S. passenger cars in service by type, 1960	
Lightweight coach/chair	2,655
Commuter/suburban coach	1,771
Standard coach	3,862
Lightweight sleeper	2,003
Standard sleeper	1,136
Diner	1,133
Parlor/lounge	686
Baggage/express	7,735
Box express	2,273
Express reefer	225
Railway Post Office	1,874
Source: AAR (via *Car Builder's Cyclopedia*)	

diesel-powered streamliners hit the rails in the years before World War II. Although the idea of articulation soon went away, lightweight construction materials and techniques became standard for new streamliners, both for entire trainsets and individual cars. Construction ceased during the war, but railroads ordered lightweight cars by the hundreds as soon as they could from the end of the war into the 1950s. These lightweight cars would serve through the end of railroad-owned passenger service, and would make up the bulk of Amtrak's initial fleet and serve for decades longer.

The "lightweight" and "heavyweight" monikers were certainly appropriate: a typical lightweight coach weighed about 60 tons, 20 to 25 tons lighter than an earlier all-steel car. This enabled lightweight trains to be longer and require less power to pull them.

A couple of notable designs appeared after World War II. The Chicago, Burlington & Quincy built the first dome car in its shops using a Budd lightweight coach. The car, dubbed *Silver Dome,* was an immediate hit, and spurred a variety of similar cars from all passenger-car manufacturers. Cars with short domes ("bubble-tops") as well as full-length cars with viewing windows were common on most name trains by the 1950s, especially in the West where clearances were less restrictive.

Another noteworthy design appeared in 1952 when the Budd Co. delivered the first of its "Hi-Level" two-deck passenger cars to Santa Fe for its all-coach *El Capitan.* Bi-level designs maximized interior space and became popular for commuter cars from the late 1950s onward, but the Santa Fe cars were the lone distance cars until Amtrak received its first bi-level Superliner cars from Pullman-Standard in 1978. Amtrak now operates bi-levels on most long-distance trains on routes that have sufficient clearance.

Passenger travel is divided by class: generally first, second, and third (coach) class. First-class is the most expensive, usually involving sleeping car

The Chicago, Burlington & Quincy built the first dome car, *Silver Dome,* converting a lightweight stainless-steel coach in its shops in 1945. Henry J. McCord

The Santa Fe placed the first bi-level passenger cars in service in the early 1950s: Budd-built Hi-Level coaches for its *El Capitan* all-coach streamliner. TRAINS magazine collection

Amtrak continued the use of double-deck cars with its Superliner equipment. Here a sleeper brings up the rear of a train at Los Angeles. Andy Sperandeo

accommodations (parlor cars for day travel) and dining service as part of the fare. Many railroads' name trains were all-first class (such as New York Central's *20th Century Limited*); other trains had mixed accommodations or were all-coach trains. Second-class was less expensive, usually in economy sleeping cars (Slumbercoaches or open section cars, where seats were turned into berths at night); dining service was available, but at extra cost. Coach (third) class is economy travel in coach seating, with food service extra. Specific accommodations and designations varied by railroad, route, and train. (See "Passenger train operations" in chapter 1.)

Passenger car components

Passenger car construction is substantially different compared to freight cars. Overall construction is sturdier, since the cars are longer and heavier and travel at higher speeds. Safety is a prime concern when carrying passengers as opposed to freight.

Couplers. Tightlock (Type H) couplers, developed in the 1930s, are used on passenger cars. The design interlocks the knuckles, preventing them from separating vertically in derailments. This increases the chances of cars remaining coupled and upright in accidents, and limits the chances of telescoping (where one car rides over the frame of another) or jackknifing.

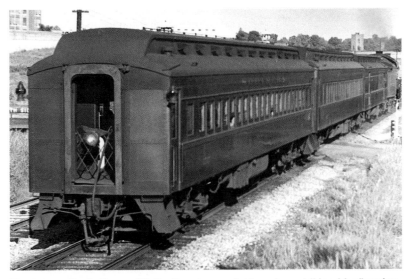

The steam and brake lines on this Southern heavyweight coach are visible, with a "monkey tail" hose allowing trainmen to control braking during backing moves. Leonard A. McClean

U.S. passenger cars in service

This shows the total number of passenger cars in service, along with the number of new cars built that year.

Year	Total	Built
1925	65,628	2,428
1930	63,444	1,534
1935	50,453	205
1940	45,224	257
1945	47,225	931
1950	43,585	964
1955	36,894	886
1960	28,396	264
1965	20,022	244
1970	11,378	318
2020	21,400	n/a

Sources: American Public Transit Association; American Railway Car Institute (via *Car Builder's Cyclopedia*); Amtrak; Association of American Railroads. Sources vary after 1970 in counting passenger cars for commuter service.

Tightlock couplers, together with buffers on the car frame ends, also eliminate most slack action, resulting in a smoother ride.

Trucks. Passenger-car trucks have longer wheelbases than freight car trucks (at least 6'-6" for four-wheel trucks) and use 36"-diameter wheels (compared to 33" for freight cars). From the late 1800s on, many longer, heavier cars rode on six-wheel trucks. These spread the weight on the track and also offered a very smooth ride. The coming of lightweight cars resulted in new four-wheel truck designs, with some diners still riding on six-wheel trucks. Passenger trucks were among the first to use roller bearings, starting in the early 1920s.

Steam and signal lines. From around 1900 into the 1970s, steam (from the steam locomotive or the steam generator on a diesel or electric) was piped through passenger cars to provide heat as well as cooling. The steam line required a pipe connection between cars (pipes with pivoting joints), with valves on each end. (It's why it's more time-consuming to switch passenger cars than freight cars.) Steam piping was insulated (with such innovative products as Johns-Manville "Asbesto-Sponge Felted Pipe Insulation"). The signal line was a separate air line connected to the brake system, allowing signals to be transmitted from the train to the locomotive. Thus each end of a passenger car has two air-hose connections and a steam pipe connection.

Head-end (electric) power (HEP). By the 1970s, railroads were turning to electricity from the locomotive to power car lights, air conditioning, and heaters. Head-end power (HEP) can come from either the locomotive's prime mover or a separate small engine/generator set. It requires electric cable connections between cars, which replace the steam pipes. Some commuter lines had HEP equipment in the 1960s, and Amtrak adopted it as standard when its first Amfleet equipment arrived in 1973.

Outside swing-hanger passenger truck

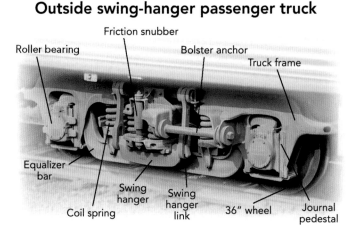

Passenger car trucks have been built in many variations. This shows the components of a lightweight four-wheel outside-swing-hanger truck. Kevin J. Holland

Air conditioning. The first passenger-car air-conditioning systems of the early 1930s used ice. Blocks of ice in under-car bunkers cooled water that was piped to the car interior, with fans blowing air across the pipes. In the 1930s, steam-ejector (also called "steam jet") air conditioning was developed. The system used steam to drive a vacuum ejector that cooled a closed water system (the Santa Fe was a major user). Mechanical refrigeration eventually became standard, with a compressor either driven directly by connection to an axle, or electro-mechanical, powered by an axle-driven generator. Air conditioning quickly proved popular. As of 1939, about 11,700 cars were equipped with AC (3,800 ice, 1,800 steam ejector, and the rest mechanical or electro-mechanical). Axle-based systems gave way to head-end power (HEP) when that became standard in the 1970s.

Lighting. Through the 1800s, oil lamps were typically used in passenger cars. Gas lighting was also used in some (with an on-board pressure storage tank), but the combination of open flames and wood car construction was disastrous in wrecks. Electric lighting has been standard since the early 1900s. The most common method was a small generator and regulator on each car, powered by an armature drive connected to a car axle by belt. A battery or batteries store power for when the car is not in motion. Some cars used battery-power only, with larger banks of cells that required recharging at terminal stops. The coming of head-end power (HEP) by the 1970s eliminated the need for generators on individual cars.

Vestibules, diaphragms. Through most of the 1800s, passenger cars had open platforms on each end, and crossing between cars was done on a small walkway between platforms. By the heavyweight era, cars had enclosed ends, with flexible diaphragms—either full width or just around the doorway—to enclose the passage between cars, making travel between cars safer and protecting passengers from the elements. The enclosed ends are "vestibules," and they feature side doors with steps to allow access on and off the car. Vestibules first appeared in the late 1880s, and were standard by the turn of the century.

Water supply, toilets. By the 1900s, coaches, sleepers, and dining cars had on-board water tanks with sinks and toilets. By the 1940s, many cars had electric water coolers. Coaches and sleepers usually had a bathroom on each end, and sleepers had various levels of amenities, with toilets and sinks (often foldable) in many rooms. Some first-class cars included showers as well. Through the 1960s, toilets (also called "hoppers" or "water closets") used water to flush, but discharged waste directly on the track. Most high-end cars used a "double pan" discharge so waste went through the upper pan, which then closed, before being dumped by the lower pan. Older single-pan toilets dumped directly and could be problematic, especially at high speeds, as wind could blow water and waste back upward. These toilets were the reason for signs in car bathrooms stating "PLEASE DO NOT FLUSH WHILE TRAIN IS IN STATION." Retention toilets became common on passenger cars starting in the 1970s.

Car types

Coach, chair car. The most common passenger car is the coach, which typically has rows of seats with an aisle down the center. Bathrooms are located at one or both ends. Commuter and short-haul cars have tighter spacing (and some older commuter cars have benches instead of individual seats); commuter cars often have "walkover" seats that allow the back of the seat to be moved to the other side. Many commuter cars since the 1950s use bi-level designs to increase capacity. Coach seats have varying levels of quality and luxury. Long-distance cars generally have reclining seats, leg rests, higher seatbacks with padded headrests, and more leg room. Some railroads called their nicer coaches "chair cars."

Parlor car. A parlor car was a step up from a coach or chair car. Parlor

This lightweight coach or chair car built for the Nashville, Chattanooga & St. Louis *City of Memphis* features individual reclining seats and lots of leg room. NC&StL

Bi-level commuter cars became popular in many areas. This Chicago & North Western car has an operator's bay and headlight for push-pull operation. Chicago & North Western

cars were first-class cars designed for day travel, and had individual seats with wider spacing than coach cars. Parlor car seats, if mounted, would often rotate; some had chairs that were moveable. Some parlor cars included a small lounge or smoking room.

Sleeping car. Sleeping cars were first- and second-class accommodations designed for overnight travel (see "Pullman Company" in Chapter 1). There have been hundreds of variations, with designs ranging from sections to enclosed rooms of various sizes and levels of luxury. Historically, the most basic sleeper of the heavyweight era was the Pullman section car. Each compartment featured an upper and lower berth, with a heavy curtain providing

Parlor cars have individual seats. This Illinois Central car shows the typical arrangement, with swiveling armchairs and a center aisle. The presence of a porter indicates first-class accommodations. Illinois Central

Pullman section

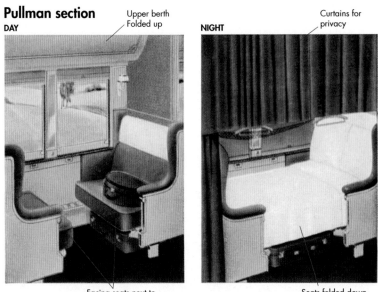

DAY — Upper berth / Folded up — Facing seats next to paired windows

NIGHT — Curtains for privacy — Seats folded down to form lower berth

Pullman sections featured facing seats in the daytime. At night, the upper berth folded down and the seats folded to form the lower berth. A curtain provided privacy. Pullman

privacy from the aisle. In the daytime, the upper berth folded upward and the lower converted to a pair of bench seats. Compartments (small rooms) and drawing rooms (larger rooms) were also available. Cars had many layouts with combinations of these accommodations, and they were described by number. For example, an all-section car had 16 sections; a 10-1-2 car—a common type—had 10 sections, 1 drawing room, and 2 compartments.

In the lightweight era, the roomette—a single small room with fold-down berth and concealed toilet and sink—largely replaced the section. A common lightweight sleeper was the 10 & 6, which had 10 roomettes and 6 double bedrooms. The mid-1950s saw the introduction of the Slumbercoach, which redesigned the layout to fit 24 small single rooms and 8 double rooms into a car.

Dining car. Full meal service began appearing on trains by the late 1800s, and through the 1950s dining cars ("diners") were staples of most long-distance trains. A typical diner has a kitchen (galley) taking up about a third of the car, with the remainder a dining room seating 36 to 48 passengers. Shorter-run trains sometimes had combination diner-lounge, lunch counters, or cafe-lounge cars with more limited menus. By the 1960s, full diners were being replaced on many routes by expanded lounge cars serving pre-packaged food and drink items, or even by vending machines.

Lounge car. Lounge cars were staples of first-class trains, providing bar service (beverages and often snacks) with couch and table seating and often a separate smoking area. The lounge could be the entire car, or could be divided with coach seating or dormitory facilities in a separate compartment.

Amtrak's Amfleet cars were the company's first new cars, arriving starting in 1973. This is a diner ("Amcafe"). The single-level cars were built by Budd. George Drury

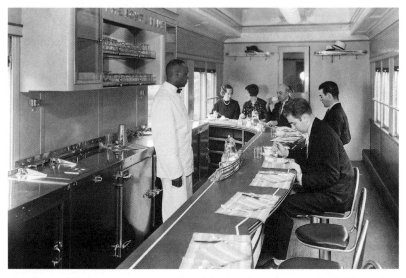

Many levels of food service were available. This is a lunch counter car on the Baltimore & Ohio *Royal Blue* in the 1940s. Trains magazine collection

Some short-haul and secondary trains had a combination diner-lounge car instead of a full-service dining car.

Observation car. The last car of most name trains usually provided an open seating area with large windows on the sides and rear. Into the early 1900s this often included an open rear platform with railing, but by the 1920s the car end was typically enclosed. Depending upon the train, this could be a first-class area or open to all passengers. The streamlined era provided many distinctive observation car designs, including Milwaukee Road's sloped "beaver tail" and skytop cars, with rounded-end cars on many railroads. Many railroads added lighted signs, called drumheads, to the rear of the observation car, highlighting the railroad herald and train name. Observation cars were often combined with other car types, including sleeper-lounge-observation and diner-observation cars.

Combination cars (combines). Although many car types were often combined, the term "combine" generally refers to coach-baggage or coach-baggage-mail cars, which have an abbreviated section for carrying baggage and express (and sometimes a Railway Post Office, or RPO) with the remainder of the car as coach seating. Combines were often used on branchline and secondary passenger trains with low ridership. They were also often tacked on the ends of mail and express trains to provide working space for the conductor and brakeman and a few seats for passengers.

A combine (coach-baggage) was common on mixed trains. This heavyweight version is on the Milwaukee Road at Mineral Point, Wis., in 1952. Paul E. Larson

Baggage-express. What was commonly called a baggage car—an enclosed car with one or two wide sliding side doors—certainly carried passenger baggage, but far more often carried express parcels and bags of U.S. Mail in storage. Through the 1960s, passenger trains carried mail under contract to the U.S. Postal Service and also express shipments for Railway Express Agency (REA). These cars traveled on set schedules and routes. Collectively this was known as head-end traffic, and it made up the entire consist of some trains.

Most baggage-express cars followed the basic design of heavyweight passenger cars, were 75 to 85 feet long, and had pairs of sliding doors on each side. Some streamlined lightweight versions were built, but they were outnumbered by heavyweight cars. Some railroads also equipped boxcars for express service by fitting them with high-speed trucks and steam and signal lines (these were sometimes painted in railroads' passenger colors as well)—they were known as "box express" cars.

A variation is the baggage-express-messenger car. These were built to have a messenger—usually a Railway Express Agency messenger—riding along, who handled deliveries and pickups at stations (including high-value express carried in a safe). These cars had a toilet, desk, light, and water, and were marked as messenger cars by having a five-pointed star on the side of each car (directly below the Railway Express Agency lettering, as on the Seaboard car pictured below).

Express refrigerators. Refrigerator cars equipped for express service (see page 223) were carried at the head end of passenger trains in the same

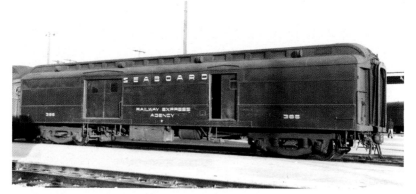

Seaboard Air Line 386 is a heavyweight baggage-express car. The star below the Railway Express Agency lettering indicates it's equipped as a messenger car. Bob's Photo

manner as mail and other express traffic. Express reefers were ice-bunker cars, and most were longer than standard reefers—50 feet—with rounded roofs and swinging plug doors. Bodies could be wood or steel; cars had high-speed trucks and steam and signal lines. Railway Express Agency also acquired a fleet of steel express reefers in the 1950s that looked more modern (like contemporary boxcars), with sliding plug doors. Express reefers carried perishable express traffic, which included most berries, early fruits of a season, and cut flowers and plants. Most of this traffic had moved to trucks by the late 1950s; remaining express reefers by 1960 were often used (without refrigeration) for standard express shipments.

Mail (Railway Post Office) cars. Not only did railroads carry a great deal of U.S. Mail—clerks aboard specially equipped Railway Post Office (RPO) cars sorted mail while trains were in motion, with mailbags picked up and dropped off as trains passed through towns. These cars were built to standard interior designs in three versions: with 15-, 30-, and 60-foot-long compartments (called "apartments") featuring sorting slots and bag holders. The remainder of the car was for mail storage; cars were often coupled next to a baggage-express car to allow moving bags to and from storage. The number of mail routes declined rapidly as passenger train numbers diminished from the 1950s into the 1960s. The postal service's move to large regional automated sorting centers in the early 1960s doomed most RPO service; almost all remaining routes were terminated in 1967 with the cancellation of almost all contracts by the U.S. Postal Service. Mail still travels by rail, but in trailers as piggyback shipments.

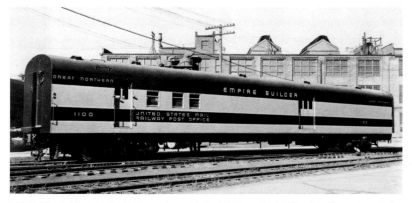

This lightweight Great Northern car has a 30-foot Railway Post Office (RPO) apartment at left with a baggage area (for stored mail) taking up the rest of the car. Great Northern

NON-REVENUE AND
MAINTENANCE-OF-WAY EQUIPMENT

The term "non-revenue" equipment applies to any rolling stock that does not bring in revenue for the railroad. The most common (and visible) example through the 1970s was the caboose (see chapter 1). Other non-revenue equipment includes snow plows, equipment in maintenance-of-way (MoW) service, and cars carrying company-owned materials and goods.

Railroads have fleets of cars assigned to company service. These can be either converted older cars that have been removed from revenue service, or new purpose-built cars. They include tank cars (for water, fuel, and lube oil), ballast cars, flatcars and gondolas (for carrying rail, wheels, and many other bulky products), side-dump gondolas, and boxcars (for any goods that require protection from the elements). Rack cars deliver welded rail to sites in quarter-mile long strings. Through the 1960s, older ice-bunker refrigerator cars were often converted to company ice service. Crews working in remote locations are often accommodated in bunk cars, typically older passenger cars or cabooses rebuilt for the service. Business cars are passenger cars that serve as rolling offices and inspection platforms for executives.

Other types of non-revenue and MoW equipment include:

Handcars. From the 1800s into the early 1900s, the handcar was the typical method of bringing crews and equipment to work areas along the tracks. They were small four-wheel vehicles with a rocking handle, powered by one or two workers who pumped the handle up and down to move the car. They could pull one or more small flatbed four-wheel trailers.

Plows. Railroads use wedge plows of many designs to clear snow. Railroads in northern climates also operate rotary plows, which use spinning blades to throw snow to the side of the tracks. These were steam powered through the 1950s, and modern rotaries are diesel powered. Jordan spreaders are a type of plow with multiple front and side blades; they are also often used to reshape the roadbed and subgrade.

Speeders. Speeders are small four-wheel rail vehicles powered by gasoline engines. They replaced handcars for local maintenance crews in the early 1900s and remained common through the 1970s, when they largely gave way to hi-rail trucks.

Hi-rail trucks. Equipping a highway vehicle with retractable rail wheels became common in the 1950s, at first with passenger vehicles and pickup trucks and eventually for full-size trucks and cranes. Hi-rail vehicles are

A pair of diesels pulls a short string of freight cars while pushing a snowplow on Conrail near Blasdell, N.Y., in 1978. Fred B. Furminger

Track speeders are small motorized vehicles that can be set on and off the rails at grade crossings or special set-outs. This is on Spokane International in 1984. Bruce Kelly

Hi-rail trucks have rail wheels along with highway wheels, and come in many configurations. This is a weed sprayer on the Santa Fe. Santa Fe

much more versatile than all-rail speeders, as they can easily get on and off the tracks at any grade crossing.

Rail inspection cars. Electrical testing of rails to find hidden defects began in the late 1920s. Sperry was the first company to provide the service, and its fleet of self-propelled defect-detector cars (and those of several other companies) provide inspection services to railroads across North America.

Rail grinders. As rail wears it loses its profile. It can be reground multiple times to reshape it, a service done by a rail grinder. A typical grinding operation has a locomotive pulling several cars equipped with grinding wheels,

Defect detectors use electrical current sent through the rails to detect defects within the rail. Jackson (shown here in 1983) and Sperry are two operators of detector cars. Paul J. Cirulli

You can see the sparks generated by the grinding wheels on this Loram rail grinding outfit. Rails are periodically reground to restore their profile and improve operations. Jeff Wilson

with a fire-suppression car at the rear to douse any fires caused by sparks from grinding. Railroads contract for grinding services, with Loram and Speno the best-known contractors today.

Dynamometer cars. Railroads use dynamometer cars to test locomotive performance. Dynamometers have stress gauges mounted through their center sills, and measure the force exerted by a locomotive against a train behind the dynamometer car.

Scale test cars. These are small, four-wheel cars of a specific weight that are used to calibrate track-mounted scales.

Track maintenance equipment. Track repair became increasingly mechanized from the 1940s onward. Equipment includes tampers (which distribute ballast and level the track), ballast cleaners/shapers, and self-pro-

Dynamometer cars are placed between the locomotive and train, and use a stress gauge to measure the force exerted by a locomotive. John Ingles; J. David Ingles collection

pelled machines that remove and install ties, spikes, and rail anchors. Cranes (steam- and later diesel-powered) were used to clean up derailments as well as for track and bridge maintenance.

Work-train cars. Work trains are moved to areas of construction or maintenance, and often serve as temporary quarters for workers, especially in remote locations. Old freight and passenger cars are often converted for work train service, and these can include bunk cars, kitchen cars, tool

Louisville & Nashville crane no. 40026, shown at DeCoursey, Ky., in 1980, is typical of cranes used for maintaining tracks and bridges and cleaning up derailments. Jim Hediger

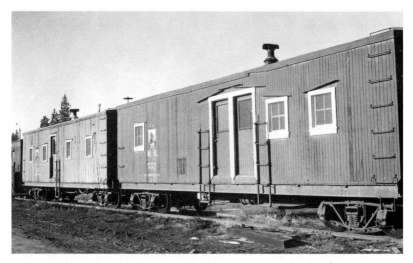

Retired freight and passenger cars are often converted for maintenance-of-way service, as these old archbar-truck-equipped wood boxcars on the McCloud River in 1964. Donald Sims

(storage) and workshop cars, and gondolas, boxcars, and flatcars for carrying equipment and supplies.

FREIGHT AND PASSENGER CAR MANUFACTURERS

Hundreds of manufacturers built cars in the wood-car era. The shift to steel construction eliminated most smaller car builders, as steel fabrication required larger facilities and a larger volume of business to be viable.

Car building is a very cyclical business. It depends heavily upon the economy, which drives traffic levels. Freight-car manufacturers in particular often find themselves in a feast-or-famine situation, seemingly either producing cars as fast as they can or having a surplus of cars and production capacity with no orders. This has led to larger companies acquiring small builders, with many smaller companies that specialized in certain car types going out of business, merging, or being bought out by larger companies. The recession of the early 1980s eliminated many builders.

Most car builders today have diversified into other related industries or are owned by parent companies that manufacture other products. Most freight-car builders have also smoothed out production cycles by also owning their own fleets of cars for leasing and by supplying parts and providing repair and rebuilding services. As of 2022, North American freight car manufacturing is dominated by six major builders: American Railcar Industries (ARI)/ACF; FreightCar America; Greenbrier/Gunderson; National Steel Car; TrinityRail; and Union Tank Car. In addition, many railroads have built cars in their own shops. Here's a summary of the major manufacturers that have produced freight and passenger cars since 1960:

American Car & Foundry (AC&F). ACF Industries (American Car & Foundry until 1955) was one of the country's largest freight and passenger car manufacturers. It was formed in 1899 with the merger of 13 companies. (Also see American Railcar Industries.)

American Railcar Industries (ARI) was formed in 1994 as the railcar-building subsidiary of ACF Industries. ARI continues to build tank and covered hopper cars based on ACF designs at plants in Paragould and Marmaduke, Ark. ACF provides parts, components, tanks, and conversion and rebuilding services at its Milton, Pa., plant.

Berwick Freight Car Company began as Berwick Foundry & Forge, acquiring ACF's former Berwick, Pa., plant after it closed in 1961. BF&F closed in 1982 and shortly thereafter reopened as Berwick Freight Car, building cars until 1993.

Bethlehem Steel Car Company's freight car division was formed in 1923 with the purchase of Midvale Steel and Ordnance. The division built freight cars until it was sold to Johnstown America in 1991; that company was renamed FreightCar America in 2004.

Bombardier began building passenger cars in the early 1970s, and has built a variety of commuter and mass transit cars as well as conventional cars. It acquired the passenger designs and assets of Budd and Pullman-Standard in the late 1980s. The company was acquired by Alstom in 2021.

Budd Company was founded in 1912, and became known for its innovative shot-welding process for welding stainless steel. It began building fluted stainless-steel passenger cars in 1934, notably Burlington's *Zephyr* and subsequent cars. Its railcar assets went to Bombardier in 1987.

CNCF (Constructora Nacional de Carros de Ferrocarril) was a Mexican company that built boxcars for IPD (incentive per diem) owners as well as Mexican railroads from 1979 through the early 1980s.

Evans Products Company, a long-time builder of car components, entered the freight car business when it bought U.S. Railway Equipment Co. in the 1960s and operated it as a leasing company. The company built cars (mainly coil steel cars, covered hoppers, and boxcars) under the Evans name. Evans also acquired SIECO in the 1970s. Evans ceased building cars in 1984.

FMC Corporation built freight cars from 1965 to 1985 at a plant in Springfield, Ore.; the facility was purchased by Gunderson in 1985.

FreightCar America (FCA) currently builds cars at a plant in Mexico. It traces its roots to Bethlehem Steel Car Co.; that company was acquired by Johnstown America in 1991. The company changed its name to FreightCar America in December 2004. FCA specializes in coal gondolas and hopper cars but also builds covered hoppers, flatcars, and boxcars.

General American Car Company was a major builder of cars through most of the 20th century. It began as the German-American Car Co., but changed its name in 1916. General American had multiple divisions and also operated a leasing company. It ceased building cars in 1984, and its designs were licensed to Trinity. Successor GATX Corp. still operates as a car leasing company.

Greenbrier, the second-largest builder entering 2020, began as a steel fabricating company owned by the Gunderson brothers in Portland, Ore., in 1919. The company began building freight car underframes under contract in 1958. The Springfield (Eugene), Ore., plant was owned by FMC Corporation from 1965 to 1985, and operated as the Marine and Rail Equipment Division of FMC. This plant was sold in 1985 to the Greenbrier Companies, which had been officially named such in 1981, and began building cars as Gunderson, Inc. The Gunderson name became The Greenbrier Companies in 1994, and the company acquired Trenton Works in 1995. Greenbrier builds cars of most types at plants in Oregon as well as in Mexico and other countries.

Greenville Steel Car Company began as Greenville (Pa.) Metal Products Co. in 1910, acquired its name in 1914, and built new cars from 1916 into the 1980s. It was acquired by Trinity in 1986.

Gulf Railcar built tank cars at the former Richmond Tank Car plant (in Houston) from 1983 into the 1990s.

Gunderson: See Greenbrier.

Hawker Siddeley Canada (later listed as Hawker Siddeley Canada Ltd., Trenton Works Division) built cars in Trenton, Nova Scotia from 1962 until 1988. It was best known for building Canadian cylindrical covered hoppers. Its plant was eventually sold to Greenbrier.

Ingalls Shipbuilding built freight cars in 1979 and 1980 for North American Car Co.

Johnstown America: See FreightCar America.

Magor Car Corp. built freight cars beginning in the 1910s. It became a division of Fruehauf in 1964 and ceased building freight cars in 1973.

Marine Industries Ltd. was a Canadian company based in Sorel-Tracy, Quebec. It built railcars from 1957 to 1986, notably Canadian cylindrical covered hoppers as well as flatcars and gondolas.

National Steel Car (NSC) is based in Hamilton, Ontario. It began building freight cars in 1912 and has the largest single-site manufacturing facility in North America as of 2020. The company built cars under license to Pullman-Standard through the 1970s and currently builds cars of all types.

North American Car Co. built freight cars and also operated as a leasing company. Its designs were sold to Trinity and Thrall in 1985.

Ortner Freight Car Co. began building cars in 1948. It was primarily known for its line of rapid-discharge hopper cars; it was acquired by Trinity in 1984.

Pacific Car & Foundry was incorporated as Seattle Car & Foundry in 1911, then merged with another builder and became PC&F in 1917. It became a subsidiary of AC&F in 1924 and specialized in refrigerator cars. Its parent company became Paccar in 1972; it ceased railcar manufacturing shortly after 1980.

Portec was known mainly for building the auto racks that are mounted to flatcars (it acquired Paragon in the early 1970s), but the company also built freight cars and components from the late 1970s into the 1980s.

Pullman-Standard was one of the country's largest freight car builders through the 1970s. It was formed by a merger of Pullman Company's freight car division and Standard Steel Car in 1930. Its designs and several plants were acquired by Trinity in 1984.

Richmond Tank Car Co. built tank cars from the 1940s to 1983 and also built some covered hoppers at its Houston plant. Gulf Railcar later took over the plant and built tank cars into the 1990s.

Siemens Mobility began building passenger cars (as well as locomotives) in the 2010s, and currently builds its Venture cars for Amtrak, VIA Rail Canada, and others. The German-based company manufactures cars in Sacramento, Calif.

Southern Iron & Equipment Co. (SIECO) was a long-time rebuilder of steam locomotives and other equipment. In 1973 the company began building freight cars and was best known for its 50-foot incentive per-diem (IPD) boxcars. It was acquired by Evans in the late 1970s.

Thrall Car Manufacturing Company was formed in 1917 in Chicago. It had become the country's no. 2 car builder when it was acquired by Trinity in 2001. Thrall built most car types except tanks, and also acquired auto-rack builders Whitehead & Kales and Portec (Paragon) in the 1980s.

Trenton Works: See Hawker Siddeley.

TrinityRail, a division of Trinity Industries, is the largest supplier of new cars as of 2020. It began as Trinity Steel in Dallas, Texas, in 1933. The company began building tank car bodies under contract to other builders in the late 1960s, then began building its own line of cars (initially tank cars and covered hoppers) in 1978. Trinity has since bought, merged, or acquired the designs and/or manufacturing facilities of General American (1984), Pullman-Standard (1984), Ortner (1984), Greenville (1986), and Thrall (2001). The company offers a full line of freight car types.

Union Tank Car (UTLX) is best known for its leasing fleet of tank cars.

The company began operating in the 1860s and designed its own cars—but did not build them—until acquiring Graver Tank Co. in 1955. Since then the company has manufactured cars for its own fleet and for sale and lease. It operates plants in Alexandria, Va., and Sheldon, Texas.

U.S. Railway Equipment Co. was a Chicago-based company (later a division of Evans) that mainly rebuilt cars, but built some new cars, from the 1950s to 1978.

AAR FREIGHT CAR CLASSIFICATIONS

BOXCAR — X, V	
XM	General service
XA	Automobile box, inside height of 10 feet or more
XAB	Automobile box, inside height of less than 10 feet
XAP	Automobile parts car with permanent interior racks
XAR	Automobile box with auto stowing equipment
XAF	Automobile/furniture car
XF	Furniture car (usually larger than a general service car)
XI	Insulated box
XT	Tank box (boxcar with one or more interior tanks)
VA	Ventilated box for fruits and vegetables
VM	Ventilated box, partially insulated
VS	Ventilated box, insulated with swinging side doors
* An "H" suffix with any of these indicates heating equipment	
REFRIGERATOR CARS — R	
RS	Ice-bunker car
RSM	Ice-bunker car with meat rails
RA	Brine-tank car (usually for meat service)
RAM	Brine-tank car with meat rails
RB	Bunkerless (insulated) car
RBL	Bunkerless car with loading devices
RC	Car carrying insulated containers

RCD	Carbon-dioxide-cooled car
RP	Mechanical refrigerator car
RPA	Mechanical car powered by mechanical car-axle drive
RPB	Mechanical car powered by electromechanical axle drive
RT	Milk bulk car

TANK CARS — T

TM	General service, unlined, non-insulated car
TA	Acid-service car (no bottom outlet)
TL	Car equipped with special lining
TG	Glass-lined car
TP	Pressure tank
TW	Car with one or more wooden or metal tanks or tubs

* An "I" suffix with any of these cars indicates an insulated car

HOPPER — H

HM	Twin-bottom car
HMA	Twin-bottom car with lengthwise (between-rails) doors
HE	Non-self-clearing car
HT	Three (or more)-bottom car
HTA	Three (or more)-bottom car with lengthwise (between-rails) doors
HD	Two (or more)-bottom car with lengthwise (outside of rails) doors
HK	Two (or more)-bottom car with lengthwise (between or outside rails) doors

COVERED HOPPER - LO

GONDOLA — G

GB	Mill gondola with fixed or drop ends
GT	Coal gondola, high sides and fixed ends
GA	Drop-bottom (between rails) car with fixed ends
GE	Drop-bottom (between rails) car with drop ends
GH	Drop-bottom (outside of rails) car with drop ends
GS	Drop-bottom (outside of rails) car with fixed ends
GRA	Drop-hopper-bottom car with fixed ends and sides
GD	Side-dump car
GW	Well-hole car

STOCK CARS — S

SM	Single-deck car
SF	Double-deck car
SC	Convertible double-deck car

SD	Car with drop-bottom doors in floor
SH	Horse car
SP	Poultry car

FLATCARS — F

FM	General service car
FC	Piggyback car
FD	Depressed-center car
FB	Barrel-rack car (skeleton car)
FL	Logging car

ADDITIONAL DEPARTMENT OF TRANSPORTATION (1966) AND AAR (1996) TANK CAR CLASSIFICATIONS:

Class	Pressure	PSI	Insulated	
DOT103*	No	35	Yes or no	Tank with expansion dome
DOT104*	No	35	Yes	Tank with expansion dome
DOT105	Yes	75-450	Yes	Steel (carbon or stainless) tank
DOT106	Yes	375-600	No	Multiple removable tanks
DOT107	Yes	Varies		Multiple seamless tanks
DOT109	Yes	75-225	Yes or no	Carbon steel or aluminum tank
DOT110	Yes	375-750		Multiple removable tanks
DOT111	No	35-75	Yes or no	Domeless steel or aluminum tank
DOT112	Yes	150-375	No	Steel (carbon or stainless) tank
DOT113	—	30-115	Yes	Cryogenic with vacuum insulation
DOT114	Yes	255-300	No	Steel (carbon or stainless) tank
DOT115	No	35	Yes	Insulated tank
DOT117	No	35-75	Yes	Upgraded version of DOT111
DOT120	Yes	150-450	Yes	
DOT211	No			
AAR203*	No	35	Yes or no	(matches DOT103)
AAR204	—	30-115	Yes	(matches DOT113)
AAR206	No	35	Yes	(matches DOT115)
AAR207	No	—	No	Car for granular products, pneumatic unloading
AAR208	No	—	No	Wood-stave tank with metal hoops
AAR211	No	35-75	Yes or no	(matches DOT111)

* Obsolete by 1980s

AAR PASSENGER CAR CLASSIFICATIONS

PASSENGER — CLASS P

PA	Suburban or commuter car, with seats and open platforms
PAS	Combination coach/sleeping car
PB	Coach or chair car
PBO	Coach/observation car
PC	Chair or parlor car
PD	Tavern car
PL	First-class lounge car
PO	Observation car
PS	Sleeping car with compartments (seats that can be made into berths)
PSA	Dormitory car
PT	Tourist sleeping car (second-class)
PV	Private car

DINING — CLASS D

DA	Standard dining car with kitchen
DB	Buffet car; chair car with cooking facilities
DC	Cafe car (combination lunch car/diner)
DCL	Lunch counter/lounge car
DD	Combination diner/dormitory car
DE	Dining car without kitchen
DG	Grill room car (similar to cafe car)
DK	Combination kitchen/dormitory car
DKP	Kitchen car (no dining area)
DL	Buffet/lounge car
DLC	Lunch counter car
DO	Cafe/observation car
DP	Dining/parlor car
DPA	Diner/lounge car

COMBINED CARS — CLASS C

CA	Combined coach/baggage car
CAD	Coach/baggage car with dining facilities
CO	Combined coach/baggage/Railway Post Office car
CS	Combined smoking car/baggage car
CSA	Combined baggage/dormitory/kitchen

CBS	Combined baggage/dormitory
CSP	Combined mail storage or baggage/dormitory/coach

BAGGAGE — CLASS B

BE	Standard baggage-express car with side doors
BEM	Baggage-express messenger (equipped with toilet, desk, and facilities for on-board messenger; noted by a star on the car side)
BH	Horse or horse-carriage express car (for fine stock)
BLF	Flatcar equipped to carry trailers or containers
BM	Milk car (non-refrigerated) for cans or bottles
BMR	Milk car with ice bunkers for cans or bottles
BMT	Milk car with one or more internal tanks for bulk service
BP	Refrigerator express car
BR	Refrigerator/ventilator express car
BS	Refrigerator express with brine tanks
BX	Box express (boxcar with high-speed trucks and steam line)
BXM	Box express messenger (same requirements as BEM)

MAIL — CLASS M

MA	Postal (Railway Post Office) car
MB	Combination RPO/baggage car
MBE	Three-compartment car, RPO/baggage/express
MBD	Combination RPO/baggage/dormitory car
MD	Combination RPO/dormitory car
MP	Mail storage car, for newspapers/large packages
MR	Mail storage car, for bulk mail
MS	Combination mail/storage car

Not all classifications listed; classifications sometimes changed over the years.

FREIGHT CAR TIMELINE

1923 ARA 1923 boxcar first built; it was the first common steel boxcar

1932 AB brakes required on new equipment

ACF introduces the first purpose-built covered hoppers

1941 Archbar trucks banned from interchange

1947 Metal running boards required on new cars (replacing wood)

1948 First mechanical refrigerator cars

1953 K brakes banned from interchange

1954 Union Tank Car builds its first frameless tank car

General American introduces the Airslide covered hopper car

1955 First purpose-built piggyback flatcars: 75-footers for Pennsylvania RR

Trailer Train (later TTX Co.) formed

Frameless tank cars eliminate the center sill, relying on the tank itself for strength. UTLX

Archbar trucks were common into the 1900s; they were banned from interchange service in 1941. Jeff Wilson

1956 Malcolm McLean forms Sea-Land; first ship/truck/railroad container service

1957 Cast-iron ("chilled") wheels no longer allowed on new equipment.

Flexi-Van containers rode on special skeleton flatcars. New York Central

Flexi-Van container/flatcar system is introduced

1960 First multi-level open auto rack cars placed in service

First jumbo covered hopper for grain: Southern's "Big John" 100-ton aluminum car, built by Magor

Southern's "Big John" cars were the first true dedicated grain cars. J. David Ingles collection

1963 Gross Rail Load (GRL) limits increased; 100-ton cars become effective standard

First 86-foot high-cube boxcars (for auto parts)

FREIGHT CAR TIMELINE

1964
First jumbo 100-ton wood chip gondolas are delivered

First rotary-dump unit-train coal gondolas enter service

1966
Roller-bearing trucks required on all new and rebuilt 100-ton cars

Running boards no longer required on new cars

1967
ACI (Automatic Car Identification) labels begin appearing on cars

1968
Roller-bearing trucks required on all new freight cars

ISO standards for container sizes and connectors are established

1970
Tank car size limited to 34,500 gallons

Cast-iron ("chilled") wheels banned from interchange service

ACI labels required on all cars

1971
Shelf-style couplers required on tank cars

The ACI bar-code system didn't work; grime proved an unsolvable problem.
J. David Ingles collection

1972 Consolidated stencils begin appearing

1974 Railbox pool boxcars enter service

Cars built since July 1974 can operate 50 years in interchange service

1975 ARA tank cars no longer allowed in service

1977 First significant order of center-beam flatcars delivered

ACI system abandoned

1978 Wheel-inspection dots appear on cars currently in service

Railbox cars are operated in a free-roaming pool.
J. David Ingles collection

FREIGHT CAR TIMELINE

1981 First double-stack container cars placed in service.

1983 Running boards to be removed from all house cars (originally 1974)

1985 Capacity data line no longer required on new cars

1989 First all-purpose intermodal spine cars placed in service

1990 Cryogenic refrigerator cars enter service

Cars of 110-ton capacity (286K GRL), like this ARI-built grain covered hopper on Union Pacific, are now the standard for interchange. Jeff Wilson

1994 AEI (Automatic Equipment Identification) tags required on all cars

1995 Solid-bearing trucks banned from interchange

110-ton (286,000 GRL) cars approved for interchange

1999 53-foot well cars enter service

2003 TTX begins shortening 45- and 48-foot well-car platforms to 40 feet

TBOX and FBOX boxcars begin appearing

2015 New tank car (DOT-117) specifications are released

2020 About 1.66 million freight cars are in service on North American railroads

PASSENGER CAR TIMELINE

1830 — First paid passengers travel behind the *Best Friend of Charleston*

1867 — Pullman Palace Car Co. is incorporated by George Pullman

1870s — First dining cars appear

1882 — First passenger car featuring electric lights

1907 — The first all-steel passenger cars appear, ushering in the "heavyweight era"

1921 — The Pennsylvania Railroad begins installing roller-bearing journals on many passenger cars; they soon become common on passenger equipment

1929 — First air-conditioned cars appear

1934 — The streamliner era begins as the Union Pacific's M-10000 (distillate powered) and Burlington's *Zephyr* (diesel powered) enter service.

The use of stainless steel and aluminum usher in the "lightweight era" with the introduction of streamlined cars

1937 — The first Roomette cars appear from Pullman

1945 — The first dome car, Burlington's *Silver Dome,* enters service

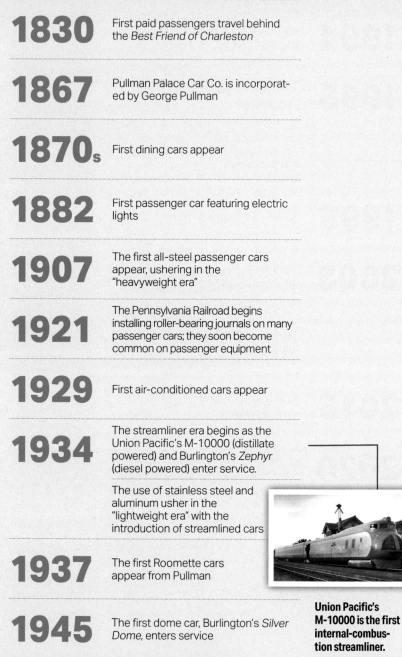

Union Pacific's M-10000 is the first internal-combustion streamliner.
Trains magazine collection

1950 The first double-deck commuter cars enter service: Budd-built cars on the Burlington Route in Chicago

1952 The first full-length dome cars appear, built by Pullman-Standard for Milwaukee Road

1956 Santa Fe buys the first double-deck ("Hi-Level") cars for long-haul service, using them on its *El Capitan*

1967 The U.S. Postal Service cancels almost all mail service contracts on railroads

1969 Metroliner high-speed electric trains enter service between Washington, D.C. and New York City

1971 Amtrak begins service on May 1, taking over most intercity passenger service in the U.S.

1973 Amtrak purchases its first new equipment; tubular, fluted-side Amfleet cars

1980 Amtrak buys the first of its double-deck Superliner passenger cars

1995 Amtrak's first Viewliner passenger cars enter service

2000 Amtrak's high-speed *Acela Express* enters service in the Northeast Corridor (the name was shortened to *Acela* in 2019)

2016 The first Viewliner II passenger cars enter service on Amtrak

The railroad right of way

■ The railroad right of way (RoW) includes much more than the track itself. "Right of way" literally means "right to make a way over a parcel of land." Most railroads received their rights to exist from government grants, giving them ownership of a path through federal- or state-owned land. Railroads can also acquire land for their track through eminent domain via state or federal laws, by purchase, or by easement, which is when a landowner grants permission to allow a railroad to use a path through the owner's land without conferring ownership.

Track is the most visible element of a railroad right of way, and can be maintained to many levels. The Illinois Terminal yard track at Springfield, Ill., in 1976 is definitely slow-speed trackage. Mike Schafer

A railroad's physical right of way is usually 100 feet wide, measured 50 feet outward from the center of the track. This can be narrower, especially in urban areas, and it was sometimes wider (the General Railroad Right of Way Act of 1875 allowed railroads to claim a 200-foot-wide path across public lands).

The most noticeable component of the right of way is the track itself. Along with the rails and ties, track details include turnouts of many types, crossings, and all related connectors and components such as joint bars, spikes, switch stands, switch machines, switch heaters, derails, guardrails, and wood and concrete ties.

The roadbed and subroadbed are key components of the RoW. Elevating the track above the surrounding ground allows smooth transition of grades and provides drainage and stability for the track structure. This includes the ballast, sub-ballast, and subgrade, including fills and cuts that allow railroad lines to smoothly pass among hills and through valleys.

Other RoW features include highway and street crossings (with their warning signs, gates, and crossing signals), pole lines (for communication, signaling, and power), various types of signals and signal bridges, equipment cases, battery vaults, phone boxes, defect detectors, signs, microwave towers, antennas, retaining walls, culverts, bridges, tunnels, fences, and depots and other structures.

TRACK

Gauge

The standard track gauge—the width between inside edges of the rail-heads—in North America is 4'-8½". This was effectively established with the Pacific Railway Act of 1862, which chartered the first transcontinental railroad. The early days of railroading saw railroads using a wide variety of gauges. Five feet was common in Southern states, with six feet on some Northern lines, notably the Erie. Many narrow gauge lines were built with gauges of two feet (primarily in Maine) and three feet (Midwest and West). Narrow gauge lines were less expensive to build—especially in rugged territory—and used smaller, cheaper equipment. Their diminished capacity led to most narrow gauge lines being either abandoned or converted to standard gauge by the 1940s.

The inefficiency of having to transload freight between cars at every rail-road junction became apparent in railroading's early years, and a movement

Narrow gauge lines were less expensive to build and featured smaller equipment. This is the three-foot-gauge Rio Grande Southern at Porter, Colo., in 1952. Robert F. Collins

began to unify track gauge among railroads to allow interchange of cars. Although most northern lines adjusted to match standard gauge, many railroads in the South remained at five feet for another two decades. It wasn't until 1886 when these lines agreed to change, a project largely accomplished over two days (May 31-June 1) of that year.

Narrow gauge lines remained in some areas, primarily in Colorado, New Mexico, Alaska, and Maine, along with logging lines in several areas. Notable survivors as of 2022 include several former Denver & Rio Grande Western and Rio Grande Southern lines, Alaska's White Pass & Yukon, and the East Broad Top in Pennsylvania.

Rail

Rail has evolved substantially since the 1800s, increasing in size as loads became heavier. And although it can't be seen, rail has changed with advances in metallurgy and steel production processes to improve resistance to wear and stress.

The first rails of the early 1800s were iron straps fastened to longitudinal timbers. Even with the light equipment of the early 1800s, this didn't work well, as the iron straps tended to separate from the timbers and curl up as

EARLY RAIL CROSS SECTIONS

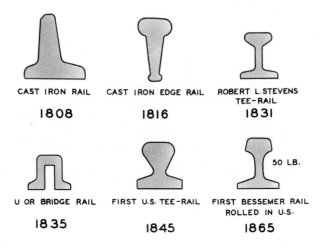

CAST IRON RAIL
1808

CAST IRON EDGE RAIL
1816

ROBERT L. STEVENS
TEE-RAIL
1831

U OR BRIDGE RAIL
1835

FIRST U.S. TEE-RAIL
1845

FIRST BESSEMER RAIL
ROLLED IN U.S.
1865

50 LB.

Several types of iron rail were used before steel T-rail became standard. Rail would continue evolving, with many profiles used. Bethlehem Steel

cars passed over them. The solution was solid iron rails with a T-shaped cross-section, which first appeared in England in 1831 and were first rolled in U.S. mills in 1845. The first steel rails began appearing in 1865.

The basic rail shape, or cross-section, has remained similar since the mid-1800s. The large, flat bottom is the base; the vertical section is the web, and the wide part at the top upon which the wheels ride is the head. The size of the rail has increased substantially, with heavier (wider and taller rail) able to support heavier loads and faster train speeds. By the 1890s, manufacturers were producing rail in 119 different profiles and 27 weights. Rail designs were eventually standardized under the direction of the American Railway Association (ARA) starting in 1905 (the Association of American Railroads after 1934).

Rail size is rated by weight, in pounds per yard. Early rail was light, only 36 to 60 pounds per yard. By 1900, new mainline rail was typically 80 or 90 pounds, with 112-pound rail by the mid-1930s. In 1921, the average rail weight on Class I railroads was 82.8 pounds; by 1956 it was 105 pounds. Rail at 132 pounds was used on heavy-traffic lines by the 1940s, and the Pennsylvania Railroad was noted for its massive 152-pound rail that it began using on some major routes in the 1930s. Today, most mainline rail is 136 or 141 pounds, but there is still plenty of lighter rail on secondary lines, branch

RAIL HEIGHT VARIATIONS

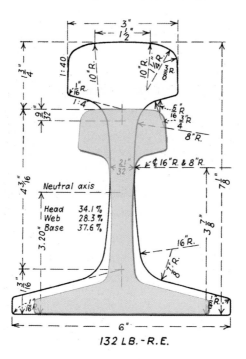

132 LB. - R.E.

Rail size is measured by weight in pounds per yard. The outline shows 132-pound rail (7⅛" tall); the shaded profile is 90-pound rail (5⅜" tall). Kalmbach Media

lines, passing sidings, and industrial tracks.

Differences in rail profiles include depth of the head and width of the web and base. The drawing above shows the dimensions for 132-pound rail, which is noticeably taller at 7⅛" than the 90-pound (5⅝" tall) shown with it. Modern 141 pound RE rail is 7⁷⁄₁₆" tall.

The length of individual rail sections on prototype railroads has always been based on the length of standard gondola cars of each era. This meant 15- to 20-foot sections in the 1800s, extending to 33 feet by 1898. The common 39-foot length, adopted in 1925 and still found on railroads across the country, was designed to fit in a 40-foot gondola; most new jointed rail was this size through the 1960s. Today, rail is typically offered in 70- and 80-foot sections, although 39-foot rail is still produced.

Welded rail is used on most modern main and secondary lines. This is Union Pacific's double-track main line in Nebraska. Jeff Wilson

Welded rail

Rail joints are problematic in many ways. That familiar "clickity-clack" is the sound of wheels battering at rail ends as they cross joints, causing chipping, wear, and vertical deflection. Bolts on joint bars require periodic tightening, and can crack. Along signaled lines, each joint requires a bond wire between rails to ensure electrical conductivity. Every mile of track with conventional 39-foot lengths of rail has 270 rail joints—135 on each rail— which means 540 joint bars, 2160 bolts, and 270 bond wires to be installed and maintained.

The ultimate solution to the problem of rail joints was continuous welded rail (CWR), also called "ribbon rail." It's made by factory-welding individual sections of rail into quarter-mile-long pieces, which are then carried to installation locations on special rack cars that hold multiple lengths of rail. Once laid, the rail is then field-welded to even longer stretches—often several miles, with the length generally determined by the length of signal blocks or distance between turnouts.

Along with lowered maintenance costs in both labor and materials, CWR significantly improves operations. It provides a smoother ride with less wear and damage to rolling stock, loads, and locomotives from wheels hitting rail joints, allowing higher train speeds in many cases.

The Central of Georgia in 1933 was the first to install a significant length

Quarter-mile sections of welded rail are being pulled from rack cars and placed between the existing jointed rails in preparation for replacement. Mike Small

of CWR on mainline track—through a couple of tunnels—and Delaware & Hudson followed with 42 miles of CWR through the 1930s. Welded rail remained relatively rare through the 1950s, with less than 1,000 total miles in service by 1955. Tunnels were popular initial locations, along with street trackage, station platforms, and other areas where routine track maintenance could be difficult.

The main challenges in laying welded rail were developing effective methods for welding the butt ends of rail, then controlling the long rail's expansion and contraction caused by changes in temperature, which can be extreme (120 degrees or more) in some areas. This can cause rail to fracture or pull apart joints in extreme cold and buckle or kink in extreme heat. This was the main reason it took 30-plus years for CWR to become common.

To combat this, rail is pre-stressed (heated and cooled in a controlled manner), and then installed at a "rail-neutral" temperature to avoid extreme forces in either direction. This is optimally about 30 to 40 degrees below the maximum rail temperature at the installation location, which keeps the rail in slight tension at most times.

The other key is to anchor CWR more securely than standard rail—concrete ties are often used—and give track a deeper ballast profile. Firmer anchoring keeps the rail in place and prevents it from moving lengthwise once installed. Improvements in welding (thermite welding is now standard), along with stronger joint bars and connectors at the end sections of CWR (particularly insulated joints) have increased reliability.

As technology advanced, CWR mileage increased considerably. The first year that saw more than 1,000 miles of CWR installed was 1959; by the 1970s, railroads were adding 4,000 to 6,000 miles of CWR annually. Total CWR mileage in 1976 was about 60,000; by the 2000s it was over 100,000 miles.

Ties

Railroads use a lot of ties: In 2020, North American railroads purchased about 20.5 million wood ties, plus several hundred thousand concrete ties. Wood still retains 93 percent of the new-tie market, although concrete ties have grown in popularity since the 1980s. Other materials, including steel, resin, and composite (plastic-encapsulated wood) have been used, but in very small numbers.

Crossties perform several vital functions. As their name implies, they "tie" the rails together, keeping them aligned and in proper gauge. They support the weight of the rails and the loads they carry, providing a broad footprint to dissipate the load over a larger area. And ties also allow the track structure to be resilient, providing some "give" to the dynamic forces of moving trains.

The first railroads of the early 1800s had rails resting on stone bases, or sleepers (as they're still called in Europe). This didn't work well, as the stone

Wood ties are standard on most track. Here a four-hole joint bar secures a rail joint, with multiple bond wires connecting the rails. The tie plates on this secondary track are small single-shoulder models. Trains magazine collection

was prone to shifting in the ground. Railroads soon adopted wood timbers placed crosswise under the rails, which have been the standard ever since.

Early untreated wood ties required frequent replacing, often lasting less than 10 years. By 1900 most ties were pressure-treated with creosote, helping them withstand damage from water, insects, and decay. Exactly how long individual ties last in service depends upon the type of wood they're made of, the type of treatment they receive, the traffic level they support, and local ground and atmospheric conditions. There are ties still in service on secondary and branch lines that are 75 or more years old; even on heavy service lines, 30 years isn't unusual.

Through the 1800s, ties were often sawed or hewn on two sides only (top and bottom), with widths that varied. Since the early 1900s, ties with all four sides sawed/hewn have been standard. Early ties were usually 8'-0" long; most modern ties are 8'-6" long, but some railroads prefer 9'-0" ties. Tie height and width vary from 5" to 7" tall and 5" to 10" wide, with sizes falling into numbered standard dimensions from No. 0 to No. 6 (thickness x width): No. 0: 5 x 5; No. 1: 6 x 6; No. 2: 6 x 7; No. 3: 6 x 8; No. 4: 7 x 8; No. 5: 7 x 9; No. 6: 7 x 10. As train speeds and weights have increased, tie size has likewise increased, with Nos. 4 and 5 ties now the most commonly used. A new treated wood tie weighs about 235 pounds.

To stabilize ties and keep them from splitting, checking, or cracking, most ties have metal reinforcements on their ends called "tie irons" (also sometimes called "S irons" or "end plates"). These are sometimes S-shaped metal shapes driven into the ends; they can also be spiked metal mesh driven onto the end. These began appearing in the 1940s.

Tie spacing varies based on era, traffic, and loads. On modern main lines a 19.5" center-to-center spacing is typical for wood ties, meaning about 3,250 ties per mile of track. Industrial spurs, yard tracks, sidings, branch lines, and older installations often have wider spacing. A contemporary Canadian National specification sheet for new industrial trackage calls for 20" spacing on lead tracks and 22" on body (storage or loading) tracks.

Concrete ties were first tried by the Reading—a 200-tie test installation—in 1893. Several other manufacturers and railroads designed, patented, and tested various designs in the early 1900s, but none made it past the experimental stage, mainly because concrete ties were significantly more expensive than wood versions, which were readily available, cheap, and worked well.

By the late 1950s, rising prices of treated-wood products led the Associa-

Concrete ties have a thinner profile between the rail seats. They are wider than wood ties and use clips instead of spikes to secure rail. Jeff Wilson

tion of American Railroads (AAR) to encourage manufacturers to try again, and several designs of precast, prestressed concrete ties were developed and tested starting in 1957. Variations included tie shape and methods of securing rails.

Concrete's positive attributes include overall strength; resistance to decay and deterioration caused by insects, water, and other weather factors; and the ability to manufacture ties to specific, consistent dimensions and quality. The main challenge of concrete is its lack of flexibility, which can lead to cracking and abrasion; concrete ties also remain more expensive per unit than wood ties. A goal with concrete ties was that they be longer-lasting, countering their initial expense.

The first test sections of the new tie designs were installed in 1960 and 1961 on Atlantic Coast Line, Canadian National, St. Louis-San Francisco, and Seaboard Air Line. However, the ties quickly showed problems, primarily cracking (in the middle from flexing or under the rail seats) and wear/abrasion under the rail seats.

The best of the initial designs was modified, with changes including increasing the amount of prestress during casting and altering the tie profile, mainly by deepening the tie at the rail pads. The changes improved their durability, and by the late 1960s about a million concrete ties were in service in additional locations. Although reasonably successful, a high percentage still suffered various failures (mainly cracking).

Manufacturers continued redesigning the ties, mounting pads, and rail clips, leading to improved performance. Installations increased in the 1980s and later, and as of 2020 more than 35 million concrete ties were in use on North American railroads. Although wood ties still dominate the market, concrete—with about 6 percent of total market share—has become the choice of many railroads for their heavy-haul and high-speed traffic lines.

Modern concrete ties are wider than wood ties (11" compared to 8" or 9"), are long (9 feet), weigh about 850 pounds, and allow wider spacing: 24" to 30" center to center. This mitigates the initial expense somewhat, since several hundred fewer ties are required per mile compared to wood. The Railway Tie Association estimates that overall installation costs per mile for wood ties is 60 to 80 percent of concrete.

Spikes, joint bars, and hardware

Rails were initially spiked directly atop crossties. As cars and locomotives became heavier, this arrangement proved unsatisfactory, as the base of the rails would dig into the wood ties over time, often skewing and losing alignment as well. The solution was the tie plate, a steel plate that fits atop the tie between it and the rail base. The top has longitudinal ridges that keep the rail aligned, with square holes next to the rail allowing spikes to pass

Tie plates and spikes secure the rail on wood ties and keep track in gauge. Rail anchors (on either side of the left and right ties) keep rail from creeping. Jeff Wilson

through while keeping them in alignment as well. Along with alignment, the tie plate spreads the weight of the rail and load over a broader area.

Plates are either single-shoulder (with one alignment ridge, used on the outside of the rail) or double-shoulder (ridges on both sides of the rail). They have four square holes for spikes, two on either side of the rail, and most larger plates have four additional holes outside the shoulders to anchor the plate to the tie.

Cut spikes are standard in North America for securing rails to wood ties. These have a square shaft with a chisel-shaped tip, and are driven into place with a spike maul or mechanical hammer. The square shaft resists twisting, aiding stability, and the angle of the head clamps the base of the rail, keeping it firmly in place and in gauge.

On most trackage, one spike is used on each side of the each rail per tie. Additional spikes are sometimes used on curves where a lot of lateral thrust (centrifugal force) would tend to broaden the gauge. Standard placement is to have spikes staggered on opposite sides of each rail.

A variation is the screw spike, which has a bolt-style head and threaded shank. These are most often used to secure tie plates to ties and switch stands to headblocks, but are sometimes used to secure the rails as well. They are installed with power wrenches into pre-bored holes in the tie.

Spring clips of various designs are sometimes used to secure rails, most of-

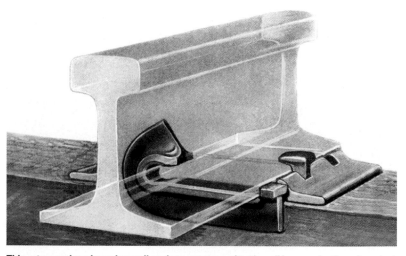

This cutaway view shows how rail anchors are secured to the rail base under the rail against the side of the tie. They are made in several designs. P&M Co.

Insulated joint bars have non-conductive pads between the bar and rail, as well as insulated liners in the bolt holes and an insulating pad between rail ends. Jeff Wilson

ten with concrete ties. Clips (and additional braces) are often used in special trackwork on wood ties, such as crossings and turnouts.

Rail anchors are used on most mainline tracks. These are C-shaped metal pieces that wrap around the underside of the base of the rail, anchored firmly to the rail on either side of a tie. Their purpose is to keep rail from "creeping," which is longitudinal movement that can be caused by train movement

Turnouts allow trains to travel on multiple routes. The switch stand at left controls it; an electric lock secures it. This is a passing siding on the Wabash in the 1950s. William D. Middleton

of various types (such as by braking forces on downhill grades). Some lines have anchors at every tie; others have them every other tie.

Joint bars ("fishplates") are steel members bolted to the web on each side of each rail at end-to-end joints. They're secured by bolts that pass through holes in the joint bars and rail web. Most are 24" long with four bolt holes, but 36"-long, six-hole versions are used on high-traffic lines. Joints are staggered between rails.

Compromise joint bars join rail of different sizes, such as where an industrial spur with light rail meets a main line with heavy rail. Compromise bars have a distinctive stepped profile that allows the top and gauge side of each railhead to match.

Insulated joint bars are used where signal blocks meet and where track-based signal circuits must be isolated. These have insulating pads between the joint bar and rail web, insulated linings in the bolt holes, and an insulating pad between the butted rail ends. Insulated joints are often painted white or orange to mark them.

Bond wires are used to connect rails electrically at joints. They consist of heavy-gauge wire either welded or tapped with pins or screws at each rail end.

Turnouts, crossings

Turnouts are the track devices with moving rails that allow trains to take multiple routes. Since the late 1800s, the "split" (or "split-rail") turnout has

TURNOUT COMPONENTS

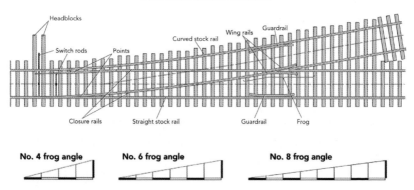

This drawing shows the components of a split-rail turnout. Turnouts are measured by the angle of the diverging track. Kalmbach Media

been the standard design. The components of a turnout are shown in the drawing on the previous page. The stock rails are the solid outside rails that follow the straight and curved (diverging) routes. The frog is where the inner rails from each route meet, forming the point of a "V." The points are the two moving rails that taper at one end to meet the stock rails; the other end of the points ("heels") are joined in a butt joint with the closure rails, which connect the points and frog. The wing rails are extensions of the closure rails that bend to form flangeways on each side of the frog. Guardrails are located inside the stock rails opposite the frog. They aid in keeping wheel flanges traveling on the proper path through the frog.

Switch rods are located between the point rails, keeping them in proper alignment and gauge. The head rod is located between the headblocks (the two long ties where the points meet the stock rails), with the end of the rod extension connecting to either a manual switch stand or powered switch motor. One or more back rods are located farther inward; they help distribute the force of the motion of the head rod and also keep the points in gauge. Some turnouts—especially at modern high-speed locations—have wing rails that slide to close the gap at the frog; these are called closed-frog turnouts.

A note on terminology: The terms "switch" and "turnout" are sometimes used interchangeably, but they have different meanings. The switch refers to the moving parts (points and assemblies)—the part that actually switches the routes—while the turnout is the entire assembly through the frog and diverging tracks.

Stub turnouts were the standard design into the 1870s. These were controlled by moving the butt ends of the approach rails side-to-side to align with rails of either the main or diverging route. They were trouble-prone: they required precise alignment to operate well. If the approach rails were off even slightly, the result was rough operation as the wheels hit the joint, or at worst, a derailment. Wheels continually battered the rail ends, causing downward rail deflection. Summer heat could cause expansion that closed the operating gap and either stuck the rails in one position or didn't allow enough clearance to move rails into the other position. Some stub turnouts could still be found on slow-speed and seldom-used track, including industrial spurs, into the mid-1900s.

Turnout size is measured by the sharpness of the angle of the diverging track at the frog, measured by number in terms of the number of units of length per one unit of separation at the frog (see the drawing). For example,

With stub switches, the rail ends of the approaching track are aligned with either route. They were obsolete by 1900, but some survived longer on slow-speed track. Paul H. Schmidt

a turnout that diverges one foot over 10 feet of length is a no. 10 turnout, and so on. Broader turnouts allow higher speeds with fewer mechanical issues and restrictions regarding length of cars and locomotives. A no. 10 turnout is considered sharp, with speed limited to about 20 mph. High-speed turnouts on mainline tracks are often nos. 18 or 20.

Switch stands are manual devices, mounted to the headblock, that move the points back and forth. Moving a lever on the stand rotates a series of gears and links that pull or push the switch rod, moving the points and holding them in position. Padlocks secure the lever in position; as an additional measure of safety, turnouts on mainline tracks have electrically powered locks (controlled by the dispatcher) as well.

Electric switch machines are used on remotely controlled turnouts, such as those at the ends of passing sidings or at junctions in Centralized Traffic Control territory. These are boxy assemblies located atop and adjacent to the headblocks.

Spring switches allow trains from either route to pass through without throwing the switch. The points are spring-loaded, so the wheel flanges push them aside to pass through. They're most often used at the ends of passing

This is a manual high-level switch stand with an electric lock (controlled remotely by the dispatcher) and control box on a pedestal. Union Switch & Signal

Modern switch stands typically have large loop-style handles that are easy to operate. Note the padlock securing it in position on this industrial track. Paul Dolkos

Turnouts that are controlled remotely by dispatchers are powered by electric switch machines. Gordon Odegard

sidings and at the beginning and end of double-track territory, so that trains do not have to stop to reset the switch after clearing it. They are marked by a sign on the switch stand (usually an "S" or "SS").

Three-way turnouts have two pairs of switch points, and allow any of three routes to be chosen. They are most common in yards and industrial

Crossings (also called "diamonds" for their shape) allow two rail lines to cross at grade. The frogs are high-wear components. Linn Westcott

Slip switches are crossings that also allow taking a different route. This is a single-slip switch. It allows trains to move between the tracks at the right of the crossing. Gordon Odegard

trackage (see the hump yard photo in Chapter 1).

Crossings allow two rail lines to cross without being able to change routes. Rails of the routes meet at four frogs, with flangeways and guardrails. Crossings are measured by the angle of the crossing.

Slip switches are a combination crossing/turnout. Two tracks cross at a shallow angle; pairs of points allow trains to change routes along either one side (single-slip switch) or both sides (double-slip switch) of the crossing. Slip switches are complex, slow-speed trackage. They are most often found in yards, especially in passenger terminals.

Ballast/roadbed

The drawing on page 284 shows how the ballast, sub-ballast, and subroad-bed work together to support the track. The roadbed supports the track and

BALLAST AND ROADBED PROFILE

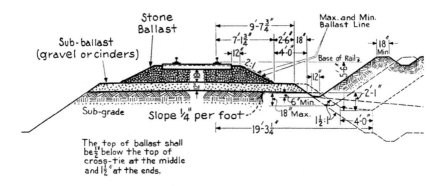

This shows how the ballast, sub-ballast, and sub-grade all support the track. The ditches and slope help aid in drainage. Pennsylvania Railroad

distributes its weight more evenly across the subroadbed. It locks ties into position, keeping them from shifting, but it also lets the track flex with train movement, allows track to be easily adjusted and realigned if needed, and protects track from frost heaves and other shifts in the surrounding ground. It also resists vegetation growth.

Crushed rock has long been the most-common ballast material—often quartzite, granite, or limestone—sized to about 1.5"-3.5" for individual pieces. Another material that's still used is crushed steel slag, a byproduct of the steel-making process. The keys are that ballast be hard enough to resist breaking or abrasion and have sharp edges that lock together well when tamped and distributed around the crossties.

In the 1800s—and on some lines, well into the 1900s—cinders were widely used for ballast. They were readily available, inexpensive, and although much smaller than crushed rock, held their shape and still allowed drainage. Cinders can still be found as roadbed on some branch lines and older industrial spurs.

Track was sometimes laid directly on the ground or subgrade, with no ballast. Into the early 1900s this was common for branch lines, yards, and industrial tracks. Over time, these tracks tend to sink into the ground, until at some point all that's visible are the rails (and they're often obscured by grass and other overgrowth). The increasing weight of cars into the early

After new ballast has been applied and tamped, a ballast shaper leaves a clean slope on the ballast profile, with a shoulder stepping down to the sub-grade. Erie

diesel era made this impractical, as too much maintenance was required to keep unballasted track in useable condition.

The depth of ballast varies by era and by the amount and type of traffic carried. Heavy-haul, high-speed main lines have 12" to 24" of ballast between the bottom of the ties and the subgrade. This creates a distinctive, tall profile. Secondary lines and passing sidings generally have 6"-10" of ballast. The ballast often rests atop a layer of sub-ballast, which can be cinders or finely crushed rock up to 6" deep.

With the passage of hundreds of heavy trains, ballast tends to settle, break down, and lose its profile. It becomes contaminated with fragments of itself (from crushing due to track movement) as well as soil and other impurities. To combat this, railroads use a variety of mechanical devices. Tampers travel along the track, elevating it while redistributing the ballast under and between the ties while leveling the track (when needed, new ballast is dumped directly atop the track prior to tamping). Ballast cleaners take that a step further by pulling out ballast, cleaning it, and redistributing the ballast behind it, restoring its profile.

Subroadbed

The subroadbed, also called subgrade, is earth that's been graded to support the roadbed and track. In some cases the ground itself was simply graded to prep for the track and roadbed—think a late-1800s low-budget line, or a short spur to an industrial area. In most cases, the subroadbed is elevated with earth fill above the surrounding terrain, if only by a couple of feet, to provide for drainage and to ensure that track is level.

The top of the subroadbed is generally a minimum of 20 feet wide for a single-track line (measured from shoulder edge to shoulder edge of the subroadbed) and 34 feet wide for double track. Ideally, an 18"- to 30"-wide shoulder of the subroadbed should be visible outside of the edge (toe) of the ballast slope. The subroadbed slopes outward from the shoulder, generally at a 1.5:1 pitch (horizontal to vertical). Well-maintained lines show this, although the shoulder will wear down over time if it's not re-graded and reshaped regularly, so it may not be apparent on some lines. Although it can't be seen under the ballast, the top surface of the subroadbed is crowned slightly (about 3" at the middle) to encourage proper drainage. Since the 1980s, some railroads have begun using a layer of asphalt atop the subroadbed to provide a more-solid base for the ballast.

It was common to use cinders as ballast on branch lines and industrial tracks through the early diesel era. This is on the Baltimore & Ohio at Beardstown, Ohio, in 1967. J. David Ingles

The tracks at Clayton, Ill., on the Norfolk & Western have largely sunk into the ground. There's not much ballast or subgrade visible in this 1967 view. J. David Ingles

Cuts and fills

A "cut" is where a path for the roadbed must be excavated from a hill or rise in the terrain to keep the roadbed level or at a steady grade. The cut must be broad enough to provide the necessary width of the top of the subroadbed, plus room for appropriate ditches along either side. The longer the cut, the larger the ditches must be to carry away water from rain (and snow melt)—especially if the surrounding slopes are tall. The slopes of the cut are generally kept to a 1.5:1 angle to minimize problems with sliding earth and rocks. Narrow cuts in particular can cause problems in the winter, especially in the Midwest and West where blowing snow can quickly fill a cut.

Fill is where earth is used to elevate the roadbed surface, and can be quite low or very tall. Fill is used to keep the roadbed level over undulating terrain, to provide for drainage, and on approaches to bridges. Whenever possible, the earth removed from cuts is used as fill nearby, to avoid having to transport material long distances. Fill is often needed on either side of a cut where the terrain features rolling hills or mountain foothills.

Tunnels

If a cut isn't sufficient to provide a path for the right of way, a tunnel must be bored through the hill or mountain. Excavating a tunnel is the most expensive way to create a right of way, especially if rock is involved. Tunnels present many operational, safety, and clearance challenges, so railroads will first explore all other options.

How a tunnel is built depends on the material encountered and its stability. Railroads will continue cuts with retaining walls as far as possible before starting a tunnel. The tunnel entrance itself (the portal) is often part of the surrounding retaining walls used on the tunnel approach, and keeps the opening stable by holding back surrounding earth. Timber portal construction in the mid-1800s wasn't long lasting, and was subject to fire. Cut stone and concrete became the materials of choice by the late 1800s. Vertical side walls with arched tops are most common portal design in North America. The year of construction is often engraved into the stone or concrete, sometimes along with the tunnel number, name, or milepost location. The interior walls and ceilings are lined in all but solid rock tunnels. Timber in the mid-1800s gave way to brick, stone, and then concrete by the 1900s. Multi-track tunnels exist, but are rare because of the expense involved.

Smoke in long tunnels was a major problem, especially through the steam era. Railroads used a variety of fan and exhaust systems to combat this, sometimes involving doors at the tunnel portals or vertical shafts that allowed smoke to be exhausted upward out of the tunnel. The structures that hold the exhaust equipment are located at one of the tunnel portals.

Snow sheds

Railroads at high altitudes in mountainous regions are subject to heavy snowfall, and their right-of-way is often high along mountainsides, making them subject to snowslides and avalanches. Snow sheds, first used in the late 1800s, are shelters with sloped roofs built in mountainous areas. On cuts along mountains, they have roofs sloping from the high (face) side of the right of way over the track. Their goal is to direct snowslides over the tracks and down the mountain. Other snow sheds protect tracks in long cuts that would otherwise fill with snow. Early snow sheds were all timber; many modern snow sheds have concrete walls on the face side of the track, and some feature all-concrete construction.

Curves

Railroads avoid curves whenever possible and minimize them when they're needed. Curves—especially sharp ones—create rolling resistance, require more power/energy to traverse (especially on grades), and increase wear on equipment, including rails, rail fasteners, and wheels.

This 1992 view shows Burlington Northern's well-maintained two-track main in northern Illinois. It's passing through a cut, with ditches and gradual slopes on each side. Jeff Wilson

Northern Pacific used a tall fill to approach a bridge (at right) at Logan, Mont. Here matched F units lead a freight train across the bridge and fill in 1966. J.W. Swanberg

Railroads measure curves by degrees—see the illustration on page 292—based on the degree of the angle of the curve measured over a 100-foot chord. The higher the measurement in degrees, the sharper the curve. As a comparison, a 1-degree curve has a radius of 5,730 feet, a 2-degree curve is 2,865 feet, and a 5-degree curve is 1,146 feet (doubling the number of degrees cuts the radius in half).

Railroads combat dynamic forces on curves with superelevation, the practice of raising the outside rail to 3", 4", or 5" above the inner rail (think of it

Concrete portals and lining are common for tunnels. This is tunnel 36 on the original transcontinental main line in Nevada. Ed Anderson, Library of Congress

like a banked curve on a racetrack or highway). Superelevation counteracts centrifugal forces, resulting in a more stable ride at speed while lessening wearing forces on the track, and is most common on main lines. Although tall superelevation allows higher speeds by faster trains, it can cause operational and mechanical issues with slower trains, as slow-speed operation

Rio Grande's Moffat Tunnel has a ventilation system at the east portal. Fans blow exhaust gases out of the tunnel, and a curtain covers the opening between trains. Bruce R. Meyer

results in excessive drag and unbalanced loads that lean inward, resulting in more wear and stress on the lower rail. Because of this, railroads use complex formulae to compute the ideal amount of superelevation for any given curve.

Grades

Grades are an operational challenge for railroads, as they mean trains must carry reduced tonnage and/or operate at lower speeds—a sustained quarter-percent grade can cut the amount of tonnage a locomotive can pull by half. Railroads do just about anything possible to minimize grades. Grades cause problems for trains in both directions, with downgrade trains requiring heavy braking to maintain slow, safe speeds on long slopes. Grades reduce operating speeds, increase fuel usage, present operational dangers, increase maintenance to cars (wheels, brake shoes, and couplers) and track, and can become operational bottlenecks on a main line.

Grades are measured by percentage based on the distance of rise divided by the amount of run. For example, if a track rises 1 foot vertically over 100 feet of track distance, the grade is 1 percent (1÷100=.01, or 1 percent); 1 foot of rise over 200 feet is .5 percent (1÷200=.005); and so on.

How steep is steep? On main lines, grades steeper than 1 percent are rare.

An eastbound Southern Pacific passenger train enters a snow shed approaching a tunnel at Donner Summit in California in 1951. D.W. Johnson

Even in mountainous territory, railroads try to keep grades at 2 percent or under. It's not just long, sustained mountain grades that present problems, however. An otherwise level rail line that follows the undulations of rolling farmland, for example, might have a series of up and down grades each a couple of thousand feet long and no more than a half a percent, but with long trains this will cause slack to continually run in and out as part of the train is going down while another is going up. This can damage couplers and loads, and makes it a challenge to maintain consistent speeds.

Profiles like this are most often found on branch lines and secondary lines, where short trains and slow speeds mitigate their effects. On high-traffic routes, most railroads invested in the cost of smoothing profiles, in some cases re-routing original lines to cut down on grades and/or curves.

A route's "ruling grade" is the limiting grade found on a particular line (usually a subdivision or other operating district), and is used to determine the maximum load that can be pulled (usually listed by specific locomotive type in steam days and in tons per horsepower in the diesel era). The ruling grade is not necessarily the steepest: a shorter, steeper grade may be more easily surmounted than a longer, not-as-steep grade.

Track types

Railroads must specify each line they operate as "main track" or "other than main track," but tracks and routes fall into several general classifica-

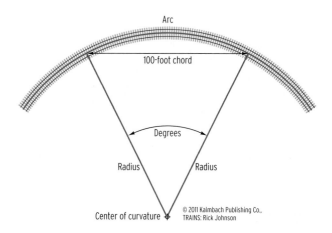

Railroads measure the sharpness of curves in degrees, based on the angle formed by a 100-foot chord and the center point of the curve radius. Kalmbach Media

Most mainline curves are superelevated, with the outer rail a few inches higher than the inside rail. Railroads use complex formulae to determine the ideal superelevation. Jeff Wilson

tions. Main lines are the main through routes of a railroad. They are maintained to the highest standards, and are often signaled. Secondary lines are main tracks that might not see as much traffic as a primary line; they may have lower speed limits or more operating restrictions compared to a railroad's primary lines, or be unsignaled. Branch lines are non-through routes that diverge off of a main line. They can be short (a few miles to a neighboring town) or be hundreds of miles long; they can be low traffic or host several trains per day. Along any of these routes you'll find passing sidings, which are double-ended tracks that allow trains to meet or locomotives to go around their train for switching; spurs, which are single-ended sidings commonly used to serve industries; and yard tracks, which are groups of tracks used to sort or store cars (see "yard operations" in Chapter 1).

Track quality and classifications

All track is not maintained to the same standards. Track ranges from smooth, well-profiled main lines to weedy, undulating branch lines and just about anything in between. The differences among types of track are defined by the Federal Railroad Administration (FRA), which publishes classifications for prototype track ranging from Class 1 to Class 9 (plus an additional "excepted" category). Each classification has a maximum allowed speed, along with minimum maintenance standards that must be followed. Each railroad determines the class of its track. Here's a summary of the classifications:

Excepted track: 10 mph freight; passenger service not allowed. (Only allowed by the FRA under narrow guidelines.)

Class 1: 10 mph freight, 15 mph passenger. This classification covers most yard and industrial trackage, along with some branch lines and short lines.

Class 2: 25 mph freight, 30 mph passenger. This includes many branch lines, short lines, and some regional railroads.

Class 3: 40 mph freight, 60 mph passenger. This includes many regional railroads and secondary main lines of Class I railroads.

Class 4: 60 mph freight, 80 mph passenger. Most Class I mainline trackage falls in this category.

Class 5: 80 mph freight, 90 mph passenger. Not as common as class 4; some high-speed passenger and freight routes use this.

Class 6: 110 mph freight, 110 mph passenger. Exclusive to Amtrak's Northeast Corridor (New York-Washington, D.C.).

Classes 7, 8, 9: Also exclusive to certain stretches of the Northeast Corridor; Class 7 allows 125 mph and Class 8 allows 150 mph; the proposed Class 9 allows 200 mph.

The requirements for each class include specifications for allowed deviations in gauge, rail joints, rail profiles, number (and condition) of ties, and devices, which become more restrictive for higher classes. Higher classes require more frequent inspections. No grade crossings of any kind (rail or highway) are allowed on Class 8 or 9 lines, and grade crossings on Class 7

The train is on one of two main tracks; other tracks include a siding and two industrial tracks, all with diminishing levels of roadbed and track quality. Jeff Wilson

lines require barrier-style warning devices.

Track can vary on any given route. For example, a main line may be maintained to Class 4 standards, but have passing sidings that are Class 2, with a local industrial lead that's Class 1.

Street trackage

Railroads sometimes share a right-of-way with streets in urban areas. Although this was relatively common into the early 1900s, railroads eventually re-routed most of these tracks because of the many safety and operational challenges in dealing with vehicular traffic. Street trackage also presents significant maintenance problems, namely the inaccessibility to ties and rail hardware and the tendency of track motion to crack and deform the paving material.

Street trackage falls into two main categories: main lines and industrial tracks. Main lines often traveled down a town's main street. Urban areas often featured industrial tracks that traversed side streets—of varying lengths, from a half a block to several blocks—to get to one or more businesses. Turnouts in pavement require throw mechanisms that are under ground level, usually with a hinged metal cover protecting it.

Train movements along street trackage are slow-speed operations. Traffic lights on major streets are synched to train operations, allowing trains to proceed directly through without stopping. On branch and industrial lines

This Minnesota Prairie Line track at Gaylord, Minn., has lots of undulations. In the early 2000s it was maintained to Class 1 standards, with a 10 mph speed limit. Jeff Wilson

where switching moves are performed, street tracks are often worked at night, when there's the lowest level of vehicle traffic.

Abandoned railroads and rights of way

Common-carrier railroads can't simply abandon unprofitable lines and routes. They need regulatory approval to do so—from the Interstate Commerce Commission (through 1995) or Surface Transportation Board (since 1996). It's a process that often took years, especially in the period before the Staggers Act of 1980. Track that is out of service may not actually be abandoned. A railroad may be granted permission to embargo a stretch of track based on various factors (shippers going out of business, damage to bridges or track, etc.), and a railroad may choose to leave track in place in case traffic resumes.

When permission to abandon is granted, what happens next often depends upon how the railroad originally acquired the land. The railroad (or a contractor) takes salvageable material—rail, ties, and other hardware. This doesn't always happen right away. Rails can sit unused for years (sometimes decades). Right of way that had been acquired via easement generally reverts to its original owners. Abandoned RoW has high value in some areas (especially in urban areas), and railroads can sell it—a yard in a city could be sold to a building developer, for example. The land sometimes goes to adjoining landowners, such as a RoW through farm fields.

Since the 1970s, many former railroad rights of way have been turned into multi-use trails. The Rails-to-Trails Conservancy is a nonprofit group that works to provide funding for this through the Railroad Revitalization and Regulatory Reform Act of 1976. The government's goal in supplying funding is to keep rail corridors open for possible future use, a procedure called "rail banking."

BRIDGES

Bridges range from culverts and small trestles to long, multi-span viaducts that cross wide canyons and rivers. Terminology varies regarding what constitutes a bridge. You will often hear and see the terms culvert, bridge, viaduct, trestle, and span; each can have multiple meanings. A bridge is any structure that carries a railroad over a river, ravine, road, railroad, or other obstacle. Span can refer to the distance between two intermediate supports, or the structure that accomplishes this. A multi-span bridge uses two or

Street trackage presents many operational hazards and maintenance headaches. This is at West Utica, N.Y., on Delaware, Lackawanna & Western. Dante O. Tranquille

more structures to cross the total span distance. A trestle is generally a wood structure with multiple supports (bents) connected by beams, while a viaduct can be either a steel version of a trestle, with multiple steel spans atop two or more steel-frame support towers, or a multiple-arch stone or concrete bridge. Bridges are either deck (with supports below the track) or through (supporting trusses or girders next to and above the track) designs; some types of bridges (truss, plate girder) can be built in either style.

Bridges require solid support. They rest upon abutments (built into the ground at each end of the total span) and piers (free-standing structures between individual spans). Piers and abutments are typically stone or concrete but can also be wood or steel pilings. Each end of a truss, girder, or beam span must rest upon an abutment or pier.

Bridges are expensive to install and require regular inspection and maintenance, so if a railroad can avoid building one, it will. In almost all cases, a railroad will choose the least-expensive, easiest-to-maintain solution when it needs to cross an obstacle. In other words, a railroad won't install a plate-girder bridge if an earth fill with a culvert would do the job just as well.

Many factors go into the selection of a bridge type, including span length and height; below-bridge clearance (especially over highways, navigable waterways, and other railroads); stability of the ground (for piers and footings);

durability; cost; amount (and weight and speed) of traffic; availability of materials; and current technological progress/standards. Individual railroads often tend to favor certain designs over others.

Bridge types

Railroads have used dozens of types of bridges, with wood, iron, steel, stone, and concrete construction. Some have been long lasting—there are stone bridges built in the early 1800s that are still in heavy mainline service. Others became obsolete rather quickly because of the materials used, their design, or because of increased train weights and speeds. Here are the most common, with information on eras used and common characteristics:

Culvert. Culverts are typically small and easy to overlook, but don't underestimate their importance. They can be stone arches, concrete or timber box structures, or many types of pipe, including clay, concrete, iron, or corrugated steel. They are the least-expensive—and thus most-common— choice for providing drainage along a right of way.

Wood trestle. Trestles have a series of vertical supports (bents), each comprising multiple vertical posts or piles, with wood beams connecting the caps atop the bents. Pile trestles have vertical posts driven into the ground; frame trestles have vertical posts that rest atop stone or concrete foundations. Trestles were the most common type of railroad bridge into the late 1900s (as of 1948, 60 percent of railroad bridges were trestles). Tall timber trestles were the bridge of choice for spanning tall valleys through the 1800s, but they gave way to sturdier, non-flammable steel viaducts by 1900. Most trestles today are low pile structures crossing shallow ditches, marshy or swampy areas, and low, slow-moving creeks and waterways. You'll still find them on main lines as well as secondary and branch lines, although concrete beam spans are now replacing many of them.

Wood truss. Truss bridges have sides made from a series of vertical, diagonal, and longitudinal members. Wood truss bridges became common from the mid- to late 1800s, and some survived into the late 1900s. Whether individual diagonal and vertical members were in compression or tension (with iron and steel rods also used) varied among designs; the most common truss designs for wood bridges were the Howe and Pratt. Many wood trusses were covered, with side sheathing and a peaked roof. This protected the truss members from the elements and extended their service lives. Covered bridges often used the Long (X truss) and Town (lattice) truss designs.

A Boston & Maine freight crosses a Warren through truss bridge and several Warren deck spans at Haverhill, Mass., in 1941. Wayne Brumbaugh

Stone arch. Arch bridges made from cut stones were common for large and small spans alike from the early days of railroading through the mid-1800s. Although strong, they were extremely labor-intensive to build, and by the post-Civil War period they had fallen out of favor to iron and then steel truss bridges, and to concrete and then steel for viaducts by the early 1900s. Their durability enabled many to serve through the 1900s, and several still see heavy traffic today, hauling loads far heavier than their designers imagined. Most are in the Northeast and other areas where early railroads were built, but examples can be found in other areas of the country.

Concrete arch. Reinforced concrete became a viable material for large structures by the early 1900s, and single-arch and long multi-arch concrete bridges were built across the country. Concrete became popular for city street and highway overpasses starting in the 1920s, with many art deco-style installations (including many combined with steel girders).

Steel truss. Iron truss bridges began appearing in significant numbers in the 1850s, with steel replacing iron by the 1890s. Their durability made them the bridge of choice by the late 1800s, especially for long spans: bridges to 300 feet became common, with some to 500 feet. The longer the span, the taller the sides and heavier the members. Truss bridges are built in three basic styles: deck, through, and half-through (also called "pony"). Deck bridges are used whenever possible, as they eliminate the clearance issues presented by through bridges, which have a portal opening at each end. Pony trusses

Culverts are the simplest and most common method of providing drainage along rights of way. This is a stone-arch culvert on Chicago & North Western in Wyoming. Library of Congress

are rare on railroads (but common as highway bridges).

Hundreds of truss designs have been patented, with the key differences the specific placement of side vertical and diagonal members, and whether they are in tension or compression. Since the early 1900s, the Warren and Pratt designs have become the most common; early designs included the Whipple, Bowman, and Fink—these were obsolete by the early 1900s.

Long truss bridges often have arched upper chords—although called "curved-chord" bridges, keep in mind that each segment and member is straight. Other variations of the truss include the continuous truss (to 800 feet), steel arch (which can cross gaps of more than 1,000 feet), and canti-

This light timber frame trestle serves a Baltimore & Ohio branch in West Virginia in 1952. By the late 1900s, railroads were replacing many trestles with bridges. Richard J. Cook

lever (to 1,800 feet). The cantilever design uses two pillars, each with one anchor arm and one free arm, with the free arms supporting a suspended span between them. Although many truss bridges are still in service, and new long ones are being built, plate-girder bridges are now used for most spans up to 150 feet.

Plate-girder. The sides of plate-girder bridges are made from multiple pieces of steel riveted (or, in the last few decades, welded) together. Their simplicity and strength made them the most popular choice for short- to intermediate-length spans by the mid-1900s. Typical use in the early 1900s was to 125 feet; modern plate-girder bridges can be 150 or even 200 long. They are built in either deck or through variations; the longer the bridge, the deeper the side girders.

Steel viaduct. Tall steel bridges became the standard method of crossing deep valleys by 1900. These bridges comprise tall towers, each made with four steel legs connected by horizontal and diagonal braces, connected by short deck plate-girder spans that also traverse the tops of the towers.

Covered wood bridges are wood truss bridges with exterior sheathing and a roof. Some survived into the mid-1900s. This is on the New Haven at Woonsocket, R.I. R.S. Allen collection

Kansas City Southern built a multi-arch concrete viaduct over a chasm and highway near Kansas City. The deck is ballasted. Kansas City Southern

Viaduct height typically ranges from 60 to 200 feet, but some are deeper, and individual towers of each viaduct can vary in height. They can be several thousand feet in length.

Beam. Beam bridges have the track structure sitting atop multiple beams made of wood, steel (I or H beam), or concrete (box, I, or T beam). Wood was common for short spans (to 15 feet), with steel to 50 feet. Concrete beams through the 1960s were typically 40 feet or shorter; modern pre-stressed concrete beam bridges can stretch to 50 feet for box girders and 100 feet for heavy I and T beams. All beam bridges are deck structures. Concrete has become the most popular choice for replacing older short-span wood trestles and beam bridges.

Moving bridges. Moving bridges are used where railroads cross navigable waterways when a conventional bridge wouldn't provide sufficient vertical clearance. Moving bridges are of three basic types:

Swing bridges are mounted on a pier and pivot horizontally to clear the waterway. They can pivot around the center, or the pivot can be closer to one end, in which case a heavy counterweight will be placed on the short end. Through truss versions are the most common, but some swing spans are

Common steel and iron truss designs

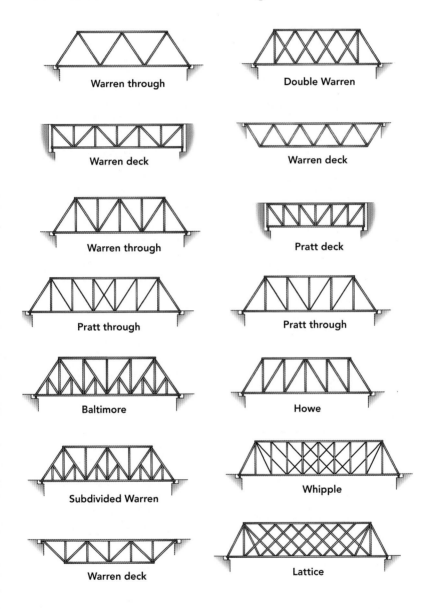

Railroads have used dozens of iron and steel truss designs since the mid-1800s. Most have been built in both deck and through variations. Kalmbach Media

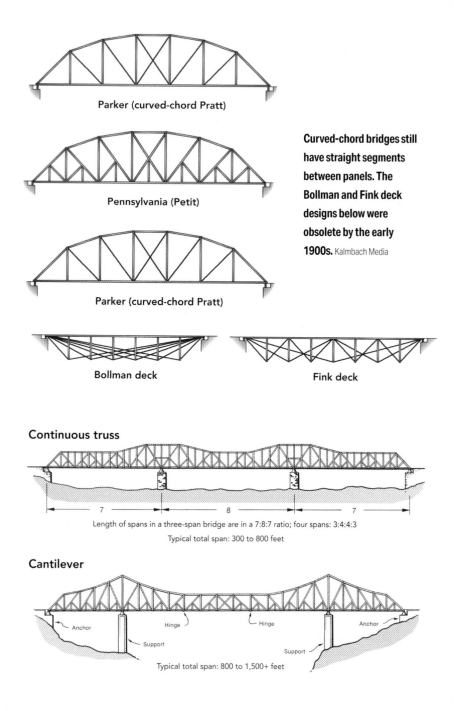

Parker (curved-chord Pratt)

Pennsylvania (Petit)

Parker (curved-chord Pratt)

Curved-chord bridges still have straight segments between panels. The Bollman and Fink deck designs below were obsolete by the early 1900s. Kalmbach Media

Bollman deck

Fink deck

Continuous truss

Length of spans in a three-span bridge are in a 7:8:7 ratio; four spans: 3:4:4:3
Typical total span: 300 to 800 feet

7   8   7

Cantilever

Anchor   Hinge   Hinge   Anchor

Support   Support

Typical total span: 800 to 1,500+ feet

Long gaps can be spanned by either continuous truss or cantilever designs. Kalmbach Media

plate-girder designs. They were the most common movable bridge through the 1800s, and many are still in service today.

Bascule bridges have one end that pivots upward—think of a drawbridge. They have the advantage of providing a clear waterway channel (with no center mounting pier as with swing bridges), and became the most common moving bridge into the early 1900s. They were built in truss and plate-girder versions.

Vertical lift bridges raise the entire bridge structure between tall towers at each end of the span. Lift bridges are the most dramatic-looking, eye-catching moving bridges, and they can be quite long (up to 500 feet). By the late 1900s, they had become the most-popular type of moving span for intermediate as well as long bridges.

Bridge decks. Bridges can be open deck (ties sitting directly atop the bridge structure) or ballasted deck. Ballasted-deck bridges have become the choice for most types, as they do a better job of dissipating weight and reducing dynamic-force stress on the bridge structure.

Bridge capacity

Determining how strong a bridge needs to be is obviously critical in ensuring safe operations. Through the mid-1800s, bridge designers often relied on experience and experimentation, but since then, engineers have

A Peoria & Eastern train crosses the Wabash River on a multi-span deck plate-girder bridge west of Covington, Ind., in 1959. Bruce R. Meyer

Great Northern's *Empire Builder* crosses Two Medicine Valley on a steel viaduct at Glacier National Park in Montana in the late 1960s. Great Northern

developed formulae to accurately determine load stresses based on specific designs. The first factor to consider is the dead load, which is simply the weight of the bridge itself. This includes the track structure (rails and ties) and for a ballasted-deck bridge, the weight of the ballast trough and ballast.

The live load is trickier to determine. This is the heaviest possible weight that the bridge is expected to carry. Determining it is a lot more complex than adding the potential weight of a locomotive and freight cars across the length of the span. Train weight is one factor, both in axle loading (the specific points upon which the weight is transferred) as well as axle spacing and the total weight of a train on the span. A key part of the live load is the impact load—for example, the actions of steam locomotive side rods pounding downward result in temporary loading significantly heavier than the locomotive itself. The rocking motion of locomotives and cars creates lateral and longitudinal forces, which are exacerbated by uneven and rough

Concrete beam spans have become popular options to replace low wood pile trestles. This is along the Union Pacific in Nebraska. Jeff Wilson

track. Flat and irregular wheels on freight cars also create a pounding effect and increased load.

Another important consideration is the effect of heavy braking or acceleration. Conventional track uses rail anchors to combat "rail creep," but that doesn't work on a bridge. Picture a train moving at 40 mph that goes into emergency braking. The weight upon all of the wheels on that train is transmitting force to the rails, with wheels trying to push the rails forward. Curves add centrifugal forces, which must be accounted for (and these stresses increase the faster a train is moving). Oh, and the potential wind

This swing bridge has an off-center pivot, requiring a counterweight on the shore (left) end. This is Chicago & North Western's Mississippi River crossing in the Twin Cities. Jeff Wilson

Bascule bridges pivot upward from one end. This two-track plate-girder bascule is on the Reading crossing Darby Creek in Eddystone, Pa. Library of Congress

load must also be factored—especially critical for moving bridges.

Cooper's Rating is a common method of expressing bridge strength. It was first developed in 1880 by engineer Theodore Cooper. Simplified, the E (equivalent) number in the rating is based on weight loading per axle: thus a modern E80 bridge can carry loads weighing 80,000 pounds per axle, while

On lift bridges, the entire span is elevated between towers at each end. This is on the Burlington at Ottawa, Ill. Library of Congress

Ballasted-deck bridges are common. They better spread the weight of loads and minimize stress on the bridge structure. Library of Congress

an older E-50 bridge is only rated at 50,000 pounds per axle. An E40 rating was standard for new bridges through 1919, the E60 rating through 1934, E72 through 1968, and E80 through today, although some new bridges are being built to E90 standards. Bridge loading was a key factor in the large-scale abandonment of branch lines from the 1960s through the 1980s. These lines typically had older bridges that simply couldn't handle the new 100-ton cars of the period, and repairing or upgrading them wasn't practical.

SIGNALS AND SIGNAL SYSTEMS

Railroad signals are similar to highway traffic signals in that they indicate to trains whether it is safe to proceed on a track. Their specific meanings, however, differ greatly. Railroad signals can be used to indicate speed and route as well as specific permission to enter a block of track. Many types of signals have been used by railroads, and signals' specific meanings vary by railroad and installation. Some signal types are particular to regions or specific railroads. Many signal types were short-lived, but other types remained in service for long periods of time (100 years or more).

Since the early 1900s, there have been two main suppliers of railroad signals. Union Switch & Signal Co. (US&S, purchased by American Standard in 1968; later Ansaldo Signal), and General Railway Signal Co. (GRS, acquired by Alstom Signaling Inc. in 1998). Although both companies have always offered similar products, many details differentiate them. Other companies have also produced signals, most notably the Hall Signal Co., which was acquired by US&S in 1925.

Chapter 1 includes information on how signals are used within several types of train and dispatcher control, including block signals, absolute-permissive block signals, Centralized Traffic Control, and interlockings (see page 78).

Signal indications

The basic colors used for railroad signals are red, yellow, and green, and some railroads use lunar (white) as well, with corresponding semaphore positions at horizontal (red), 45 degrees (yellow), and 90 degrees (green). Each signal aspect has a different meaning. Some are common among all railroads, but many are particular to certain railroads or have their own specific rules (especially at interlockings). The chart on page 312 shows searchlight signals, but the same rules follow regardless of the type of signal.

Signaling has three basic terms: aspect, name, and indication. The aspect is the actual color or combination of colors shown (or semaphore or light position)—for example, "green" or "green over red." The name is the formal name given to the aspect in that situation ("clear"). The indication is the instruction provided by the signal ("proceed"). These are easy to understand with single-head, three-aspect block signals, but can get complex on busy routes or at complex junctions with multi-head signals.

In addition, the presence of a number plate below the signal head makes a signal "permissive," while no number plate means it is an "absolute" signal. At permissive signals, trains are allowed to stop and proceed or proceed at restricted speed even with a red aspect (the name for that aspect at a permissive signal is "stop and proceed"). At an absolute signal, trains may not proceed after stopping. Absolute signals are generally found at junctions and control points (such as the end of a passing siding).

The chart shows several indications as listed in the *Consolidated Code of Operating Rules*. Signal use has evolved and rules have changed over the years, and some railroads use additional signal aspects or have variations.

Track detection and controls

By the 1870s, engineers had developed methods of detecting trains by sending low-voltage electricity through the rails. Tracks are electrically divided into blocks; when a train enters a block it closes a circuit by shunting electricity between the rails. A relay added to the system is then energized, triggering signal indications.

This signal bridge spans the three-track Burlington Northern main line at Riverside, Ill., in 1980. Searchlight signals are above each track. Ed DeRouin

Detection circuits and signals long relied on lineside wires to carry electrical messages and codes between blocks and signal locations. Every signal (lineside or highway crossing) has an equipment case either at the base of the mast or a separate nearby installation, with a cable running from the communication line to the case. New signal systems developed in the 1970s use microprocessors to generate and detect codes passed through the rails themselves, eliminating the need for lineside wires for signaling (Electro Code is one trade name). Some systems use small satellite dishes or radio signals. By the 2000s, most heavy-traffic lines had shed their lineside wires.

Power for signals has historically been one of three types: primary (battery only), primary a.c. (from power lines), or a.c. float (batteries, but with a connection to lineside power wires to charge the batteries). The type depends on power available at specific locations. A.C. float is preferred wherever electric lines are practical, with rural electrification expanding greatly in the 1920s and later. Power lines could come from railroads' own lines, from local utilities, buried cables, or solar power.

Signal types

Ball signals. The earliest manual signals at junctions were baskets elevated on masts with pulleys. Their position on the mast (high, middle, or

SIGNAL ASPECTS AND INDICATIONS

Aspects	Name and Indication

Clear. Proceed.

Approach. Approach next signal prepared to stop.

Flashing yellow

Approach medium. Approach next signal not exceeding medium speed.

Diverging approach. Proceed on diverging route at prescribed speed prepared to stop before any part of train or engine passes the next signal.

Diverging clear. Proceed on diverging route at prescribed speed.

Stop and proceed. Stop before any part of train or engine passes the signal, then proceed at restricted speed through engire block.

Permissive. Proceed at restricted speed without stopping. (May be indicated by "P" or "G" or plain yellow sign; some installations have signal heads in place of signs to indicate when permissive rule is in effect.

Stop. Stop. (The lack of a number plate below the signal head(s) makes these signals absolute.

Signals have aspects, names, and indications. Specific indications can vary among railroads, but these are among the most commonly used. Jeff Wilson

low) and color (black or white) conveyed information on train locations or permission to enter track. The baskets soon gave way to large cylinders or spheres, usually red, and they eventually acquired the name "ball signal." The number of balls on a mast varied by installation, depending upon how many indications were needed. The number of balls visible, or raised, indicated which railroad had the right of way (these signals are where the term "highball" comes from). Lanterns were swapped for the balls for nighttime operation.

Ball signals were especially common in New England. Although most were converted to other signal types, some ball signals remained in service at junctions through the late 1900s, with at least one (at Whitefield, N.H.) serving into the 2010s.

Clockwork signals. Among the first automatic signals were those with clockwork mechanisms. A passing train tripped the signal—a rotating disk in a housing—to its closed position (the disk facing the track) via a track circuit relay. A clockwork mechanism then slowly turned the signal 90 degrees to the clear (open) position. Clockwork signals first appeared in the 1870s, but were obsolete by the 1890s. Although they provided some degree of safety when trains were short and train speeds were slow, they had serious shortcomings in that they didn't accurately report whether a block was occupied—they gave approaching train crews only a rough gauge of when a preceding train had last passed.

Disc signals. Disc signals (also known as "banjo signals" for their shape) were developed by Thomas Hall (Hall Signal Co.) in 1869. They have a round head with a large clear round opening, and can show two indications. A red disc moves inside the housing to show "stop," and the disc moved out of view to the side to show "clear." A small, round lens at the top echoed the disc indication, illuminated by an oil lantern for nighttime operation. Disc signals were triggered by track circuitry and used magnets to move the disc, so did not use electric motors. Since they could only provide two indications, some railroads used a pair of signals on a mast, with the top signal the "home" signal, indicating occupancy in the next block; the bottom signal was the "distant" signal, showing occupancy

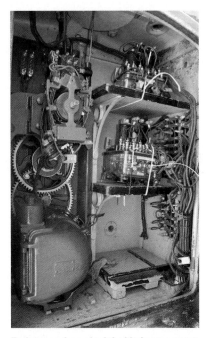

Early semaphores had the blade-movement mechanism in a case at the bottom of the signal mast (left). Relays and other wiring are at right. Trains magazine collection

two blocks ahead (usually with a yellow disc instead of red). Disc signals were obsolete by the 1910s, and most were soon replaced by electrically operated semaphores or light signals that could provide three indications. A few, however, survived in service as late as the 1950s.

Lower-quadrant semaphores. The first semaphore signals appeared in the 1860s. Early semaphores were lower-quadrant designs with two aspects: Stop was the arm at horizontal; clear was the blade lowered to a 60-degree angle. To allow for viewing at night, semaphores included glass lenses (red, green, or yellow depending upon specific useage) that rotated in front of a light source as the blade moved. Early lights with oil lanterns were replaced by electric bulbs as they became available.

Because most only allowed two indications, it was common for block signals to use two semaphores on the same mast. As with disc signals, the top signal was the "home" signal and the bottom the "distant" signal. Blade shapes also differed, often with a pointed blade for the home signal and

Ball signals were among the earliest types of signals, often used at junctions. Some, like this one at Whitefield, N.H., lasted late into the 1900s. Ben Bachman

notched blade for the distant signal. Some three-aspect lower-quadrant signals were made, but they were rare (most commonly used for train-order signals—more on those in a bit).

Semaphore blades have a heavy casting that houses the lenses and secures the blade, which is usually wood or thin sheet metal. Early installations were mechanically powered by rod linkage, usually at interlockings. Many early block signals were electro-pneumatic or electro-gas (powered by compressed carbonic gas), with electric motors becoming standard by 1900. Blades were weighted and counter-balanced so that a power failure would rotate them to the "stop" position, making them as fail-safe as possible. Lower-quadrant signals were used in new installations into the 1910s. Most were replaced by more modern signals by the 1950s; a few, however, lasted in service into the 2000s, notably on some Union Pacific (former Southern Pacific) lines.

Upper-quadrant semaphores. The first three-aspect upper-quadrant semaphores were developed by Frank Patenall in 1903, and signal designs from the two main manufacturers—US&S and GRS—in 1908 popularized the design. Upper-quadrant signals displayed three aspects: horizontal/ red; angled upward at 45 degrees/yellow, and vertical/green. This allowed

Disc ("banjo") signals use a disc behind a round glass opening. They can provide two indications. Charles S. Freed

one signal to replace two-headed lower-quadrant installations. Semaphores remained popular with some railroads even after other light-only signal types were developed, as the semaphore has redundancy—the dual aspects of a signal light plus the visual arm position. They remained the most-common signal type installed through the 1930s.

Semaphore mechanisms were labor-intensive to maintain, especially as they became older. And, since their moving parts were in the open, they could be fouled by snow and ice. The reliability and lower expense of light-only signals doomed semaphores, but many remained in

Lower-quadrant semaphores were commonly installed from the late 1800s to the 1910s; some lasted in service into the 2000s. This is on Illinois Central in the 1910s. Illinois Central

service through the 20th century. A few can still be found in 2022, although those that remain are disappearing quickly.

Railroads used a variety of blade shapes (pointed, squared-end, notched) and colors to indicate their service, with variations indicating a block signal or an interlocking distant or home signal.

Color-light signals. The color-light signal has a separate bulb for each indication, with each head usually having a red, yellow, and green lamp against a black or dark gray oval target. They began appearing around 1914, when bulb technology advanced enough to produce a long-lasting, bright filament that could easily be seen in daylight. The lenses focus the beam down the track, and shades above each lens help viewing when sunlight is shining on the target (some versions have a single large hood grouped over all the lenses).

The most common arrangement is three vertical lamps, with green on top; many railroads opted for triangular-grouped heads as well. Two-lamp targets were used in some installations (especially at interlockings or on dwarf signals), and some modern installations include four or five lights to show additional aspects. To conserve energy and increase bulb life, color-light signal installations are often "approach lit." This means that the signals are normally dark, or unlighted, and only come on when a train is in a neighboring block.

The introduction of searchlight signals in the 1920s dropped the popularity of color-light signals through much of the 1900s. However, since the 1990s, new versions of color-light signals have become the most-common signal type, and new installations—using LEDs and updated, energy-efficient technology—are rapidly replacing older searchlight, position-light, and semaphore signals.

Searchlight signals. The searchlight signal was revolutionary when introduced by Hall in 1920. It uses a single lamp in a round target head with an internal mechanism that moves one of three colored lenses in front of the lamp. An efficient reflector and highly focused (directional) lens allows a low-wattage bulb to create a bright beam that can be seen more than a mile away with low power consumption.

Even though they were the most-expensive option for new signals, many railroads soon began opting for the design. The single low-wattage bulb made them energy efficient, and the internal color-lens mechanism was protected and more reliable than a semaphore. Searchlights became the

Upper-quadrant semaphores, like these on the Santa Fe, were the most common signal type from the 1910s through the 1940s. Some are still in service in 2022. J. David Ingles

most-common signal type installed through the 1970s, replacing many semaphore and old color-light installations.

Although less troublesome than semaphore signals, their mechanisms became problematic enough on older signals that railroads in the past couple of decades have begun opting for upgraded color-light signals, and older searchlight signals are rapidly being replaced on many routes.

Position-light signals. The Pennsylvania Railroad developed the position-light signal, introducing the design in 1915. Each round target has eight lights arranged in a circle plus one in the center. Three lights provide each indication, arranged in vertical, horizontal, or either diagonal position, mimicking semaphore aspects. The lamps are a yellowish-white color designed to penetrate fog better than a single colored light. Another advantage is redundancy, in that one light (two, in some cases) could be out while still providing the signal indication. Some signal heads have individual bulb locations blanked out, or are in a different shape if only one or two aspects are needed.

The signals were used system-wide on the PRR and on affiliated lines (Norfolk & Western and Lehigh Valley). Most remained in service through successor Penn Central and into the Conrail era, but high maintenance costs and their non-standard use of colors meant many were replaced starting in the 1980s.

Color position-light signals. Baltimore & Ohio in 1921 added a twist to the position-light design, keeping the circular pattern but eliminating the center bulb and using colors (red, green, yellow) in the appropriate locations. As with the PRR's design, the B&O version has redundancy in that the pattern and color both provide the indication, and one light can be out and still allow the signal to be read. Most color position-light signals survived the Chessie System and CSX mergers, and many are still in service as of 2022.

Color-light signals have a separate bulb/lens for each color, with green on top and red on the bottom. This is on Milwaukee Road in the 1970s. Gordon Odegard

Dwarf signals. Low-level signals mounted on short masts or on ground platforms are known as dwarf signals. They are typically used on slow-speed trackage, often at the ends of passing sidings or in yards where they give permission to enter main tracks. Dwarf signals can be almost any signal type; semaphores often used rotating disks instead of conventional arms.

Smashboards. Although more common in Europe, smashboard signals could be found in some installations in the U.S. They are used in conjunction with conventional signals and have a large semaphore-like paddle that has two positions: vertical (clear) or horizontal across the track (stop). They provide both a visual and physical (sound) indication—the train striking the signal board. They're most often used at rail crossings and on approaches to moving bridges.

Train-order signals. Also called "train-order boards," these signals were located at depots or interlocking towers staffed by operators. They indicated when the operator had written orders to give to the train crew (see "time-table and train-order operation" in Chapter 1). When train movements deviated from the published schedule—changing the location of a meet, for example—the dispatcher provided written instructions to all involved crews in the form of a train order. The dispatcher dictated the orders to the station operators via telegraph or telephone. The agents would type or write the order on forms, then attach them to hoops and hand them up to engine and

Position-light signals use yellowish-white bulbs arranged in a pattern that mimics semaphore indications. This is on Norfolk & Western in 1949. Paul Gibbs

caboose crews as they passed.

Train-order signals followed many styles and designs. Most were upper- or lower-quadrant semaphores, but some railroads opted for searchlight or color-light signals. Most railroads used signals with two aspects: Green meant no orders to pick up; red meant picking up orders on the fly. Some railroads used Form 31 train orders in certain situations; these required trains to stop and sign for them. These railroads required three-aspect train-order signals—yellow meant picking up orders on the fly; red meant stopping to sign for orders.

Motor-car signals. Motor-car signals are small, low-mounted signals that indicate track occupancy to work crews aboard motor cars and hi-rail trucks. They are small dials mounted on masts or relay cases, often no more than four to six feet above the ground. Their faces rotate, simulating semaphores or position-light signals (as opposed to lights). They're used because speeders and high-rail vehicles don't trigger signal circuits, so they won't trigger approach-lit signals, and trains will not be aware of their presence on a track. They generally provide two indications: occupied and not occupied.

Baltimore & Ohio modified the position-light signal by adding color to the indications and omitting the center bulb.
Brian Schmidt

Dwarf signals are at ground level. They can be in any style, as this color-light version. Many, like this one, only provide two indications. Jeff Wilson

LINESIDE AND TRACK DETAILS
Communication lines

Telegraph systems had been established in the U.S. by the late 1840s, and railroads began using telegraph messages to dispatch trains in 1851. Railroads soon installed poles carrying telegraph wires along most rights of way, and railroad stations became the offices for commercial telegraph services (mainly Western Union) as well as their own lines.

By the 1880s, automatic signal systems controlled by rail-based detection

Smashboard signals are used in conjunction with other signals (note the dwarf at right). They extend over the track, providing a physical reinforcement of the indication. J. David Ingles

circuits were being installed on more and more major routes. These required additional lineside wires for carrying codes among signal installations, and by the 1900s the lines also carried electricity to power them. At the same time, telephone service expanded, and railroad pole lines soon carried their own as well as commercial phone lines.

Trackside pole lines were a good indicator of the traffic level of a railroad. A one-train-a-day branch might have simple two-wire poles carrying a telegraph circuit along the line, or perhaps a single crossarm with four to six wires. A busy main line, on the other hand, may have poles with three or four crossarms to carry telegraph, telephone, power, and signal lines. Pole lines were expensive to maintain and were subject to damage from storms (especially ice and wind), vandalism, theft, and accidents.

Some railroads continued using telegraph for dispatching and other communications through the 1940s, but by the 1950s the telephone and teletype had become dominant. Most railroads discontinued telegraph operations by the end of the 1960s. Railroads began using microwave communications in the late 1950s, eliminating many wires. Further advances in radio communication and the introduction of signal systems that use the rails themselves to transmit codes eliminated more wires, and by the 1990s, pole lines were being completely removed from a majority of routes.

Pole and line construction: Pole height varies depending upon terrain and locale (rural or town/city). From the ground to the bottom arm, a mini-

Train-order signals were located at depots. At this shared Rock Island/Minneapolis & St. Louis depot in Grinnell, Iowa, the Rock used semaphores (left) and the M&StL (right) color-light signals. Trains magazine collection

mum clearance of 18 feet is required over roadways and 25 feet over railroads. Poles are tapered, meaning they're heavier at the base (14"-18" diameter) than at the top (10"-14"). Crossarms are seated into notches ("gains") cut into the poles. The top crossarm is located 8"-12" from the top of the pole, with 24" spacing between multiple arms. The vast majority of poles along U.S. lines had one or more 10-pin crossarms, but not every pin position held an insulator, and not all positions were used. Some branch lines had single-arm poles with 4, 6, or 8 pins. Spacing between poles varied by railroad, with 40 poles per mile common (132-foot spacing; every four poles is a tenth of a mile), but some railroads used other spacing, including 50 poles per

Motor-car signals are low-mounted devices that show block occupancy. Most have rotating faces that mimic semaphore or position-light designs. Union Switch & Signal

mile (106-foot spacing). Poles often held mile-marker signs.

Arm and pin locations were divided and specifically assigned by the service they provided. Each pin location on a pole is numbered, starting with 1 to 10 on the top pole and moving downward. The bottom arm was generally devoted to communication, which could include multiple wires for telegraph circuits and telephone lines. Up from that was one or more arms dedicated to signal system code lines. Centralized Traffic Control installations required the most wires. Yet another arm can carry commercial circuits being leased to companies, such as Western Union telegraph or public telephone utilities.

Low-voltage electric wires—used to power signals and other lineside equipment—rest on their own pins. If high-voltage wires (750 to 2,300 volts) are used, they're carried on a separate two-pin arm at least four feet above the next-lowest communication arm.

Communication wires were subject to interference ("crosstalk") from neighboring lines if they maintained the same relative positions over long distances. Railroads fought this by transposing pairs of wires every few poles, and transposing other pairs at varying distances. This was done with a four-insulator transposition bracket or by brackets that held an insulator below the crossarm, allowing neighboring wires to swap positions.

The amount of traffic along a route could often be judged by the number of wires on the lineside poles. Many have been eliminated on this route. Gordon Odegard

Signal and communication lines must be connected (dropped) to trackside structures and devices such as lineside signals, crossing signals, stations, interlocking towers, powered turnouts and derails, phone booths, relay cases, and instrument cabinets. At these locations, wires are tapped as needed at a neighboring pole and routed to the device. This was usually done by a bundled, insulated cable strung to an extended pole atop the relay case or structure.

Defect detectors

Into the early diesel era, spotting problems with moving trains—such as overheated bearings, dragging or broken equipment, and shifted loads—was dependent upon human observation from the caboose as well as lineside from station operators, section gangs, and other employees. Unfortunately, crews and trackside observers were often unable to spot problems until damage had already occurred—by the time smoke was rising from a hot bearing, it was often too late. Railroads now use a wide variety of automated detectors to catch problems before they become serious.

Dragging-equipment detector. These began appearing in the the 1940s, and improved designs led to their increased use in the 1960s and later. Initial designs used a thin, breakable wire or bar between the rails just below railtop level—called a "brittle bar"—that carried a low-level electrical current. A low-hanging obstruction would break the bar, breaking the circuit and alerting the dispatcher. By the 1960s, detectors were redesigned with a series of moveable, sprung paddles outside and between the rails. The paddles extend from a rod under the base of the rail upward to just below rail-top level. Broken equipment will push a paddle over, as will the wheel of a derailed car, triggering the detector. This design requires less maintenance

Cables are routed ("dropped") from pole lines to signals and relay cases. This is along the Santa Fe in the 1940s. Library of Congress

and was more effective than earlier designs. Early systems used lineside signals to warn train crews, but by the 1990s, most detectors reported their findings (problem and axle number) by radio.

Hotbox detectors. Overheated axle bearings—"hotboxes"—were a major problem for railroads in the days of solid-bearing journals. If a journal box ran dry and overheated, the result could be an axle failure and derailment. The coming of roller bearings in the 1960s greatly reduced the problem, but they can fail as well. Hotbox (hot-bearing) detectors began appearing in the mid-1950s, using infrared sensors in a scanner head mounted outside each rail. They provide an alarm if a bearing is above a certain temperature (usually 180 degrees above ambient temperature). Modern infrared detectors can now also identify overheated wheels, which can indicate sticking brakes.

Acoustic bearing detectors. Since 2000, several additional types of detectors have begun appearing along railroads. Acoustic bearing detectors and multiple high-speed, high-definition cameras capture the sounds and appearance of passing cars; a microprocessor compares the detector's results to standards. This allows identifying many defects before they become hazards, such as worn bearings, misaligned or defective trucks, loose hopper gates, and flat and defective wheels.

Wheel-impact load detectors (WILD). These use rail-mounted strain gauges to measure impact forces of each passing wheel, detecting damaged wheels by the increased force they transmit (think of the "wham-wham-wham ..." of a flat wheel passing by on a train).

Load detectors. High-and-wide load detectors use stereo imaging to accurately plot the overall dimensions of passing cars. They can flag cars that are too tall or wide to clear upcoming obstructions (such as tunnels or underpasses) and identify loads that have shifted on open cars.

Slide fences. In many mountainous areas or along rock cuts, rocks and boulders can fall and land on the track. Slide fences are located along these rock walls. Slide fences have a series of closely spaced horizontal wires that carry a low-voltage current. If a rock falls and breaks a wire (or, on some systems, causes a wire to be unplugged from its socket), the detector activates a red signal in advance of the area.

Detector locations. Dragging-equipment and hotbox detectors are often grouped together at the same location. Specific placement and frequency varies by railroad and region; high-traffic main lines often have detectors every 12 to 20 miles. Other specialized detectors are placed as needed.

Dragging-equipment detectors have pivoting paddles between and along the rails. The sensor outside the rails at upper left counts passing axles. Tom Kline

ACI and AEI scanners

The first attempt at automatically tracking and identifying freight cars in motion was the Automatic Car Identification (ACI) system, developed by GTE and (marketed as KarTrak), which debuted in 1967. It required bar-code-style plates (10" x 22") with reflective color stripes mounted to all rolling stock and locomotives. The bar codes included the car's reporting marks, number, and type. By 1975, about 90 percent of cars were equipped. Trackside optical scanners were installed on main tracks approaching yards and junctions where trains originated and terminated. The scanners were located in boxes mounted on posts, with a hood over the scanner opening.

The ACI system was unsuccessful; in particular the fail rate in reading passing cars was 20 percent. The system's biggest problem was dirt, as the optical readers simply couldn't read grime-covered barcodes. The system was abandoned in 1977.

The solution came in 1991 with the AEI (automatic equipment identification) system, which uses passive radio signals (radio-frequency identification, or RFID) instead of optics. Data tags—passive radio transponders enclosed in hard-plastic housings—are affixed to the frame on each side of all freight cars. The data includes reporting marks, car number, and equipment type.

Hotbox detectors use infrared sensors outboard of each rail to detect overheated bearings. The angled ramps protect the detector from dragging equipment. Jim Hediger

This is a BNSF wheel impact load detector (WILD) at Cochrane, Wis. It measures forces of wheels on the track to spot defective wheels and trucks. Steve Glischinski

Slide-detector fences, like this one on Norfolk Southern near Elkhorn, W.Va., have multiple low-voltage electric wires that trip signals when broken by falling debris. Samuel Phillips

The AEI readers are boxy structures mounted on stands; they're often located near other detector equipment. More than 3,000 trackside scanners were in service by 2000. The system has been extremely successful, with an accuracy rate of nearly 100 percent.

Equipment cases

They're often called "relay cases," but equipment sheds, cabinets, and cases hold all manner of electrical control equipment, keeping it safe from the elements but accessible for maintenance. Every location with powered signals—block signals, Centralized Traffic Control signals, grade crossing gates and flashers, and powered turnouts—requires one or more nearby equipment sheds to hold equipment. Near each equipment shed will be a battery well (or "vault" or "cellar"). Signals are powered by batteries, but since the 1930s most also have have a.c. line power to charge batteries and provide a constant backup (called "a.c. float"). The battery well is a reinforced, waterproof concrete box, usually cylindrical—although some are square—with a locked cover.

Communications

Communication between train crews and the dispatcher and local operators have always been important. Phone booths and boxes were a common lineside detail, and were especially important into the 1960s before direct radio communications between dispatcher and train crews became common and reliable. Phone boxes are typically located at the ends of sidings, at junctions, crossings, and other interlockings, at defect detectors, and many

The ACI system used optical readers (left) to scan colored bar-code plates on passing freight cars. Grime doomed the system; it was abandoned in 1977. Sylvania Electric

signals—locations where a train might be stopped or delayed.

The coming of radio and microwave communication led to installation of antennas and dishes of various types along the right of way. The recent adoption of Positive Train Control (PTC; see Chapter 1) has led to even larger installations.

Structures and facilities

Railroads have used a number of buildings and structures to assist operations, facilitate repairs, and serve customers. Here's a summary of the most common structures and facilities along a railroad:

The AEI (automatic equipment identification) system uses radio signals to read small data tags on passing equipment. The system's accuracy rate is near 100 percent. Russell Lyon

Stations and depots. The two words are often used interchangeably, but a depot is the actual building and "station" can refer to either the structure itself or a named location (which may or may not have an accompanying structure). Historically the function of a depot was to provide an office for an

Every signal (lineside, crossing, Centralized Traffic Control) has one or more nearby equipment cabinets. A round battery vault is at left. Jeff Wilson

The more complex the installation, the larger the equipment case. Walk-in sheds have become common at many locations.

Gordon Odegard

operator, whose responsibility was to communicate with the dispatcher and relay information to trains; provide an office for the agent, who deals with shippers and other customers; and provide a waiting room and ticket office for passengers. Early depots often provided living space for operators. Most depots in towns and small cities were "combination stations," which had attached freight rooms for handling express and less-than-carload (LCL) shipments. Small buildings that served operators only (with no passenger or agent duties) were "train-order offices." Depots declined in number by the 1960s and later with the move to radio-based dispatching, remote agents, and the decline of passenger and LCL traffic. By the 1990s, most station buildings were being torn down, used as maintenance buildings, or sold for private use.

Passenger terminals, union stations. Passenger-only stations were found in larger towns and cities, and are still common. Large-city terminals were often the fanciest, most ornate structures on a railroad. They often have

multiple tracks and yards serving them. Commuter lines often have smaller shelters at station points. Union stations are passenger terminals that serve multiple railroads—in the days before Amtrak, they were typically co-owned by the participating railroads, and large ones might be served by a separate terminal railroad (also owned by the railroads owning the station).

Freight houses. Freight houses (freight stations) handled less-than-carload traffic at larger towns and small cities where a combination station wasn't large enough. Depending upon the amount of local LCL traffic handled, a freight house may send

Telephone boxes were vital at key locations, especially before radio communication became common. Gordon Odegard

A BNSF train passes a PTC (Positive Train Control) and microwave installation at East Siberia, Calif., in 2015. Scott A. Hartley

and receive a few boxcars per day, and large-city freight houses that served as traffic hubs had multiple tracks and could handle more than 100 inbound and outbound cars each day. Railroad LCL traffic declined sharply from the 1950s into the 1960s; most was gone (to trucks) by 1970, with freight houses out of service.

Interlocking towers. Control levers at interlocking points (crossings and junctions) were usually housed in two-story structures ("towers") at the location being controlled. Single-story interlocking structures were usually called "cabins". Operators on duty at towers handled train orders in the same manner as operators at depots (see Interlockings in chapter 1) as well as operating the levers that controlled turnouts and signals. Thousands were in service in the mid-1900s, but most were gone by the early 2000s, replaced by dispatchers controlling turnouts and signals remotely.

Section houses. Through the steam era, basic track inspection and maintenance was assigned to crews based along small segments of line called sections. Each section had its own work crew (sectionmen) and their base was the section house, which housed all maintenance equipment and materials they would need. Crews (track, signal, and other departments) now work on much longer sections of line, but there are still buildings located periodically to house equipment; many old depots have been repurposed for this.

Railroad stations were once centers of activity in towns and were vital for railroad operations. This is Logan, Iowa, on Illinois Central in 1900. Illinois Central

St. Louis Union Station was among the nation's busiest rail passenger terminals through the 1950s. It once served 22 railroads. Al Rung

Turntables. A turntable is a bridge structure with track that turns in a circle, allowing locomotives to be turned. They are usually supported in the middle at the pivot and along the rim by wheels on a rail, and the turntable itself is in a depression (turntable pit). Turntables varied in size by era and need, and could be powered by hand ("armstrong") or by an electric or

Freight stations served as hubs for less-than-carload (LCL) operations into the 1960s. That traffic vanished by 1970, going to trucks. Chicago & Eastern Illinois

pneumatic motor. They could also be used to turn rolling stock (orienting piggyback, observation, or mail cars in proper direction, for example). Their need diminished with the end of steam locomotives; some still exist, but they are becoming rare.

Roundhouses, engine houses. An engine house is a structure that holds locomotives for routine and major maintenance, and a circular engine house that surrounds a turntable is a roundhouse. Roundhouses may have just two or three tracks, or can fully surround the turntable with dozens of tracks. Roundhouses and turntables can still be found, but are rare. Their need was largely eliminated by the coming of diesels, which required far less routine maintenance and which were either bidirectional or operated in sets with cabs facing both directions. Modern engine houses or shops are generally large buildings with parallel interior tracks served by ladder tracks.

Engine servicing facility. This is a group of buildings and associated equipment for maintaining locomotives. These complexes can be small or large, meant to serve a locomotive or two or dozens at a time (see Chapter 1). In the steam era this could include a roundhouse, additional shop buildings and storehouses, foundry, ash pit (for dumping ashes), coaling

Interlocking towers were located at junctions. They housed control equipment for the junction's signals and turnouts and the operator who ran them. Library of Congress

Roundhouses with turntables were common at engine facilities in the steam era. Steam locomotives required much more daily care than diesels. New York Central

tower, water tank, sand house and tower, and crew locker rooms and bunkhouse. Diesel facilities are fewer in number and spaced much farther apart, and typically include a shop building, fuel rack, and sand tower. "Ready tracks" hold locomotives ready for service.

RIP track. The name sounds ominous, but it simply stands for "repair in place." The RIP track is where rolling stock goes for quick repairs that can be done without major shop work—replacing wheels or trucks, simple body repairs, coupler repairs, and brake gear repairs.

Grade crossings

There are more than 125,000 public grade crossings in the U.S.—plus another 80,000 private crossings—where railroad tracks cross streets, roads, and highways. Getting roadways (and vehicles) safely across the tracks is a high priority for railroads as well as state and federal highway agencies.

Crossing materials. Into the early 1900s, the most common crossing material was wood: planks were laid parallel to the rails, butting against the outsides of the rails and allowing a flange gap on the insides. These evolved to purpose-built prefabricated wood crossings. Paving material (gravel, asphalt) is sometimes used, with guardrails preserving flangeways on the gauge sides of the rails. Prefabricated rubber and concrete pads were developed in the 1940s, and today are the most-common type of crossing material (especially at high-traffic crossings).

Signs and manual gates. Warning signs of many types have been used since the mid-1800s, with the now-common X-shaped "crossbuck" sign appearing by 1900 and becoming standard by the 1940s. Crossing watchmen were stationed at busy crossings by the mid-1800s, armed initially with signs and lanterns. Manually operated gates (at first hand-cranked, then electrically or pneumatically powered) first appeared around 1870, and became common through the 1940s (some lasted even longer). Manual gates were usually controlled by operators in elevated towers, which gave them a longer view down the tracks.

Bells and wig-wag signals. The first automatic crossing signal (triggered by a track circuit) was a warning bell, patented in 1889. The growing use of automobiles in the early 1910s led to the invention of the "wig-wag" signal, a round target with a red light at the center mounted on a moveable arm. When activated, the red light illuminated and the arm waved back and forth (powered by a magnet). The first successful version, built by the Magnetic Signal Co. (and marketed as the "Magnetic Flagman") appeared in California around 1914. Some lasted into the 2000s.

Automatic flashers and gates. Crossing signals with alternating/

Wig-wag signals were developed in the 1910s and some remained in service into the 2000s. This is at Van Dyne, Wis., on the Soo Line in 1993, with the Illinois Railway Museum's restored Burlington *Nebraska Zephyr* approaching on an excursion run. Jeff Wilson

flashing lights began appearing by the late 1920s. By the late 1930s, an additional set of flashing lights was sometimes added on a cantilever above the roadway—a common practice today. By the 1940s, the AAR standard was for 8" lights on 20" targets, spaced 30" center-to-center. Size was increased in the 1970s to 12" lights on 20" targets, with target size increased to 24" in the 1980s. High-intensity LEDs are now used in place of bulbs on new signals. The first automatically controlled gates appeared in 1936, the Western Model 10. Gates were painted with black-and-white diagonal stripes through the 1960s; red-and-white became standard around 1970. Crossing bells are usually included with flashers and gates. Through the 1990s this usually meant an electrically operated gong-style bell at the top of the signal mast; after that, electronic bells became more common.

Griswold signals had flashers as well as stop signs that rotated into position when a train approached. J. David Ingles

Signal and gate details varied by manufacturer. One distinct version was the flashing signal with a rotating stop sign in a bracket below the crossbuck. These were made primarily by Griswold, but Western had a version as well. As a train approached, the flashers began operating and the stop sign rotated to face traffic. When the train cleared and the flashers stopped, the sign rotated 90 degrees.

Crossing evolution. By the 1950s, separate track circuits that required insulated rail gaps were replaced by audio-frequency overlay (AFO) circuits that didn't interfere with block signals. By the 1960s, these could allow crossing signals to automatically adjust to train speed and direction as well. A modern variation that began appearing in the 1990s is the wayside horn. This is a stationary directional horn mounted on a mast next to the signal,

Directional grade crossings feature stationary horns (on mast at left) facing the roadway. This is Mundelein, Ill., on Canadian National in 2008. TRAINS magazine collection

Most modern grade crossings are made with prefabricated panels of rubber (shown here) or concrete. Erie

aimed down the roadway. It replaces the train horn; the stationary horn is louder for approaching motorists while producing less overall noise pollution, as the train horn is not sounded.

Signs

Railroads use a variety of informational and regulatory signs along the right of way. Some—especially into the mid-1900s—were styled uniquely by

Historically, crossing signs came in a wide variety of styles before today's 90-degree-angle crossbuck was adopted as standard. TRAINS magazine collection

Manual crossing gates were activated by a watchman, who also flagged the crossing with a stop sign. This is on the Reading. TRAINS magazine collection

each railroad, with some using concrete, stone, or cast-metal signs. By the mid-1900s, simple reflectorized signboards atop either wood or U-shaped metal posts became standard.

Mile markers. Railroads base their timetables on mile locations, so knowing the precise distance to a station or siding is vital to operations. In the steam era, many locomotives didn't have speedometers. Engine crews had to use their watches to count the time between mileposts to gauge their speed. And maintenance crews rely on mile markers to identify specific bridges, culverts, signals, line poles, and equipment cabinets. Markers are usually on small signboards

Manual crossing gates were usually controlled by operators in towers at the crossing. Some towers controlled multiple crossings. TRAINS magazine collection

on posts; early railroads sometimes used concrete markers or other ornate signs, or placed them on lineside communication poles.

Whistle, bell posts. Whistle posts let engineers know when to blow the whistle for grade crossings. Most railroads signify this with a W, some used an X, and others have used symbols for the whistle pattern (two longs, a short, and a long). Through the steam era, some railroads used ornate cast-iron signs (Pennsylvania's, for example, was an outlined keystone with a "W" in the middle). And yes, even though steam locomotives and whistles disappeared more than 60 years ago, they're still "whistle posts," not "horn posts." Since the 1990s, many municipalities have enacted regulations prohibiting whistle use except in emergencies, so no-whistle signs (usually a W with a slash through it) alert train crews to that effect. These are also used in areas where crossings have their own built-in directional horns.

Speed signs. Early speed limit signs could be ornate, but most are fairly simple, with the number (or two numbers if there are different limits for freight and passenger) on a signboard mounted to a post. Railroads had their own standards and rules for variations including sign color and signboard shape. Speed restriction signs (for curves, bridges, junctions, and other areas) are indicated by sign style or color, or with letters ("SR" for "speed restriction" and "RS" for "resume speed"). A plain green panel on a signboard indicates the end of the speed zone. A temporary speed-restriction sign (such as when maintenance crews are working) is a plain yellow board on a post. Trains will have also received orders and information regarding temporary speed zones via train order or other communication from the dispatcher.

Flanger posts. Railroads sometimes use plows with flangers, which have retractable blades that extend below railtop level between the rails, to clear ice and snow that can foul wheel flangeways. Flanger posts are signs that alert flanger operators when they approach between-rails obstructions, such as grade crossings, turnouts, and guardrails. The most common style is a plain black signboard at an upward angle on a post (easy to spot against a snowy landscape), but railroads have used many variations over the years.

Miscellaneous signs. Station signs indicate named locations. This can be a physical station building (depot or tower), a junction or siding, or any other location. Signs often indicate approaching locations ("JUNCTION ONE MILE," "STATION ONE MILE," "YARD LIMIT ONE MILE"). Yard limit signs mark important boundaries where specific rules involving speed and rights are applied. Other common signs involve signaling, showing boundaries of circuit-control areas, signal blocks, and Centralized Traffic Control (CTC) areas.

Conrail was formed from several bankrupt Northeastern railroads in 1976. It began turning a profit in the 1980s. Brian Solomon

Index

A Chesapeake & Ohio 2-8-8-2 leads a long freight train in the 1940s. Richard E. Prince

SELECTED BIBLIOGRAPHY

Books

Express, Mail & Merchandise Service, by Jeff Wilson. Kalmbach Pubishing Co., 2016

Freight Cars of the '40s and '50s, by Jeff Wilson. Kalmbach Publishing Co., 2015

Guide to North American Diesel Locomotives, by Jeff Wilson. Kalmbach Publishing Co., 2017

Guide to North American Steam Locomotives, Revised Edition, compiled by George Drury. Kalmbach Publishing Co., 2015

Guide to Signals & Interlockings, by Dave Abeles. Kalmbach Media, 2021

The Historical Guide to North American Railroads, Third Edition. Kalmbach Publishing Co., 2014

How Steam Locomotives Work, by Brian Solomon. Kalmbach Media, 2022

The Model Railroader's Guide to Bridges & Trestles, by Jeff Wilson. Kalmbach Media, 2021

The Model Railroader's Guide to Freight Yards, by Andy Sperandeo. Kalmbach Publishing Co., 2004

The Model Railroader's Guide to Passenger Equipment & Operations, by Andy Sperandeo. Kalmbach Publishing Co., 2006

Modern Freight Cars, by Jeff Wilson. Kalmbach Media, 2019

Piggyback and Container Traffic, by Jeff Wilson. Kalmbach Publishing Co., 2017

Steam and Diesel Locomotive Servicing Terminals, by Tony Koester. Kalmbach Media, 2018

Periodicals

Car Builder's Cyclopedia, various editions

Classic Trains, various issues

Model Railroader, various issues

Railway Age, various issues

Railway Engineering & Maintenance Cyclopedia, various editions

Trains, various issues

An eastbound Union Pacific double-stack train rolls on the far track as a westbound freight passes under a signal bridge at Rochelle, Ill., in a time exposure in 2003.

Jeff Wilson

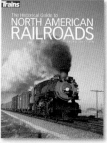

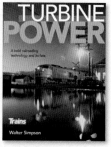